The Hemmings Book of
PLYMOUTHS

Library of Congress Card Number: 2002100090

One of a series of Hemmings Motor News Collector-Car Books. Other books in the series include:
The Hemmings Book of Postwar American Independents; The Hemmings Book of Buicks; The Hemmings Motor
News Book of Cadillacs; The Hemmings Book of Postwar Chevrolets; The Hemmings Motor News Book of Corvettes;
The Hemmings Motor News Book of Chrysler Performance Cars; The Hemmings Book of Prewar Fords; The
Hemmings Motor News Book of Postwar Fords; The Hemmings Book of Mustangs; The Hemmings Motor News
Book of Hudsons; The Hemmings Book of Lincolns; The Hemmings Book of Mercurys; The Hemmings Book of
Oldsmobiles; The Hemmings Motor News Book of Packards; The Hemmings Motor News Book of Pontiacs; The
Hemmings Motor News Book of Studebakers.

Copyright 2002 by and published by Watering, Inc., d/b/a Hemmings Motor News and Special Interest Autos. All
rights reserved. With the exception of quoting brief passages for the purpose of review, reproduction in whole or in
part is forbidden without written permission from the Publisher of Hemmings Motor News, P.O. Box 256,
Bennington, VT 05201.

Hemmings Motor News
Collector Car Publications and Marketplaces
1-800-CAR-HERE (227-4373)
www.hemmings.com

Some words and brand names, for example model names, mentioned herein are the property of the trademark holder and are used by the publisher for identification purposes only.

The Hemmings Book of

PLYMOUTHS

Editor-In-Chief
Terry Ehrich

Editor
Richard A. Lentinello

Associate Editors
James Dietzler; Robert Gross

Designer
Nancy Bianco

Front cover: 1965 Plymouth Belvedere II. Photo by David Gooley
Back cover: 1935 Plymouth Deluxe. Photo by Bud Juneau

This book compiles driveReports which have appeared in *Hemmings Motor News*'s *Special Interest Autos* magazine (SIA) over the past 30 years. The editors at *Hemmings Motor News* express their gratitude to the following writers, photographers, and artists who made this book possible through their many fine contributions to *Special Interest Autos* magazine:

William Bailey	Robert Gross	Michael Lamm
Terry Boyce	Bob Hovorka	Rick Lenz
Arch Brown	Tim Howley	Vince Manocchi
James Dietzler	Bud Juneau	John G. Tennyson
David Gooley	John Katz	Russell von Sauers
		Vince Wright

We are also grateful to David Brownell, Michael Lamm, and Rich Taylor, the editors under whose guidance these driveReports were written and published. We thank Chrysler Corporation, Chrysler Historical Collection, Image International, Motor Trend and Petersen Publishing Co. for graciously contributing photographs to *Special Interest Autos* magazine and this book.

CONTENTS

Special Interest Autos (SIA) magazine's back issues are referred to in this book by issue number. If in stock, copies may be purchased directly from Hemmings Motor News at 800-227-4373, ext. 550 or at www.hemmings.com/gifts.

Originally published in Special Interest Autos #158, Mar.-Apr. 1997

1929 Plymouth

Walter P. Chrysler Invades the Low-Priced Field

by Arch Brown
photos by Bud Juneau

IF the first Chrysler automobile, back in 1924, could be said to have been a product of *creation*, the work of the talented engineering team of Fred Zeder, Owen Skelton and Carl Breer, the Plymouth was clearly one of *evolution*.

It all started with the Maxwell Motor Company, a veteran firm dating from 1905 and reorganized in 1921 under the leadership of Walter P. Chrysler, former president of GM's Buick Division. In the five years prior to Chrysler's arrival on the scene, the Maxwell had plummeted from fourth to tenth place in the sales race. The books were awash in red ink, and the company was saddled with 26,000 apparently unsalable cars, as well as a dismal reputation resulting largely from the Maxwell's deplorable habit of snapping axles.

Walter Chrysler, who had left General Motors in a policy dispute with the mercurial Billy Durant, was called in by the bankers to mount a rescue effort at Maxwell. The offending cars were recalled to the factory for axle reinforcements, then sold, reportedly at a minuscule profit of five dollars each. And when the 1922 models were introduced, they were billed as "The Good Maxwells," which tells us all we need to know about the earlier models.

Meanwhile, Walter Chrysler had charged the engineering team of Zeder, Skelton and Breer—the men he called his "Three Musketeers"—with the design of a new six-cylinder car that would proudly bear his own name.

The original Chrysler automobile, the first mass-produced American car to feature four-wheel hydraulic brakes, was introduced during January 1924, and soon went on display in Maxwell showrooms nationwide. The newcomer's popularity soon overtook that of the four-cylin-

der Maxwell, despite some important improvements made to the older marque. Then with the arrival of the 1926 model year, in mid-1925, the Maxwell underwent a metamorphosis, to emerge as the Chrysler 58, a car that initially was little more than a facelifted Maxwell.

In the meantime, on June 6, 1925, the newly chartered Chrysler Corporation took over the Maxwell business interests, and on January 1, 1926, the four-cylinder Maxwell-cum-Chrysler was fitted with two-wheel hydraulic brakes replacing the old Maxwell mechanical binders.

For 1927 there was a smaller, lighter, less expensive four-cylinder Chrysler known as the Series 50. A three-eighths-inch reduction in the stroke cut the engine displacement from 185.8 to 170.3 cubic inches, though advertised horsepower remained at 38. Prices started at $750, down from $895 for both the 1925 Maxwell and 1926's Series 58 Chrysler.

A year later the four-banger had a new title. Known now as the Chrysler 52, its compression ratio was increased from 4.1:1 to 4.6:1, raising the horsepower to 45. Prices were cut once again, to as little as $670 this time. And it was this car that paved the way for the introduction, on June 7, 1928, of the first Plymouth, the Model Q.

Lest there be any doubts about its origin, the radiator badge on the new car read "Chrysler Plymouth"; and it was handled exclusively, at first, by Chrysler dealers. (By March

1930, however—perhaps in response to pressures resulting from the ever-deepening depression—the franchise was granted to DeSoto and Dodge dealers as well.)

Six body types were offered in the initial Plymouth line. The roadster came at first as a two-passenger job, though a rumble seat was soon added, accompanied by an increase in price from $670 to $675. For fresh-air aficionados there was also a five-passenger touring car, but from the start closed models constituted the bulk of Plymouth's production. There was a two-passenger standard coupe, priced at $670, as well as a $720 deluxe coupe, equipped with a rumble seat. Five-passenger models included a two-door sedan priced at $690 and a four-door type offered at $725.

The new Plymouth was clearly based upon the Chrysler 52, which was phased out at this time. There were a couple of important differences, however. Specifically, the Plymouth's wheelbase was stretched to 109.75 inches, a 3.75-inch increase, and it came equipped with four-wheel internal hydraulic brakes, something previously unheard-of in a moderately priced automobile. Styling was radically altered, for the Model Q was very nearly identical in appearance to the six-cylinder Chrysler 65, introduced concurrently. Featured were a slender-profile radiator shell, full crown fenders and fashionable bowl-

5

1929 Plymouth

shaped headlamps. Altogether, the Plymouth was a handsome automobile whose impressive appearance belied its modest price.

Nineteen twenty-eight was a big year for the Chrysler Corporation. Not only was the Plymouth introduced that summer, but on July 30th, less than a month after the Plymouth's debut, Walter P. Chrysler was able—after several years of negotiation—to purchase the Dodge Brothers organization from the banking firm of Dillon, Reed & Co., in a $170 million exchange of stock. And shortly afterward, the Chrysler Corporation would introduce yet another new marque: the DeSoto. (See SIA #59.)

The purchase of Dodge was of critical importance to the Chrysler Corporation, for not only did it greatly expand the company's dealer network, it also supplied the fledgling automaker with a badly needed foundry and a forging shop. But of course, our concern here is with the Plymouth.

Langworth and Norbye recount the story that "the third [Plymouth] completed was personally driven off the line by Walter Chrysler, who immediately headed west and pulled up in front of the Ford Motor Company offices in Dearborn about a half-hour later. He proudly invited Henry Ford and his son Edsel to inspect and drive the car, and the three spent most of that afternoon together. After the demonstration drive, Henry earnestly confided, 'Walter, you'll go broke trying to break into the low-priced market....' As a parting shot, Walter gave the Plymouth to the Fords and took a taxi back to Highland Park."

It may be that the story is largely apocryphal, but it is known that Henry Ford did indeed warn Walter Chrysler of the perils involved in trying to penetrate the low-priced field. And as a matter of fact, depending upon body style, the first Plymouth was priced anywhere from $70 to $150 higher than the Model A Ford. The difference wasn't hard to justify, for the Plymouth was a significantly larger, heavier car. Its wheelbase, for example, was 6.75 inches longer than that of the Ford; so Chrysler was

able to advertise it without exaggeration as "America's lowest-priced full-sized car."

There is more than one account of how the Plymouth got its name. A 1929 sales brochure explains that "the Plymouth has been so named because its endurance and strength, ruggedness and freedom from limitations so accurately typify that Pilgrim band who were among the first American Colonists." But Joseph W. Frazer, vice president and general sales manager of the Chrys-

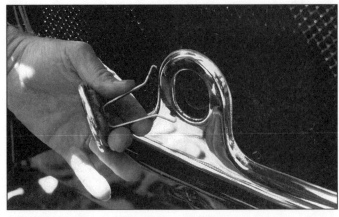

*Top: Plymouth has pleasant, uncontroversial lines. **Above:** No lack of ventilation if wanted. **Right:** Plated cover hides crankhole.*

ler Corporation at the time of the Plymouth's debut, offered a more colorful explanation. According to Frazer, Walter Chrysler was anxious to break into the lucrative rural market, then dominated by Ford. Name identification was obviously of critical importance, and, as Joe Frazer observed, "Every god-damn farmer in America's heard of Plymouth binder twine."

Walter Chrysler's Plymouth couldn't quite match the Chevrolet's price, let alone that of the Ford. But at $690 for the two-door sedan, down from $735 for the 1928 Chrysler 52 from which it was derived, it was a very attractive buy nevertheless, offering features — notably the hydraulic brakes — that could not be matched by any other car at anywhere near the Plymouth's price. "So much worth has never been bought for so low a price," proclaimed the ads; and *Time* magazine was moved to comment that "Chrysler had gone into the low-priced field with the throttle wide open."

The Chrysler-Plymouth Model Q was officially considered to be a 1929 model, despite its mid-1928 introduction. But then without fanfare, during February 1929 the Model U appeared. Virtually identical in appearance to the Q, except that hubcaps were enlarged, bumpers were altered somewhat and the Chrysler name no longer appeared on the radiator medallion, the Model U featured a number of important improvements, particularly with regard to the engine. A heavier crankshaft was employed, along with new crankcase reinforcements and a redesigned oil pan. The stroke was lengthened an eighth of an inch, increasing the displacement to 175.4 cubic inches, though advertised horsepower remained at 45. Thermo-siphon cooling, an anachronism inherited from the old Maxwell, was retained, however. Not until mid-1930 would a centrifugal pump be added to the Plymouth's cooling system.

Prices were reduced slightly on several of the Plymouth U models. The tab for the four-door sedan, for example, was cut from $725 to $695, while that of the coupe was reduced from $670 to $655.

The Plymouth's durability was convincingly demonstrated in a record-breaking endurance test in which a Model U sedan was run nonstop for 632 hours, 36 minutes. The run covered 11,419 miles, and the car was reportedly operating perfectly when the test was voluntarily stopped. (Whether the Model Q's engine could have stood up to this sort of punishment may be open to question, but there could be no doubt of

Top and left: Lamps are steel shells instead of brass. *Below left:* Artillery wheels were standard. *Right:* Rumble seat's a cozy fit for two. *Below:* Top operation is simplicity itself.

specifications

illustrations by Russell von Sauers, The Graphic Automobile Studio

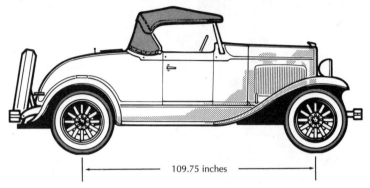

109.75 inches

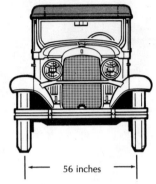

56 inches

1929 Plymouth, Model U

Original price	$695
Standard equipment	Automatic windshield wiper; speedometer, ammeter, oil gauge on dash; complete set of tools; fuel gauge on tank
Options on dR car	White sidewall tires; clock mirror
Non-stock alterations	Downdraft carburetor; electric fuel pump; 19-inch wheels

ENGINE

Type	4-cylinder, L-head, cast en bloc
Bore x stroke	3.625 inches x 4.25 inches
Displacement	175.4 cubic inches
Compression ratio	4.6:1
Horsepower @ rpm	45 @ 2,800
Torque @ rpm	N/A
Taxable horsepower	21.03
Valve lifters	Hydraulic
Main bearings	3 (precision type, bronze-backed, babbitt lined, interchangeable)
Fuel system	Originally Carter 1.125-inch up-draft carburetor, vacuum feed; now downdraft carburetor, electric fuel pump
Lubrication system	Pressure to crankshaft, camshaft and connecting rod bearings; timing gears
Cooling system	Thermo-siphon
Exhaust system	Single
Electrical system	6-volt battery/coil
Other engine features	Aluminum alloy pistons, Silcrome steel exhaust valves, rubber engine mountings

TRANSMISSION

Type	3-speed sliding gear type, floor-mounted lever
Ratios: 1st	3.04:1
2nd	1.82:1
3rd	1.00:1
Reverse	3.65:1

CLUTCH

Type	Single dry plate
Diameter	8.875 inches
Actuation	Mechanical, foot pedal

DIFFERENTIAL

Type	Spiral bevel
Ratio	4.30:1
Drive axles	Semi-floating
Torque medium	Springs

STEERING

Type	Worm-and-sector, semi-irreversible
Turns lock-to-lock	2.25
Ratio	13.0:1
Turning diameter	37 feet 11 inches

BRAKES

Type	4-wheel internal hydraulic
Drum diameter	11 inches
Effective area	114 square inches

CHASSIS & BODY

Construction	Body-on-frame
Frame	Pressed steel, 5-inch channel iron, 4 crossmembers
Body construction	Composite metal and wood
Body type	2/4 passenger roadster

SUSPENSION

Front	I-beam axle, 35.5-inch x 1.75-inch semi-elliptic springs springs; link stabilizer
Rear	Rigid axle, 53.5-inch x 1.75-inch semi-elliptic springs
Wheels	Wood artillery
Tires	4.75/20 originally; now 5.50/19

WEIGHTS AND MEASURES

Wheelbase	109.75 inches
Overall length	169 inches
Overall width	67.5 inches
Overall height	65 inches
Front track	56 inches
Rear track	56 inches
Min. road clearance	9.5 inches
Shipping weight	2,195 pounds

CAPACITIES

Crankcase	6 quarts
Cooling system	14 quarts
Fuel tank	11 gallons
Transmission	.75 quart
Differential	1.75 quarts

CALCULATED DATA

Horsepower per c.i.d.	.257
Weight per hp	48.8 pounds
Weight per c.i.d.	12.5 pounds
P.S.I. (brakes)	19.3

This page: Clock/mirror combo is a neat period option. *Facing page, top:* Plymouth has no shock absorbers but nevertheless corners and handles well. *Below center:* Unusual accessory shift knob/thermometer. *Bottom:* Instruments convey basic info.

1929 Plymouth

the sturdiness of the Model U.)

The Model U, represented here by our driveReport car, came in the same six body types, initially, as the Model Q. Then during October 1929 a dressed-up deluxe sedan, priced at $745, joined the roster. The base four-door sedan formed the basis of a taxicab, a market that Plymouth would vigorously pursue in later years. The deluxe coupe, equipped like the roadster with a rumble seat, had a soft top and was styled to resemble a convertible, though its top was actually stationary. Not until the introduction of

the Model 30U, in April 1930, would Plymouth offer a true convertible.

In keeping with industry practice at that time, bumpers were extra, at $15.00 the set. The spare tire and tube also came at additional cost, presumably in order to enable Chrysler to lower the advertised price—a practice common throughout the industry in those days. Other options included an underfloor hot air heater ($30); an eight-day, rim-wound clock, mounted in the headboard of closed models ($12.50); left fender well with tire and tube ($25); dual sidemounted spares ($50, including tires and tubes); five wire wheels with rear-mounted spare ($35); six wire wheels with sidemounted spares ($90 including tires and tubes); folding trunk

rack ($20, only for cars equipped with sidemounts); trunk ($12); windshield wind wings, open models only ($10.00); combination cigar lighter and utility light, a rather clever idea, when one thinks about it ($12); spring covers, set of four ($8); and for the roadster, a top boot ($10) and top bow rests ($8 the set of four).

The Plymouth was well received by the public. Production for calendar 1929, the Plymouth's first full year, came to 93,592 cars, enough to position Chrysler's moderately priced newcomer in tenth rank, ahead of such veteran marques as Studebaker, Graham-Paige and Hupmobile, as well as corporate siblings Chrysler and DeSoto.

Model years were not always clearly

1929 Plymouth Prices and Weights

I. Chrysler-Plymouth, Model "Q," produced 6/14/28 to 2/4/29

	Price	Weight
Roadster, 2-passenger	$670	2,210 lb.
Roadster, 2/4 passenger	$675	2,210 lb.
Touring, 5-passenger	$695	2,305 lb.
Standard coupe, 2-passenger	$670	n/a
Deluxe coupe, 2/4 passenger	$720	2,345 lb.
Sedan, 2-door, 5-passenger	$690	2,485 lb.
Sedan, 4-door, 5-passenger	$725	2,570 lb.
Total North American production, Model Q: 62,444		

II. Plymouth, Model "U," produced 1/7/29 to 4/5/30

	Price	Weight
Roadster, 2/4 passenger*	$675	2,195 lb.
Touring, 5-passenger	$695	2,260 lb.
Business coupe, 2-passenger	$655	2,280 lb.
Deluxe coupe, 2/4 passenger	$695	2,335 lb.
Sedan, 2-door, 5-passenger	$675	2,380 lb.
Sedan, 4-door, 5-passenger	$695	2,460 lb.
Deluxe sedan, 4-door, 5-pass.	$745	2,540 lb.
Total North American production, Model U: 108,350		

* DriveReport car

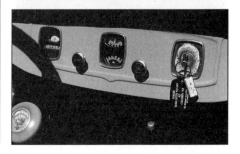

Flathead four-banger pumps 45 bhp from 170 cubes. **Facing page:** *No glove box, but deep door pockets for oddments.*

1929 Plymouth

delineated in those days, and the Model U enjoyed an extended run, with cars built after July 18, 1929, titled as 1930 models. Production terminated on April 5, 1930, when the Model U was succeeded by the slightly modified Model 30U. By that time, 62,444 Model Q and 108,350 Model U Plymouths had been produced. It was a promising start for a new marque entering a very tough market.

Driving Impressions

As noted in the accompanying sidebar, our driveReport Plymouth has spent all of its 67 years in the Sacramento Valley town of Chico, California. It has had only three owners in all that time, and all three of them are still living in Chico. Service records indicate that by August 1941 it had logged 58,000 miles in the hands of its original owners, Al and Irene Staples, an average of less than 5,000 miles a year. Thirteen years later that figure had risen to 72,000, and even today the car has covered only about 75,000 miles.

Emmett Skinner, the roadster's second owner, repainted it in its original color, mounted a set of white sidewall tires, and started the mechanical restoration, but a lot of work remained to be done when the car was acquired by

Gerry and Kathie Watson, the present owners. The engine vibrated severely, which meant that it had to be balanced—flywheel, crankshaft, rods, pistons, the works—when the block was rebored. The old four-banger runs as smoothly now as a new engine. Gerry replaced the kingpins, rebuilt the brakes, and opened up both the transmission and differential for inspection. Fortunately, all the gears proved to be in virtually mint condition.

The fuel system on this car was modified by Emmett Skinner. Like most 1929 models, it was equipped originally with an updraft carburetor, fed by a vacuum tank, but as it stands it has a more modern downdraft pot and an electric fuel pump. These items are not authentic, of course, but they do enhance the Plymouth's performance.

We found the roadster to be a pleasant car to drive. Like most open cars of its time (and a lot of closed models as well),

Plymouth Versus The Competition
A Comparison of Low-Priced 1929 Roadsters

	Plymouth	Chevrolet	Ford
Base price, roadster	$675	$545	$485
Shipping weight (lb.)	2,195	2,230	2,066
Wheelbase	109.75″	107″	103.5″
Engine	L-head 4	Ohv 6	L-head 4
Bore	3.625″	3.3125″	3.875″
Stroke	4.125″	3.75″	4.25″
Stroke/bore ratio	1.138:1	1.132:1	1.097:1
Displacment (cu. in.)	170.3	194.0	200.5
Compression ratio	4.30:1	5.01:1	4.22:1
Horsepower/rpm	45/2800	46/2600	40/2200
Lubrication system	Pressure	Splash	Splash
Cooling system	Thermo-siphon	Pump	Pump
Fuel feed	Vacuum	Mech. pump	Gravity
Axle ratio	4.30:1	3.82:1	3.70:1
Tire size	4.75/20	4.50/20	4.50/21
Brakes	Hydraulic	Mechanical	Mechanical
Area (sq. in.)	118	173	225 1/2
Steering	Worm/sector	Worm/gear	Worm/sector
Springs	Longitudinal	Longitudinal	Transverse
Horsepower/c.i.d.	.264	.237	2.00
Weight (lb.) per hp	48.8	48.5	51.7
Weight (lb.) per c.i.d.	12.9	11.5	10.3

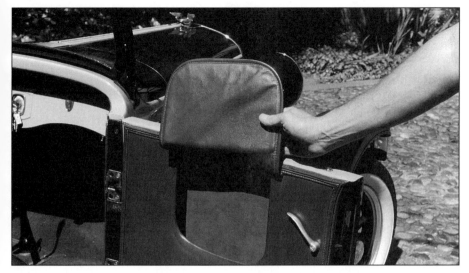

it has a fixed-position seat, and as expected, leg room is no more than adequate for a tall person. But the seat is comfortable and supportive. The engine starts promptly, almost eagerly. The clutch is chatter-free, and the Plymouth accelerates in fairly brisk fashion. With a little practice, the straight-cut gears can be upshifted without clashing. Downshifts—from high to second, for example—are somewhat more tricky. We weren't able to fully master the knack during our comparatively brief test drive.

Steering is quick; just two and a quarter turns take the wheel from lock to lock. Yet it's lighter than many cars of the Plymouth's era. The body is tight; we heard no squeaks or rattles.

Plymouth did not supply shock absorbers back in 1929, but we found the ride to be less choppy than we had anticipated. The car corners with aplomb, and it goes down the road smoothly and quietly at speeds of 40 or 45 miles per hour, which was about as fast as traffic normally moved in 1929.

Dashboard instruments include, in addition to the speedometer/odometer, an ammeter and an oil pressure gauge. (Unlike its low-priced competitors, the Plymouth was supplied with full pressure lubrication.) The fuel gauge is on the tank, requiring the driver to disembark in order to read it, and there is no temperature gauge. Fortunately, according to Gerry and Kathie Watson, who have taken the roadster on several trips up into the Sierras, the four-banger displays no tendency to overheat. This, despite the fact that in 1929 Plymouth still relied on the old-fashioned thermo-siphon cooling system,

Sixty-Seven Years in the Same Town
by Dave Brown
(based on interviews with the Plymouth's various owners)

Almost any 67-year-old car has an interesting history. Trouble is, most of its past is typically unknown to the current owner.

This roadster's history, remarkably enough, is known—in part because its owners remain living and are known to each other; and all live today in the same community where the car was originally sold.

First owners were Al and Irene Staples. This young, recently married couple purchased the car in November 1929 for $870, from Ralph S. Watkins, of Chico, California, a Dodge/Plymouth dealer who remained in business here until 1960. It was their first new car. Perhaps Al chose this model because he had previously owned a Maxwell touring car, an ancestor of the Plymouth. Irene, who is now widowed, recalls traveling to Portland, Oregon, in the car, during December 1929. It must have been an exciting trip, taken in an open car

during what was a particularly cold and snowy month in the western United States.

The Plymouth was the couple's only car until 1934, when they purchased a new Chevrolet. Thereafter it became a shop car for Al's upholstery business, located seven blocks from the Staples's home. It had been driven approximately 58,000 miles when, in 1941, Al purchased a truck for the business. For some time thereafter the roadster was used strictly to drive back and forth between the business and home; then it was placed in storage for many years.

While the Stapleses owned the car, Al changed to non-standard, later model wheels, added a cover for the rumble seat, and changed the carburetor from an updraft to a downdraft model. A clock was also added. The car was stored in a detached garage at the family home.

For many years, Irene Staples was employed by Emmett Skinner, a local farmer. After a lengthy attempt to persuade the couple to part with the Plymouth, Skinner was able to purchase it in 1968. In part, the old car was intended to keep his adolescent sons busy during the summer. Emmett oversaw a partial restoration. A repaint was done by Cooks Auto Body, duplicating as closely as possible the original specifications. While being driven by one of the Skinner sons the car was involved in a rear-end collision, but the only appreciable damage was to the rear-mounted gasoline tank.

The roadster has been driven several times in Chico's annual spring Pioneer Day parade. In January 1994 it was sold to Gerry and Kathie Watson. The Watsons have had engine and other mechanical work done, and additional restoration work is in progress as this is written. The car has now traveled 76,000 miles.

Above: *Steering wheel construction is all wood. Front seat is fixed in position but comfortable for most drivers.* **Below:** *Contrasting body moldings help give good definition to Plymouth rear styling.*

1929 Plymouth

inherited from the Maxwell.

The biggest surprise, and certainly one of the Plymouth's strongest points, had to do with the brakes. They are excellent, comparable to those used on 1950s-era cars. We have driven a number of cars of the Plymouth's vintage, ranging from Chevrolet and Ford through Pontiac, Nash, Buick, Studebaker, and on to LaSalle and Packard, along with a number of others. None could equal the Plymouth's stopping power. Even the Gardner and the Windsor (driveReport subjects in *SIA* Numbers 61 and 64, respectively), both of which were equipped with hydraulics, couldn't compare with the Plymouth in this respect. (This is easy enough to understand when one recalls that the juice brakes employed by these two excellent but obscure makes were of the external contracting variety, rather than the more effective internal expanding type employed by Plymouth.)

At $675 the roadster was priced higher in relation to the competition than most Plymouth body types. Ford, for instance, sold the roadster for $485 (including rumble seat), while at Chevrolet the comparable car cost $545 — undercutting the Plymouth by $190 and $130, respectively. Among the four-door sedans, on the other hand, the difference was much less, with the Plymouth costing $70 more than the Ford "fordor" and just $20 more than the Chevrolet version.

So the question arises, Was our driveReport car worth the premium price paid by its original owner? Taking into account its greater size, generally high quality and smooth performance, and especially those excellent brakes, to the buyer who wanted — and could afford — something a little extra, we'd say it was worth every penny of the purchase price, and then some. &

Acknowledgments and Bibliography

Automobile Trade Journal, *various issues*; Automotive Industries, *various issues*; Breer, Carl, The Birth of Chrysler Corporation and Its Engineering Legacy; Butler, Don, The Plymouth and DeSoto Story; Kimes, Beverly Rae and Henry Austin Clark, Jr., Standard Catalog of American Cars, 1805-1942; Langworth, Richard M. and Jan P. Norbye, The Complete History of Chrysler, 1924-1985; Plymouth factory literature.

Our thanks to Jim Benjaminson, Cavalier, North Dakota; Dave Brown, Durham, California; Karl and Diana Hannah, Sacramento, California; Lois Pantel, Chico, California; Gary Scholar, Chico, California; Everett Skinner, Chico, California; Irene Staples, Chico, California. Special thanks to Gerry and Kathie Watson, Chico, California.

1929

To most people, 1929 is remembered for the spectacular Wall Street debacle that signaled the start of the Great Depression. And rightly so; for the crash was certainly the defining event of the year — and indeed of the decade.

But there were other things going on in the world during 1929. Some of them were events that marked turning points in our history; others were landmarks in science, literature or the arts. It was on November 29th of that year, for instance, that Commodore Richard Evelyn Byrd, flying a Ford/Stout Tri-Motor airplane, discovered the South Pole, a feat for which he was later elevated to the rank of Rear Admiral. And in May of that year, Colonel Charles Augustus Lindbergh, still regarded in those days as America's most popular hero, married Anne Morrow, daughter of the United States Ambassador to Mexico.

Air travel was very much on the public's collective mind at that time, though the majority of Americans displayed no compelling desire to participate in it as yet; and the question of whether conventional airplanes or lighter-than-air dirigibles represented the wave of the future was as yet unresolved. The most famous of the latter was Germany's huge Graf Zeppelin. Carrying just 20 passengers, this great ship successfully circumnavigated the globe in three weeks, including a three-day stopover at Lakehurst, New Jersey.

Radio was coming into its own, and that August saw the inauguration of the sensationally popular nightly show, *Amos 'n Andy*. Blatantly racist by any measure, though most people were quite unaware of it at that time, the broadcast became so popular that at its peak, many motion picture theaters actually stopped their projectors for 15 minutes in order to tune in the broadcast, so that the audience should not miss the latest installment! But June saw a much more significant broadcasting development when color television was successfully demonstrated in the Bell laboratories.

It was a good year for literature. *The Roman Hat Mystery*, first in a long line of Ellery Queen mysteries, was published. William Faulkner gave us *The Sound and the Fury*; Sinclair Lewis published *Dodsworth*; Lloyd C. Douglas, a preacher turned novelist, wrote *Magnificent Obsession*; and *A Farewell to Arms* came from Ernest Hemingway. But arguably the most influential, or at least the most disturbing novel of the season was Erich Maria Remarque's *Im Westen Nichts Neues*, translated from the German as *All Quiet on the Western Front*.

It was a banner year on Broadway, with shows that included *My Girl Friday*, *Street Scene* (a Pulitzer Prize winner), *Journey's End*, and *Death Takes a Holiday*, the latter starring Ethel Barrymore. Musical presentations on the Great White Way included *Hot Chocolates*, an all-black revue that gave the world a number of enduring popular songs including Fats Waller's "Ain't Misbehavin'." Other musical shows that year included *Bitter Sweet*, with a fine Noel Coward score that included "I'll See You Again"; "Sweet Adeline," with some lovely Jerome Kern/Oscar Hammerstein II songs such as the poignant "Why Was I Born" and the tender love song, "Don't Ever Leave Me"

The film *Hollywood Review of 1929* gave us "Singin' In the Rain," revived a generation later by Gene Kelly; and *Gold Diggers of Broadway* introduced "Tip Toe Through the Tulips," a nice little number that was all but destroyed many years later by Tiny Tim. But the most enduring song hit of the year was clearly Hoagy Carmichael's "Stardust."

"Sound" motion pictures had all but crowded the "Silents" off the silver screen. Among the major films of 1929 were *Disraeli*, starring George Arliss in the title role. *Innocents of Paris*, paired Maurice Chevalier with Jeanette MacDonald; *Rio Rita* starred John Boles and Bebe Daniels; and Ronald Coleman appeared in *Bulldog Drummond*, a hard-hitting murder mystery.

Meanwhile, and perhaps most surprisingly, in the world of sports, Connie Mack, manager of the Philadelphia Athletics, was awarded the $10,000 Edward W. Bok prize for distinguished service to the city — an honor previously reserved for scientists, educators, artists and philanthropists.

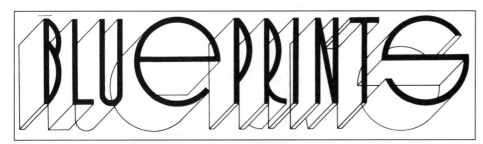

BLUEPRINTS

1933 Plymouth
by Bob Hovorka

CHRYSLER Corporation had great hopes for its 1933 Plymouths. They were totally redesigned, cost less, had more power, more cylinders, and were still the only cars in the low-price field to feature hydraulic brakes.

Unfortunately, the new six-cylinder models were built on a five-inch-shorter wheelbase than the four-cylinder cars they replaced. And while the overall size difference was about the diameter of a pre-Depression silver dollar, the cars looked much smaller. With President Roosevelt's New Deal policies pledging an end to the country's doldrums, people wanted more — not less. Sales were poor. Something had to be done to upgrade the car's looks.

Dealers suggested sidemounts. Plymouth hadn't offered the popular option on the new PC model because the side-mounted tires wouldn't fit on the 107-inch wheelbase. A quick, one-inch stretch squeaked them in but made the stubby hood look even shorter. Chrysler cut prices to spur sales. Plymouth was now offering more for the money than ever before, but the buying public wasn't buying.

Two-page ads appeared in *The Saturday Evening Post* extolling the spacious new interior. "You said it — We need a BIG CAR!" Pictures showed a family of six — mom, pop and the four kids — comfortably snuggled in a new Plymouth. The bottom of the page told another story. "New Prices — 4-door Sedan Now $90 Less." Nothing seemed to help.

In April, Chrysler halted production of the 1933 Plymouth, replacing the ill-received PC series with a new, 112-inch-wheelbase Deluxe PD. At the same time, a new PCXX model was introduced. In reality, it was little more than a base ver-

sion of the original PC, revamped to resemble the larger PD.

If all this seems confusing to you, just imagine what was going on at Chrysler. Plymouth was now offering a lower-priced car, on a fractionally longer wheelbase than the more expensive De Soto. Well, you get the idea.

And the idea worked. The new Plymouth PD outsold both the original PC and the new PCXX by nearly 90,000 cars. With all the extra length added ahead of the windshield, the new PD looked quite elegant. Fitted with optional Goodyear Airwheel tires and artillery wheels, it was about as up to date as you could get for the dollars.

To go along with its sporty exterior, the dashboard was also revised. A large center oval panel housed a circular speedometer, and twin gas/amp and temperature/oil pressure gauges. Passengers sat before a smaller oval glove compartment that was mimicked by a non-functional oval panel in front of the driver. Instead of a glove box pull, the driver's panel contained a light switch.

However. the biggest news was Plymouth's new six-cylinder engine. While it was a half dozen cubes smaller than the four-cylinder it replaced, its 189 cubic inches produced 70 horses. More important, it proved so reliable that its basic design went on to power Plymouths through 1959. Not too bad for a car so poorly received that it was phased out of production in less than six months. ☙

1935 Plymouth

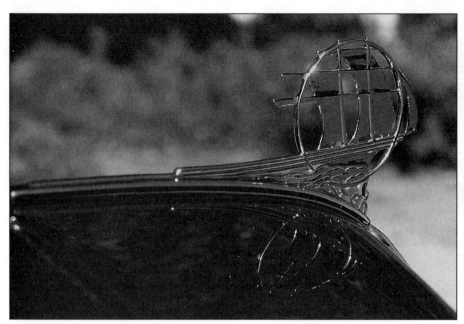

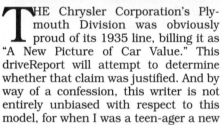

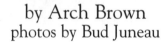

T HE Chrysler Corporation's Plymouth Division was obviously proud of its 1935 line, billing it as "A New Picture of Car Value." This driveReport will attempt to determine whether that claim was justified. And by way of a confession, this writer is not entirely unbiased with respect to this model, for when I was a teen-ager a new

by Arch Brown
photos by Bud Juneau

1935 Plymouth very nearly became our family car. So of course I was anxious to slide behind the wheel of this fine example and see what it is really like.

Veteran readers of this publication will recall that I have often griped about the lack of space between seat and doorframe in so many cars, making it difficult for me to slide my size twelves into the driver's compartment. No such problem here. There's plenty of space. Ample leg room as well, and a very comfortable and supportive seat.

I can't imagine that very many motorists would undertake to hand-crank a 1935 Plymouth engine. Given the 6.70:1 compression ratio, that task would require a rather strong arm. Nevertheless, the Plymouth's grille is fitted with a removable crank-hole cover, "just in case."

Ventilation is facilitated by an intriguing feature. When cranks are turned for the front door windows, the glass slides back an inch or so before commencing its descent. This was evidently Chrysler's answer to General Motors' "Fisher No-Draft" ventilation system. It's not as effective as the GM arrangement, but it does quite effectively draw smoke out of the car. And if the driver is really into fresh air, the windshield can be cranked out, admitting more air than most of us need.

From the start, the Chrysler Corporation has prided itself on advanced engineering, and this Plymouth certainly serves to prove the point as far as the 1935 line was concerned. The aluminum pistons were fitted with four rings apiece; full-length water jackets were used; and full-pressure lubrication was featured (this, in marked contrast

"A New Picture of Car Value"

1935 Plymouth

to Chevrolet's splash system).

The clutch in our driveReport car, ventilated in the interest of longer life, is smooth. Plymouth claimed (rightly, I think) a 30 percent reduction in pedal pressure, compared to previous models. The "synchro-silent" transmission was brand new for 1935. Synchronization is very effective. Throws are noticeably longer than those of the 1934 gearbox, and action is more crisp and precise than I expected. "Floating Power" engine mounts virtually eliminate vibration; and horsepower was increased by about six percent over the previous model.

The Plymouth's acceleration won't send anybody to the chiropractor with whiplash, but for a car of its class and time, it is more than adequate. The engine in this car, which was carefully balanced during the restoration, sounds busy, yet it is smooth and not excessively noisy, even at highway speeds. Owners Bob and Sue Galloway report that they have cruised the car for considerable distances at 65 miles per hour with no sign of strain. This suggests to me that this unit must be fitted with the 3.7:1 axle ratio which was normally reserved for the business coupes, rather than the 4.125:1 gearing that was standard throughout the rest of the line.

Plymouth had offered independent front suspension in its Deluxe line during 1934, but for 1935 this system was abandoned in favor of semi-elliptic springs and a tubular front axle, similar to that employed by the Airflow DeSotos and Chryslers. Presumably this represented an economy move; and by 1939—doubtless under pressure from Chevrolet—Plymouth returned to IFS. But we found this car to have a surprisingly comfortable ride. A 1935 Plymouth sales brochure explains: "The great difference between higher price cars and

Top: Despite beam axle and semi-elliptic springs up front, Plymouth's cornering is exceptionally good. Center: Part of grille divider can be removed for crank insertion. Right: Hood treatment is pure art moderne. Facing page, top left: Quality materials enhance rumble seat area. Right: Spare cover has lock as well as "trap door" to access valve stem. Bottom: A classy-looking coupe by any measure.

those of lower price was always in the matter of the ride. Wheelbase was considered the explanation, but the fact was that the front springs, being short, were stiff. Plymouth has now produced the first short spring in automobile history that is soft and resilient, but long-lived. It is an utterly new design, and it required the use of a new spring steel." The brochure goes on to explain that "front end bounce is controlled by *double-acting* (emphasis theirs) shock absorbers on the front springs."

The Plymouth corners exceptionally well. Again, the sales brochure explains the reason: "Sidesway is eliminated by the use of a torsion spring at the front, which keeps the car level under all conditions," adding that "Even on straight driving you will be astonished by the feeling of "steadiness" provided by this great new development in riding comfort."

All of which sounds like what Dr. Cross, my old Economics professor, might have called a "puffing statement." But it seemed to me to be pretty close to the truth.

Steering is fairly precise, reasonably quick at three and a half turns lock-to-lock, and not unduly heavy by the standards of a time when power steering was no more than a pipe dream to most people (though, as recounted in *SIA* #49 to

Plymouth Versus The Competition
A Comparison of 1935's "Low-Priced Three"

	Plymouth Deluxe Six	Chevrolet Master Six	Ford Deluxe V-8
Price, coupe/rumble seat	$630	$600	$570
Wheelbase	113″	113″	112″
Shipping weight (lb.)	2,730	2,940	2,647
Engine c.i.d.	201.3	206.8	221.0
Horsepower @ rpm	82/3,600	80/3,300	85/3,800
Compression ratio	6.70:1	5.60:1	6.30:1
Valve configuration	L-head	OHV	L-head
Main bearings	4	3	3
Lubrication	Pressure	Splash/pressure	Pressure
Carburetor	Single downdraft	Single downdraft	Dual downdraft
Clutch diameter	9 1/4″	9″	9″
Final drive ratio	4.13:1	4.11	4.11:1
Steering	Worm/roller	Worm/roller	Worm/segment
Brakes	Hydraulic	Mechanical	Mechanical
Braking area (sq. in.)	158.5	170.2	186.0
Tire size	6.00/16	5.50/17	6.00/16
Indep. front suspension?	No	$20 extra	No
Horsepower/c.i.d.	.407	.387	.385
Weight (lbs.)/hp	33.3	36.8	31.1
Weight/c.i.d.	13.6	14.2	12.0
Stroke/bore ratio	1.40:1	1.21:1	1.22:1

illustrations by Russell von Sauers, The Graphic Automobile Studio

specifications

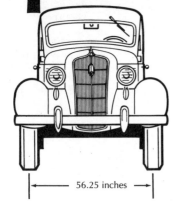
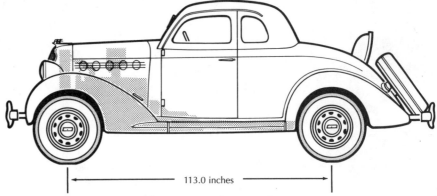

56.25 inches

113.0 inches

1935 Plymouth Deluxe

Price	$630 f.o.b. factory
Mandatory factory equipment	Front and rear bumpers, spare tire and tube, metal spare tire cover ($33 extra was charged). All Deluxe Plymouths also carried the clipper ship radiator ornament, for which a $3.50 additional charge was made.
Standard equipment	Single windshield wiper, single interior sun visor, single taillamp
Options on dR car	White sidewall tires, bumper guards, spare tire lock; Duplate safety glass in all windows, after-market exhaust extension

ENGINE

Type	6-cylinder, L-head, in-line
Bore x stroke	3.125 inches x 4.375 inches
Displacement	201.3 cubic inches
Compression ratio	6.70:1
Horsepower @ rpm	82 @ 3,600
Taxable horsepower	23.44
Valve lifters	Mechanical
Main bearings	4
Fuel system	Ball & Ball 1.25-inch single downdraft carburetor, camshaft pump
Lubrication system	Pressure to main, connecting rod and camshaft bearings and timing chain
Cooling system	Centrifugal pump; full-length water jackets
Exhaust system	Single
Electrical system	6-volt battery/coil

TRANSMISSION

Type	3-speed selective, floor lever, synchronized 2nd and 3rd speeds

Ratios:	1st	2.57:1
	2nd	1.55:1
	3rd	1.00:1
	Reverse	3.48:1

CLUTCH

Type	Single dry plate
Outside diameter	9.25 inches
Actuation	Mechanical, foot pedal

DIFFERENTIAL

Type	Spiral bevel
Ratio	3.70:1
Drive axles	Semi-floating
Torque medium	Springs

STEERING

Type	Gemmer worm-and-roller
Turns lock-to-lock	3.5
Ratio	18.2:1
Turning diameter	36 feet 7 inches

BRAKES

Type	Lockheed 4-wheel internal hydraulic
Drum diameter	10 inches
Effective area	158.5 square inches

CHASSIS & BODY

Construction	Body-on-frame
Frame	Rigid-X double drop with box section channels
Body construction	All steel
Body style	2/4 passenger coupe

SUSPENSION

Front	Tubular axle, 37.25-inch x 1.75-inch semi-elliptic 9-leaf springs; sway eliminator
Rear	Rigid axle, 53.375-inch x 1.75-inch semi-elliptic 9-leaf springs
Shock absorbers	Double-acting
Tires	6.00/16 4-ply
Wheels	Pressed steel

WEIGHTS AND MEASURES

Wheelbase	113 inches
Overall length	189.625 inches
Overall width	68.5 inches
Overall height	68.5 inches
Front track	56.25 inches
Rear track	58 inches
Min. road clearance	8.25 inches
Shipping weight	2,730 pounds
Weight distribution, f/r	49%/51%

CAPACITIES

Crankcase	5 quarts
Cooling system	15 quarts
Fuel tank	15 gallons
Transmission	2.5 pounds
Differential	3.25 pounds

CALCULATED DATA

Stroke/bore ratio	1.40:1
Engine revs per mile	3,086
Horsepower per c.i.d.	.407
Weight per hp	33.3 pounds
Weight per c.i.d.	13.6 pounds
Weight/sq. in. (brakes)	17.2 pounds

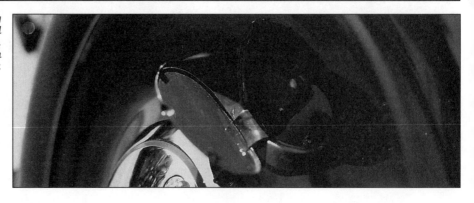

Right: Spare cover allows easy tire pressure checking, provided you've put the cover on precisely. **Facing page:** Woodgrained dash adds warmth to interior.

1935 Plymouth

Pierce-Arrow engineer Francis W. Davis, it was already a reality.)

The hydraulic brakes are very good, better than the binders on many 1935 automobiles selling at several times the Plymouth's price, and certainly far superior to the mechanical brakes that were still retained by both Ford and Chevrolet as well as Hudson's low-priced Terraplane and Nash's LaFayette.

The instrument panel layout is functional, legible, and very attractive. Directly in front of the driver are two large circular glass panes. Behind one of these is an instrument layout consisting of ammeter, oil pressure, temperature and fuel gauges; while the other houses the speedometer/odometer. All controls come easily to hand.

Plymouths came in two trim levels as far as the American market was concerned. The base series, known as the Business Six, was offered as a two-passenger coupe as well as two- and four-door sedans. In addition, two commercial units were built on this chassis. These were a Commercial Sedan (think of it as a Sedan Delivery, except that unlike most such units, this one had a removable rear seat) and a seven/eight-passenger Westchester Suburban ("Woody") station wagon, fitted with a body by the US Body & Forging Co., of Tell City, Indiana.

The Business models were "plain Jane" cars, fitted with black fenders (regardless of body color), black painted grilles, painted rather than chromed headlamp shells, and 5.25/17 tires.

But the bulk of Plymouth's customers opted for the Deluxe line, which encompassed nine body types including two on a stretched (128-inch) wheelbase. Also a member of this series was the rumble seat coupe illustrated here, as well as a dashing convertible. But the most popular of the lot was the touring sedan, featuring a built-in trunk, a relatively novel feature at that time. 6.00/16 tires were supplied with these cars.

A third series, known simply as the Plymouth Six, was assembled in Canada and intended primarily for the Canadian market. Consisting of just three body styles, it was priced only slightly lower than the Deluxe cars. Production was limited (see sidebar, this page.)

The Deluxe cars came with Duplate safety glass windshields, but those who wanted shatterproof glass throughout the car (as most buyers apparently did) had to pay extra for it. All Deluxe cars left the factory with a "mandatory option" package consisting of front and rear bumpers, spare tire and tube and metal spare tire cover (except on the trunk-back "touring"

models). For this, an extra $33.00 was charged. In addition, all of the Deluxe cars came with the clipper ship radiator ornament, for which $3.50 was added to the price tag. (This "padding" practice was common throughout the automobile industry during the 1930s, presumably in order to keep the advertised price as low as possible.)

Even with these "mandatory options" included, the 1935 Plymouths (along with their competitors) came rather

sparsely equipped. For instance, only one windshield wiper, one inside sun visor and one taillamp were supplied. Dual equipment was available, but it cost extra. And of course neither radio nor heater came with the advertised price. The reader will observe that our driveReport car carries none of these optional items. The absence of "extras" was actually quite typical during the 1930s, for times were still pretty tough in those days.

1935 Plymouth Prices, Weights and Production

	Price	Weight	Production
PJ Business Six, 113-inch wheelbase			
Business coupe, 2-passenger	$510	2,635 lb.	16,691
Sedan, 2-door, 5-passenger	$535	2,680 lb.	29,942
Sedan, 4-door, 5-passenger	$570	2,720 lb.	15,761
Commercial sedan, 1-passenger	$635	2,735 lb.	1,142
Westchester Suburban (wagon)	$765	n/a	119
Total Production, PJ Business Six			63,655
PJ Plymouth Six, 113-inch wheelbase			
Business coupe, 2-passenger	$565	2,665 lb.	6,664
Sedan, 2-door, 5-passenger	$615	2,670 lb.	7,284
Total Production, Plymouth Six			13,946
PJ Deluxe Six, 113-inch wheelbase			
Business coupe, 2-passenger	$575	2,685 lb.	29,190
RS coupe 2/4 passenger	$630	2,730 lb.	12,118
Convertible coupe, 2/4 passenger	$695	2,810 lb.	2,308
Sedan, 2-door, 5-passenger	$625	2,730 lb.	12,424
Touring sedan, 2-door, 5-pass.	$650	2,790 lb.	45.203
Sedan, 4-door, 5 passenger	$660	2,790 lb.	66,083
Touring sedan, 4-door, 5-pass.	$685	2,834 lb.	82,068
Total Production, PJ Deluxe, Standard w/b			249,394
PJ Deluxe Six, 128-inch wheelbase			
Sedan, 7-passenger	$895	3,130 lb.	350
Traveler sedan, 5-pass.	N/a	N/a	77
Total Production, PJ Deluxe, LWB:			427
Chassis (all PJ sub-series)	N/a	N/a	2,680
Grand total, 1935 model year production:			330,104

*Above: Doors have plated hardware and pulls but no armrests. **Facing page, above:** Rear window cranks down for even more fresh air as well as conversation with rumble seat passengers. **Bottom:** Driver's provided with complete set of gauges.*

1935 Plymouth

This particular car was delivered by a Berkeley, California, dealer to a medical secretary named Ruth Reed. It served as Ruth's daily driver for thirty years, covering some 157,000 miles over that period of time. At that point, Miss Reed purchased a two-year-old Buick; but instead of disposing of the Plymouth, she kept it, possibly out of sentiment, and "exercised" it occasionally until illness forced her to give up driving.

Miss Reed continued working well beyond retirement age, but in 1986 she was diagnosed with a brain tumor. Bob Galloway, husband of Ruth's niece, Sue, had for years expressed an interest in the Plymouth; so with the end of her life approaching, Ruth gave the car to Bob. She died not long thereafter, at the age of 82.

A complete restoration was required, for the Plymouth was, in Bob Galloway's words, "pretty rough." The work got under way during 1988. The engine was re-bored .040 over, meticulously rebuilt and carefully balanced by Ernie's Machine Shop, in the Galloways' home town of Martinez, California. Bob asked the machinist whether hardened valve seats should be fitted, in order for the engine to cope with unleaded gas. The machinist replied that this would not be necessary, for the block was actually harder than any new valve seats that he might install.

A body-off cosmetic restoration was undertaken by Auto Europa, another Martinez shop. The red finish is a little lighter than the original maroon. Wood-graining was done by Craig Clemons, a well-known Oakland artisan, and new upholstery was fitted by Ken Nemanic, of Vintage Automotive Upholstery in Walnut Creek. In each instance, the workmanship is flawless. And as a finishing touch, Bob Galloway found a set of 1935 license plates at a Pleasanton swap meet.

It's a beautiful car. Only occasionally, during the 70-year history of the marque, has Plymouth been noted for outstanding styling; but this 1935 coupe, reportedly designed by Phil Wright, working under the supervision of Ralph Reed at Briggs Body, is stunning, from its tall, narrow grille to its gracefully tapered rear.

The restoration having been completed, in 1996 Bob and Sue Galloway took "Aunt Ruthie's" best friend for a ride. It had been in Ruth's car that this lady had learned to drive, back in 1936. (Incidentally, she was so impressed with it that she bought a new Plymouth coupe for herself.) The lady's reaction to the restoration is worth sharing: "Ruthie would be delighted to see her car in such beautiful condition. But she would turn over in her grave if she knew how much money you spent on it!"

And then the Galloways took the Plymouth on the show circuit, where it has done exceedingly well for itself:

• Silverado Concours d'Elegance, 1996: First in class.
• Lafayette Concours d'Elegance, 1996: First in class.
• California Chrysler Products Club Meet, 1996: President's Choice.
• Greater Valley Concours d'Elegance, Fresno, 1997: First in class.
• Santa Rosa Concours d'Elegance, 1997: First in class.
• California Chrysler Products Club

1935

Nineteen thirty-five: Was there ever such a year for the motion picture industry? Greta Garbo starred in *Anna Karenina*, and Fred Astaire and Ginger Rogers found new popularity in *Top Hat*. (I loved that one when it was new, and enjoyed it even more, nearly ten years later when I was serving with the Navy on a remote island in the Philippines.) Then there was *Mutiny on the Bounty*, with Charles Laughton, Clark Gable and Franchot Tone. And *Les Miserables*: Charles Laughton again, along with Fredric March and Sir Cedric Hardwicke. And then Laughton again, this time playing the lead in *Ruggles of Red Gap*, backed up by Mary Boland and Charlie Ruggles.

There was more. Shirley Temple won our hearts in *Curly Top*, while Eleanor Powell danced her way to stardom in *Broadway Melody of 1936*, co-starring, of all people, Jack Benny. The Marx Brothers gave us *A Night at the Opera*, with Alan Jones in the role of straight man, singing the lovely "Alone." And Bette Davis starred in *Dangerous*. But when it came to bringing a classic novel to life, few films have ever matched the 1935 production of Charles Dickens's *David Copperfield*, with an enormous, all-star cast that included Lionel Barrymore, Basil Rathbone, Freddie Bartholomew, Alison Skipworth, Edna Mae Oliver, W. C. Fields and Oliver Hardy. One of the remarkable things about this excellent film was the opportunity to see two of the nation's top comedians — Fields and Hardy — in dramatic, rather than comedy roles. Both performed magnificently.

It was a great year for popular music as well, with all of us enjoying such songs as Irving Berlin's "Cheek to Cheek" and "Isn't This a Lovely Day" (both from *Top Hat*); Cole Porter's "Just One of Those Things"; Jerome Kern's "Lovely to Look At"; Noel Coward's "Mad About the Boy" and Harry Warren's "Lullaby of Broadway" — to name but a few. And of course, 1935 was the year that George Gershwin's great folk opera, *Porgy and Bess* was first produced.

Then there was the automobile industry. It would be difficult to find a five-year period in which the family car underwent more improvements than those which took place between 1930 and 1935. High-compression engines came into general use even among inexpensive machines, and most cars could cruise comfortably at sixty miles an hour, up from about forty-five, half a decade earlier; and to match the higher speeds, hydraulic brakes were increasingly popular. General Motors pioneered both independent front suspension and the seamless steel "turret" top. Nearly all transmissions featured clash-free "synchro-mesh," a blessing to those many motorists who, like my parents, never quite mastered the art of double-clutching.

Recovery from the Depression was still incomplete to say the least; but seemingly hard times had only served to spur the industry on to better and better products.

And to those of us who were young then, 1935 was, as ol' Blue-Eyes used to say, "A Very Good Year."

Meet, 1997: First in class.
- Ironstone Harvest Concours, Murphys, CA, 1997: First in class.
- Lafayette Concours d'Elegance, 1997: Second in class.
- Greater Valley Concours d'Elegance, Fresno, 1998: First in class.
- Shriners Hospital Concours d'Elegance, Folsom, CA, 1998: First in class and David R. Beeman Memorial Award.
- Chico Concours d'Elegance, 1998: Second in class.
- 70th Anniversary Plymouth Club National Meet, Plymouth, MI, 1998: Second in class.

In short, what we have here is an outstanding example of what was, in its own time, a highly advanced automobile, well engineered, beautifully styled and sturdily built. It served its original owner for many years, covering a lot of miles along the way. And now it has commenced a successful new career in the hands of its proud second owners.

Did the 1935 Plymouth live up to its billing as "A New Picture of Car Value"? We'll let the reader be the judge. But with a base price of $630, it appears to this writer to have been an outstanding buy—even though it cost a few dollars more than its closest competitors. ✍

Acknowledgments and Bibliography

Automobile Trade Journal, *March 1935;* Automotive Industries, *February 23, 1935; Don Butler,* The Plymouth and DeSoto Story; *Richard M. Langworth and Jan P. Norbye,* Complete History of Chrysler; *Motor, January 1935; Plymouth factory literature.*

Our thanks to Dave Brown, Durham, California; Bud Juneau, Brentwood, California. Special thanks to Bob and Sue Galloway, Martinez, California.

1939
PLYMOUTH

Originally published in Special Interest Autos #22, May-June 1974

Plymouth's first power top worked by vacuum.

DON'T FORGET Plymouth's fantastic Depression sales success. It's almost beyond explaining that Plymouth could tap Buick on the shoulder in 1931 and so easily become one of the Big 3. Plymouth was barely 3-1/2 years old at the time.

If you're still not impressed, think of the hordes of long-established cars killed off by the Depression. Then consider the late-comers like Ruxton, DeVaux, the Cord L-29, Continental, etc., that were born just before or during the Depression. Finally, think about the low-priced offspring of established makes—Studebaker's Erskine and Rockne, Buick's Marquette, and Nash's LaFayette. These makes could reasonably have expected to do as well as the Plymouth, but they certainly didn't.

So what happened? Why did Plymouth succeed so well and the others fail so miserably? We have no answer, but the fact remains that Plymouth held #3 without interruption for 23 years, 1931-54, and again 1957-59 and in 1970.

In 1939, which is the year we'll concentrate on here, you got pretty much the same car whether you bought a new Plymouth, a new Dodge, De Soto, or Chrysler. Chrysler Corp. had been moving toward standardization of bodies and powertrains early in the Depression, and at possibly a little faster rate than General Motors.

We tend to forget that the U.S. had only two big multi-make auto producers during the 1930s. These were GM and Chrysler. Ford wouldn't join until the 1939 Mercury. And Auburn-Cord-Duesenberg can't be considered in the same league (besides, A-C-D cars were so different, one from the other, that they couldn't have indulged much in component interchangeability, even if they'd wanted to).

The big year for standardization was 1937. That's when GM went to its A-B-C body program for its six lines—and Chrysler settled on one basic body for all four of its nameplates. Chrysler Corp. went a lot further than GM in standardizing not only bodies but engines, transmissions, chassis, suspension systems, etc. Engine swappers soon learned that any flathead 6 from any 1933-59 Mopar product slipped easily into any other—

that you could put a 1959 Dodge or Plymouth 6 into a 1933 Plymouth or vice versa.

Standardization had to come, and it came for two basic reasons: 1) the Depression, which pushed new-car prices down to $500-$600 for the Low-Priced 3, and 2) the need for high-volume mass production so the automakers could turn profits at those low prices. The more identical cars a manufacturer could produce, the cheaper each one became.

Ford Motor Co., being essentially a one-make car company, already had its standardization built in. The millions upon millions of Ford V-8s built between 1932 and 1949 were all basically alike in everything except body. And when Mercury came along in 1939, it, too, shared nearly everything except bodies with Ford (and between 1941 and 1948 Merc shared even those). As for Lincoln, its pre-Zephyr losses didn't much affect overall company economics, nor did Lincoln's post-Zephyr profits.

General Motors, on the other hand, built six major car lines during the Depression: Chevrolet, Pontiac, Oldsmobile, Buick, La Salle, and Cadillac. (We're ignoring GM's short-lived companion makes.) During the Depression's bottom, 1932-34, when decisions toward standardization had to be made, only Chevrolet was selling in anything like volume. Buick and Olds were barely squeak-

ing through, and Pontiac, Cadillac, and La Salle were doing so poorly that there was serious talk of dropping them.

As a compromise and to increase production volume per component, GM decided to launch its A-B-C body program. Pontiac and Chevy had already been sharing sheet metal stampings, as had Olds, Buick, and Cad (plus independent front suspension parts, transmissions, chassis components, etc.), but in 1937 the idea of sharing entire bodies went into effect. Chevrolet and Pontiac then shared the A-body; Olds, Buick, and La Salle shared the B; and Cadillac had the C. Later (1940, for instance), everyone but Chevy shared the B-body, and the big Buicks, La Salle, and Cadillac shared the C. In 1941, even Pontiac used the C.)

Yet, each GM nameplate, except in rare instances, had its own engines, and GM's engines were quite different, one from the other, as were most drivetrain components.

Meanwhile Chrysler Corp. was carrying out its own standardization program, and from the evidence it's obvious that Chrysler had the canniest engineers of all. We've talked about that great engineering triumvirate, the Three Musketeers—Skelton, Breer, and Zeder—so no need to give their biographies again (see 1934 Chrysler Airflow driveReport, *SIA* #16). These men, along with Walter P. Chrysler himself, company presi-

Vacuum top whooshes up and down with amazing speed, folds flat in its shallow well behind seat.

This Plymouth's owner/restorer, Bert McMillan, illustrates that narrow rumbleseat makes a cozy fit for two. In front of him, central top-locking handle serves all latches on windshield header.

The year 1939 marked the height of the "prow-nose" front end. Below is a quarter-scale clay proposed for the 1939 Plymouth by the Briggs Mfg. Co. Briggs, of course, built Plymouth bodies. Chrysler Corp. had standardized its bodies for all lines beginning with the 1937 model and had made them interchangeable between Plymouth, Dodge, De Soto, Chrysler, and Imperial. Year-to-year differences lay mostly in front ends.

Major Mopar change for '39 was new fastback sedan roof. Cars kept 1937 lower panels. Front ensemble proposal above emanated from Ray Dietrich's tiny Chrysler design staff. Note Merc-like model on shelf.

Plymouth's Mayflower appears 10 times on the car.

Here's another Mayflower. Two more appear in the taillight lenses.

Except for rear doors and floor lengths, all 1937-39 Mopar bodies interchanged. Briggs delivered Plymouth bodies to main assembly plant.

24

Engine access is hampered by bolt-on hood sides. Plymouth offered this long-lived 6 in three stages of tune for '49—65, 82 and 86 bhp.

1939 Plymouth Shipments & Prices

	Calendar year prod'n.	Model year prod'n.	Price f.o.b. Detroit
Road King (P-7) series			
Standard coupe	18,885	21,567	$645
Standard 2-dr sedan	4,373	6,590	685
2-dr. trunk sedan	35,695	41,255	699
Standard 4-dr sedan	1,192	1,680	726
4-dr. trunk sedan	11,613	16,998	740
Panel delivery sedan	438	2,099	N/A
Utility sedan	438	340	685
Bare chassis	5	17	N/A
DeLuxe (P-8) series			
Standard coupe	34,512	41,055	$725
Rumbleseat coupe	4,973	1,194	755
Convertible coupe	6,396	5,807	895
Standard 2-dr. sedan	1,379	2,170	761
2-dr. trunk sedan	70,168	79,361	775
Standard 4-dr. sedan	1,179	1,745	791
4-dr. trunk sedan	143,109	161,632	805
7-pass. sed. & limo	520	608	1005*
Station wagon	2,229	1,679	930
Convertible sedan	314	352	1,150
Utility sedan	13	13	N/A

Notes: Model year ran 8/1/38 through 7/31/39. **Source:** Chrysler Historical Collection, courtesy John Bunnell. Asterisk (*) denotes that 7-pass. limo sold for $1,095. Prices courtesy J. Ross Moore insurance figures.

One of Plymouth's big 1939 features was column shift, which we found to work well in Bert McMillan's convertible. Another talking point was the safety dash design—no projections and speedo warning lights.

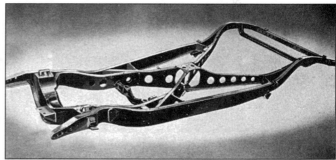

Beefy X-member frame with deep siderails and twin kickups provides more than enough torsional strength for Plymouth's convertible body.

dent K.T. Keller, chief body engineer O.H. Clark, and experimental engineer A.G. Herreshoff, spearheaded the move toward standardization.

During the early Depression, Carl Breer and O.H. Clark had tried to introduce standardization of a slightly different sort. They standardized body dies—for instance in the 1934 Airflow—so that the same basic die could, with minor alterations, serve for making a sedan's left front door as well as the right rear one. Similarly, front fender dies got minor changes to become rear fender dies. This saved some money in a car's development, but it proved a weak effort when compared with complete body interchangeability. After it became clear to Chrysler management that dual-purpose dies meant only modest savings, the company decided to concentrate on one body that could serve all four of its car lines.

Before the 1935 models, MoPar's production bodies had been designed mostly by Breer, Clark, and their engineers. They got some help, particularly in ornamentation, from the company's fledgling Art & Colour section. Raymond H. Dietrich, the famous designer/coachbuilder, had been hired in 1932 by Walter Chrysler to create a strong styling group within the corporation. Before that could happen, though, the Briggs Mfg. Co. (see *SIA* #19) had a hand in Chrysler

CHRYSLER HISTORICAL COLLECTION

Corp. styling. The corporation's 1935-36 models were, in fact. strongly influenced by Briggs' styling staff. Says A.B. (Buzz) Grisinger, who became a charter member of Chrysler's Art & Colour section in 1932, "Actually, according to the older engineers, the 1935-36 Briggs body wasn't a well engineered body, and they had a lot of problems with it. After that, the Chrysler engineering group had control again and designed the 1937-and-later bodies under Ray Dietrich's supervision."

It's the 1937 body that marked Chrysler Corp.'s first across-the-board standardization. That same body served all four lines (Plymouth, Dodge, De Soto, and Chrysler) for three years, through 1939, for a total, sustained run of nearly two million units.

The Plymouth bodies were all built by Briggs, and so were many for the other lines. The main body section was virtually identical in all these cars, the main differences being in floor and door lengths. Except for rear-seat leg room, if you were sitting in a 1937-39 Plymouth, you were also sitting inside a 1937-39 Dodge, De Soto, and Chrysler body.

Thanks to clever styling, though, each year, each model, and each car line had a different "face." The 1939 Plymouth's face was entirely unlike the '38's.

For 1939, Plymouth got what's called a "prow nose"—sort of a boattail effect up front. All 1939 Chrysler products shared that same basic prow effect, but they used it just that one year. 1939 might be called year of the prow, because Ford had it, as did Chevrolet, Pontiac, Cadillac, Graham, Studebaker, Hudson, Nash, and many other makes. The prow, combined with in-fender headlamps, derived from the 1936 Lincoln Zephyr and a design created by Bob Koto of Briggs. Ford adapted it for 1937, and by 1939 it peaked as an industry-wide trend. In that pre-Sealed Beam year, headlights took on imaginative shapes—rectangles, teardrops, squares, etc.

Ray Dietrich headed Chrysler Corp.'s exterior design department from 1932 through late 1938, so he oversaw the 1937-39 bodies. Dietrich reported to O.H. Clark, Chrysler's chief body engineer. It's hard to fathom that before the war, Chrysler Corp.'s entire design staff, including clay modelers and draftsmen, numbered no more than 26 people. Today, of course, each corporation might have 1,000 or more. But the nucleus that created the prow nose for all 1939 Mopar lines (plus trucks) numbered exactly seven: Dietrich, Buzz Grisinger, Herb Weissinger, Rhys Miller, and Ed Sheard on exteriors; Tom Martin and Henry King on interiors.

At that time, with the basic body remaining the same from year to year and car to car, the trick was to restyle the front-end ensembles. The 1939 Plymouth's prow nose meant a 10-inch-longer hood than the 1938 model. The new V'd windshield added 6.25 inches to the passenger compartment length. And with a new roof and rear deck stampings, the "fastback" 1939 Mopar sedans in all lines took on an entirely different look. In these, though, the lower doors, cowls, inner fenders, etc., were all identical to 1937-38 models—only the uppers were changed.

The car we borrowed for this driveReport belongs to Bert McMillan, an insurance appraiser who also owns a car rental company. Bert lives in Stockton, and *SIA* has watched the Plymouth's restoration for some months. Bert discovered the car in Merced in 1972. The odometer said 41,000, and although the car looked pretty shabby, 41,000 seemed to be the first time around. Bert did everything but upholstery and chroming himself:

This was Plymouth's first year for two important features—column gearshift and power (vacuum) top on the convertible coupe. In addition,

55-mph limit puts the Plymouth at its ideal cruising speed—the engine gets a little busy above that. Rectangular headlights preceded Sealed Beams.

Front quarter panes bolt on with special brackets, cut drafts even with top down. Hood ornament helps center car in lane. Bert's convertible's black lacquer finish shows how ripple-free body is. Bert painted it.

Red leather seatbacks tilt forward to reveal spare tire and storage shelves for tools and small cargo. Leatherette curtains hide area, but it's easy to get at when you need to.

specifications

 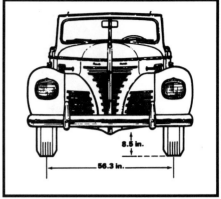

1939 Plymouth P-8 DeLuxe convertible

Price when new	$895 f.o.b. Detroit (1939).	**DIFFERENTIAL**		Tires	6.00 x 16, 4-ply whitewalls.
Options	Pushbutton radio, leather upholstery, whitewalls, spotlight.	Type	Hypoid.	Wheels	Pressed steel discs, drop-center rims, lug-bolted to brake drums.
		Ratio	4.10:1.		
		Drive axles	Semi-floating.		

ENGINE

Type	L-head, in-line 6, water-cooled, cast-iron block, 4 mains, pressure & splash lubrication.
Bore & stroke	3.125 x 4.375 in.
Displacement	201.3 c.i.d.
Max. bhp @ rpm	82 @ 3,600.
Max. torque @ rpm	146 @ 1,200.
Compression ratio	6.7:1 (7.0:1 opt.).
Induction system	Single 1-bbl. downdraft carburetor, mechanical fuel pump.
Exhaust system	Cast-iron manifold, single muffler.
Electrical system	6-volt battery/coil.

CLUTCH

Type	Single dry plate, molded & woven asbestos lining.
Diameter	8.25 in.
Actuation	Mechanical, foot pedal.

TRANSMISSION

Type	3-speed manual, column lever, synchro 2-3.
Ratios 1st	2.57:1.
2nd	1.55:1.
3rd	1.00:1.
Reverse	3.48:1

STEERING

Type	Worm & roller.
Turns, lock to lock	4.25.
Ratio	18.2:1.
Turn circle	38.1 ft.

BRAKES

Type	4-wheel hydraulic drums, internal expanding.
Drum diameter	10.0 in.
Total lining area	144.0 sq. in.

CHASSIS & BODY

Frame	U-section steel, central X-member, 4 crossmembers.
Body construction	All steel.
Body style	2-door, 4-passenger convertible coupe with rumbleseat.

SUSPENSION

Front	Independent A-arms, coil springs, tubular hydraulic shocks.
Rear	Solid axle, semi-elliptic longitudinal springs, tubular hydraulic shocks.

WEIGHTS & MEASURES

Wheelbase	114.0 in.
Overall length	194.25 in.
Overall height	65.7 in.
Overall width	73.5 in.
Front tread	56.3125 in.
Rear tread	59.9375 in.
Ground clearance	8.5 in.
Curb weight	3,044 lb.

CAPACITIES

Crankcase	5 qt.
Cooling system	14 qt.
Fuel tank	18 gal.

FUEL CONSUMPTION

Best	18-21 mpg.
Average	15-17 mpg.

PERFORMANCE (from factory proving-grounds data):

10-60 mph	11.6 sec.
Top speed (av)	80 mph.

1939 was the only year Plymouth used a 114-inch wheelbase and the last year for this particular body style. In 1939, Plymouth revived the convertible sedan, and since Chevrolet had no convertibles at all that year, people who traditionally bought open body styles in the low-price field had to choose between Plymouth and Ford.

We were very impressed with the Plymouth's general feel, its silence and smoothness, and its very spunky performance. The starter—a rather long pedal near the accelerator—takes some foot contortion, but the gearshift shifts very well and without the sloppiness of most early column levers. So often the rubber grommets deteriorate, but Bert must have just replaced his, so shifting felt fine.

The car accelerates quickly and cruises easily at 55 mph, which seems its comfortable limit. Above that we felt we were pulling too many revs.

The instruments—all working gauges—stand in a rectangular cluster in front of the wheel. The speedometer needle rotates in a round Lucite disc, and in this disc there's a little clear plastic dot. It's implanted in the shank of the needle. At night, with the dash panel lighted, different-colored lights shine through the plastic dot—green up to 30 mph, amber between 30 and 50, and red above 50. Kitsch, granted, but cute nonetheless.

The vacuum top is something to see. It's very fast going up or down, and it leaps into action with a whoosh. Built-in quarter panes, plus the rather tall windshield, keep front riders from hair tussling, but there's a constant gale for rumbleseaters.

We didn't get a chance to corner this car except in normal driving, so we can't tell how it feels under stress. Going down the road, though, and even in parking, it steers with a light touch, seems alert and responsive to the slightest correction, certainly doesn't wander or need constant watching, and the relationship of wheel to seat is great. The seat adjusts for rake, and as it moves forward, it automatically also rises. That's a boon for short drivers.

In addition to the 82-bhp engine that came standard in both Road King and DeLuxe series (Road King was the cheaper, but except for details, all 1939 Plymouths were identical), there was an "economy" version of the 6 with 5.2:1 compression and 65 bhp. This engine saw duty in countries with low-octane gasoline. Then there was also a high-compression version of the same engine that rated 86 bhp at 3,600. Bert's car used the standard 82-bhp 6.

Bert's convertible gives ample testimony toward explaining why Plymouth hung onto third so long and so easily. If the year were 1939 and if, as Mr. Chrysler had suggested in 1932, we "tried all three," we could well imagine settling on Plymouth, especially a black convertible with red leather upholstery. 👓

Our thanks to Bert McMillan, Stockton, California; Raymond H. Dietrich, Albuquerque, New Mexico; A.B. Grisinger, Mission Viejo. California; Holden Koto, Boynton Beach, Florida; John Bunnell and Don Butler, Chrysler Corp., Detroit; members of the WPC Club, 17916 Trenton Dr., Castro Valley, CA 94546; W.A.C. Pettit III, Louisa, Virginia; Rhys Miller, Walnut Creek, California, Strother MacMinn, Pasadena, California, and Burt Weaver, Oakland, California.

Strong, Simple And All Steel

The wonder of it, really, is that somebody didn't think of it years earlier. Here was a plain, practical little utility automobile that made no pretense of being anything other than what it was: a steel-bodied, two-door station wagon. No fancy stuff; no wood; no imitation wood, either. Just a trim little box on wheels.

Plymouth, in introducing the new model in June 1949, touted it as "the industry's first all-steel station wagon. It wasn't, of course (see sidebar, p. 33); but no matter. The Plymouth Suburban was the car that opened a whole new chapter in the saga of the station wagon, and a whole new market as well.

For the "Big Three" manufacturers, the 1949 cars were the first real postwar models. Until then, they had been serving up warmed-over 1942 cars—and selling them as fast as they could turn them out. Most of the independents, Nash excepted, had introduced new models well ahead of their larger rivals. Then came Ford, displaying its 1949 models in mid-1948, followed by General Motors a few months later.

Chrysler was tardy. The corporation announced 1949 models on December 1, 1948, all right; but they were the same old cars. Only their registration served to differentiate them from the '48s. The real 1949 models came along later, commencing in March, and at least one body style was introduced as late as the following July.

"The Great New Plymouth," as it was billed, was built—for the first time since 1934 (apart from a handful of seven-passenger jobs)—on two distinct wheelbases. That of the larger car, designated the P18, measured 118.5 inches, while the smaller P17 spanned 111 inches. Compared to the P15 series of 1946-48,

1949 PLYMOUTH SUBURBAN

By Arch Brown
Photos by William Bailey

the P18 was shorter overall, despite a 1.5-inch increase in the wheelbase, and narrower as well. Nevertheless, it afforded more interior room in every dimension than its predecessor. Reflecting the thinking of Chrysler president K.T. Keller, the new Plymouth's styling was conservative, even boxy—but practical. But as Don Butler has said, "The new practicality was of good sense and purpose, but it did not allow an attractive image.... Alongside their competitors, the cars appeared stubby on each end, and too high and narrow."

Most critics agreed, and the public's reaction was mixed at best. Yet the car sold well. Plymouth scored a 47.5 percent production increase for 1949, compared with a 31 percent boost for the industry as a whole. If that was a vote of confidence on the part of the motoring public, Plymouth deserved it, for the '49 model was an excellent automobile.

Improvements, on what had already been a very good car, were everywhere to be seen. The windshield area, 37 percent larger than before, was swept by wipers that cleaned 61.5 percent more surface. A small increase in weight, a longer wheelbase and diagonally mounted shock absorbers combined to give the Plymouth a smoother ride than ever before. A new, fresh-air heater, evidently patterned after Nash's excellent "Weather Eye," kept the occupants warm and comfortable. Redesigned oil rings and chrome-plated top piston rings provided better oil control, while a new intake manifold made possible quicker warmups and faster throttle response. And thanks to a slight boost in the compression ratio, horsepower was up from 95 to 97.

The P18 was available in two trim levels. Deluxe and Special Deluxe. (By that time everyone but Ford had evidently concluded that the public didn't cotton to anything that bore the label "Standard"!) Sedans and club coupes were available in both models, while the convertibles and hardwood-bodied station wagons were confined to the Special Deluxe.

The shorter P17, also bearing the Deluxe label, came in three body styles, one of which—our driveReport subject—turned out to be a genuine "sleeper." There had been a good deal of speculation in the trade journals when it had become known that Plymouth was planning to introduce a smaller car. Leonard Westrate, writing in the February 1, 1949, issue of *Automotive Industries*, noted that while prices had not yet been revealed, "the implication in both size and general appointments is inescapable that it is slanted directly to a

 Originally published in Special Interest Autos #72, Nov.-Dec. 1982

Price and Production Table
1949 Plymouth (second series)

Body Style	P-17 Deluxe (111″ wheelbase) Price	Production	P-18 Deluxe (118.5″ wheelbase) Price	Production	P-18 Special Deluxe (118.5″ wheelbase) Price	Production
Sedan, 4-door			$1,551	61,021	$1,629	252,858
Club coupe			$1,519	25,687	$1,603	99,680
Sedan, 2-door	$1,492	28,516				
Business coupe	$1,371	13,715				
Convertible coupe					$1,982	15,240
Station wagon, 4-door					$2,372	3,443
Suburban, 2-door	$1,840	19,220				

(Prices include federal excise tax)

Source: *Don Butler, The Plymouth and De Soto Story*

Right: Few wagons today offer the straightforward loading ease of the Suburban. Fundamental drop-down tailgate gives increased capacity for long loads. Below: Body styling may not win awards for elegance, but squared-off design fits the concept of a station wagon perfectly. Bottom: More simplicity. Sliding windows instead of roll-downs for back-seat ventilation.

new, low price market.... [The P17 is] aimed at capturing the buyer who feels he has been forced out of the higher price markets."

Not so! When announcement time came, the P17 was actually priced about $70 higher than the base Ford or Chevrolet, and only $27 less than Plymouth's P18 Deluxe, whose mechanical components it shared. There were three body styles, including a smart little business coupe and a fastback two-door sedan, which showed the influence of Chevrolet's popular Fleetline model. The latter was the most popular of the trio, even outselling the P18 Deluxe club coup—though with its price so nearly identical to that of the smaller car, the latter appears to have been a much better value.

But it was the third body style that was the truly significant one. Plymouth had seized the initiative by introducing a new kind of utility car, a thoroughly non-traditional variation on the station wagon theme, the Suburban. In the process they undercut by several hundred dollars the price of every other station wagon on the market, save only the Willys. Plymouth continued to build an eight-passenger "woody" in the Special Deluxe series, but it was priced at $532 (which is to say 28 percent) higher than the Suburban. The little newcomer outsold the traditional wagon by a ratio of six to one!

The woody was typical of the station wagons of the forties in that the rear seats had to be unbolted and removed in order to take advantage of the space for hauling purposes. It was a cumbersome task. The Suburban changed all that. The rear seat folded flat, with a minimum of effort, instantly providing a cargo area five feet, eight inches in length. The spare tire, meanwhile, was stowed beneath the floorboards. And while it lacked the glamour of the woody, the Suburban was a trim-looking little number, fit to be seen in the best of company. Perhaps its most endearing feature lay in the fact that the constant maintenance of the wooden-bodied wagon was a thing of the past, along with the squeaks and the rattles, the leaks and the swelling that had often characterized the hardwood jobs.

The station wagon had come of age.

For years, Ford had been the nation's wagonmaster, dominating that segment of the market—such as it was—almost completely. From 1946 through 1948, for instance, Ford turned out 41,976 station wagons, a country mile ahead of Chevrolet, with 15,887, and Plymouth, with 12,913.

The Suburban upset that particular apple cart. By 1950 Plymouth was producing 59 percent more station wagons than Ford, with Chevrolet coming in a poor third. Not until the advent of Gordon Buehrig's stylish Ranch Wagon in 1952 (see sidebar, p. 34) would Ford

Left: Despite vastly more advanced all-steel construction, Suburban was Plymouth's bottom of the line wagon in '49. Special Deluxe woody cost $532 more, at a time when $532 meant a considerable amount of money. **Below left:** *The theme of simplicity and durability continues inside with nearly unadorned vinyl upholstery.* **Below:** *No three-way atomic-powered tailgates here. You lift the rear window and secure it with a knurled knob.* **Bottom:** *Plymouth's venerable flathead six was upped to 97 horsepower for '49.*

regain the lead in wagon sales. And even then, Plymouth's Suburban was far outselling its rival from Chevrolet.

And station wagons were representing an increasingly significant share of the market in the 1950s, thanks to the impetus provided by Plymouth. The Suburban's popularity is not difficult to understand. Besides being smart, practical and cheap ($1,840 f.o.b. the factory), it was a creditable little performer. Its power-to-weight ratio of 37.2 pounds per horsepower wasn't far behind that of the Ford V-8's 35.3, and it was much more favorable than Chevrolet's 43.1. And for customers who had to travel back-country roads, Plymouth even offered 18-inch wheels in lieu of the standard 15-inch numbers.

Driving Impressions

Finding a Plymouth Suburban in suitable condition to be a driveReport subject proved to be more of a challenge than your editors had anticipated.

People don't generally preserve, much less restore, steel-bodied station wagons, it seems. Instead, they beat 'em to death!

1949 Plymouth Suburban
Compared to Other Low-priced Station Wagons

Specifications	Plymouth Suburban	Chevrolet Styleline Dlx.	Ford Custom	Plymouth Special Dlx.	Willys Jeep
Wheelbase	111"	115"	114"	118.5"	104"
Overall Length	185 3/16"	196 13/16"	196 4/5"	191 1/2"	174 13/16"
Construction (body)	Steel	Steel[1]	Wood	Wood	Steel
Shipping weight	3,105 pounds	3,450 pounds	3,563 pounds	3,341 pounds	2,587 pounds
Number cylinders	6	6	8	6	4[2]
Valve arrangement	L-head	In-head	L-head	L-head	L-head
Engine displacement	217.8 cubic inches	216.5 cubic inches	239.4 cubic inches	217.8 cubic inches	134.2 cubic inches
Bhp @ rpm	97 @ 3,600	90 @ 3,300	100 @ 3,600	97 @ 3,600	63 @ 4,000
Final drive ratio	3.90:1	4.11:1[3]	3.73:1[3]	3.90:1	4.88:1[3]
Braking area	158.0 square inches	173.5 square inches	176 square inches	158.0 square inches	133.7 square inches
Price[4]	$1,840	$2,278	$2,264	$2,372	$1,781

[1]Wooden body available at same price; 50-pound increase in weight.
[2]Six-cylinder model also available.
[3]Other ratios available.
[4]Prices include federal excise tax and handling charges.

Source: *Automotive Industries*, June 1, 1949.

illustrations by Russell von Sauers, The Graphic Automobile Studio

© copyright 1982, Special Interest Autos

specifications

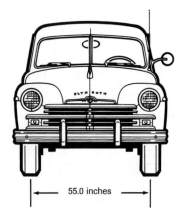

55.0 inches

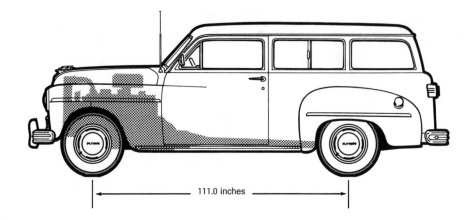

111.0 inches

1949 Plymouth Suburban

Price	$1,740 f.o.b. factory, plus federal excise tax

ENGINE

Type	6-cylinder, in-line, L-head
Bore x stroke	3.25 inches x 4.375 inches
Displacement	217.8 cubic inches
Compression ratio	7.0:1
Max. bhp @ rpm	97 @ 3,600
Max. torque @ rpm	175 @ 1,200
Taxable horsepower	25.3
Induction system	Carter 1.5-inch single down-draft carburetor
Electrical system	6-volt; 40-amp generator

TRANSMISSION

Type	3-speed selective, column-mounted control; synchronized 2nd and 3rd gears
Ratios: 1st	2.57:1
2nd	1.83:1
3rd:	1.00:1
Reverse	3.48:1

CLUTCH

Type	Single dry disc
Diameter	9.25 inches

DIFFERENTIAL

Type	Hypoid
Ratio	3.9:1
Drive axles	Semi-floating

STEERING

Type	Worm-and-roller
Turns lock-to-lock	4.25
Ratio	18.2:1
Turn circle	37 feet, 8 inches

BRAKES

Type	4-wheel internal hydraulic
Drum diameter	10 inches
Total swept area	158 square inches

CHASSIS & BODY

Frame	Box-section type
Body construction	Rigid all-steel
Body style	2-door station wagon

SUSPENSION

Front	Independent, coil springs
Rear	Longitudinal leaf springs, diagonally mounted shock absorbers
Shock absorbers	Delco-Lovejoy single-acting hydraulic

Tires	6.40 x 16 inch 15-ply
Wheels	Pressed steel, 4.5" x 15", safety rims

WEIGHTS AND MEASURES

Wheelbase	111 inches
Overall length	185.3125 inches
Overall height	65 inches
Overall width	72 inches
Length, cargo area	42.25 inches (rear seat up)
Length, cargo area	68 inches (rear seat down)
Length, cargo area	89 inches (tail gate down)
Height, cargo area	39.25 inches
Width, cargo area	55 inches
Tailgate height	27 inches (from ground)
Front track	55 inches
Rear track	56 inches
Ground clearance	7.9375 inches
Shipping weight	3,105 pounds

CAPACITIES

Crankcase	5 quarts (6 with filter)
Cooling system	15 quarts
Fuel tank	17 gallons

In the end, we used two cars. In Oak Park, Michigan, we found a gem of a '49 Suburban belonging to John D. Robertson. Problem was, Royal Oak is a couple of thousand miles away from the writer assigned to the story. But then we found an equally nice '50 Suburban owned by Len Kolodziejski of San Jose, California. The two models are virtually identical. the principal difference being the more tailored-looking grille of the later car.

Since the 1949 Plymouth Suburban was the car that might be said to have started the station wagon "craze," that's the one that is the principal photographic subject for this driveReport. The actual driving impressions, however, were recorded from the 1950 model.

There was more than a little déjà vu when we boarded Len Kolodziejski's Plymouth Suburban. Years ago we owned a '51 Plymouth—different body style, but virtually identical in most respects. It was one of the most comfortable automobiles we've ever had, and one of the most serviceable as well. So the deep-cushioned, chair-height seats and the ample leg room of the Suburban were pleasantly familiar. So was the characteristic sound of the starter.

The old Plymouth "sixes" had the reputation of being hard to start in cold weather, but this was a cold winter's day only by California standards—45 or 50 degrees. perhaps—and the Suburban responded promptly when the key was turned. Acceleration from rest is relatively brisk. Older readers may recall that the short-wheelbase Plymouths of 1949-52, in coupe configuration, knocked over a few stock car records in their day. Real sleepers, they were. This one hauls around more freight, of course; the Suburban is 180 pounds heavier than the coupe. Still, there's nothing sluggish about it!

The clutch is nice; easy pressure, no hint of chatter. Shifts are smooth, and nearly effortless. The column-mounted

lever doesn't "drop" when it is moved from first to second gear, as it does on most makes of car. We'd forgotten about that feature, which we always rather liked. Steering is easy, too, at least for a non-power setup, and while it is far from quick, it's not unduly slow either. And the car will idle along willingly and smoothly in top gear at speeds as low as ten miles an hour!

Proposition 13 has taken its toll of the city streets in most California communities, and in this respect San Jose is no exception. The Plymouth reacts to the uneven pavement with a certain choppiness that we don't recall in the old club coupe, but of course our car was built on the 118.5-inch wheelbase. Once on the freeway, the Suburban's ride smooths out, however, and is very comfortable indeed, The flathead engine is busy, though, and there's no sound insulation worth mentioning. Nothing really obtrusive, but you're aware of what goes on in the engine room.

It's a tight car in every way; no squeaks, no rattles, no loose linkage, and an engine that sounds exactly as a Chrysler-built flathead should. Even the windows are tight, although the channels are original. The odometer read 75,000 miles when Len rebuilt the engine several years ago and reset it to zero. Today it registers a little over 20,000.

Len Kolodziejski bought his Suburban some ten years ago, in decent original condition. Since that time, it has undergone an almost complete restoration, with Len himself doing the mechanical work. Only the paint and upholstery jobs were farmed out. The finish, by the

*Above: Probably the only thing that would have made the Suburban even more useful was the addition of rear doors. **Left:** Another step away from the woody wagon concept; spare tire is stored under the cargo floor.*

The Suburban's Precursor
1947 Willys Jeep Station Wagon

When the Chrysler Corporation proclaimed its 1949 Plymouth Suburban to be "the industry's first all-steel station wagon," you can bet that some hackles were raised at the Toledo, Ohio, headquarters of Willys-Overland. For in fact, that organization's Jeep Station Wagon, also of all-steel construction, had preceded the Plymouth Suburban by two-and-a-half years! And for a time—1947 and thereabouts—the little Willys was the best-selling station wagon of them all!

In its effort to capitalize on the reputation of its famous wartime Jeep, Willys really stretched a point by applying the latter's name to the company's first postwar passenger vehicle, a simple, utilitarian little station wagon. In no sense was it what we think of as a "Jeep"; no transfer case, no four-wheel drive; just a light pickup/passenger-car chassis with a conventional drivetrain and a pressed-steel body whose architecture managed, thanks to the genius of Brooks Stevens, to resemble the Jeep while suggesting (without quite imitating) the traditional wooden construction of the typical station wagon of that day.

In any number of respects, it was a practi-cal little vehicle, and it was relatively cheap as well. The cargo deck, even with the rear seat removed, wasn't big enough to accommodate loads of any great length; but it did have the advantage, from the standpoint of hauling cargo, of rather considerable height. Only 14½ feet long, the wagon stood more than six feet tall.

Of course, that very height made the Jeep Station Wagon somewhat top-heavy. It was also, unfortunately, grossly underpowered. For under the hood was the tiny, 134-cubic-inch four-banger of the military Jeep—an engine derived directly from that of the 1927 Whippet (see *SIA* #66). When fitted to the station wagon, that little engine had to lug around some 54 pounds of weight for each horsepower it generated. Only the Crosley had a less favorable power-to-weight ratio.

All of which takes nothing away from the Willys concept of a cheap, durable, practical, no-nonsense utility vehicle. The idea was a stroke of genius!

It remained for Plymouth to take that concept to its next logical step, with the introduction of the Suburban.

Full instrumentation in easy-to-read round housing makes life informative and easy for the driver.

Take the Suburban
And Add the Magic Touch of Gordon Buehrig....

Two-and-a-half years after the introduction of the Plymouth Suburban, Ford got into the act with its now-famous Ranch Wagon. Designed by Gordon Buehrig, the near-legendary architect of the 810 and 812 Cords—and a number of other strikingly beautiful automobiles including "The Best-Looking Model A Ever Built" (see *SIA* #65)—the Ranch Wagon carried the Suburban's concept one step further by making the all-steel station wagon as handsome as it was practical.

It was *SIA*'s good fortune to visit with Mr. Buehrig while this driveReport was in preparation, our second interview with him in recent months.

SIA: To what extent was the concept of your 1952 Ford Ranch Wagon influenced by the 1949 Plymouth Suburban?

Buehrig: Oh, it influenced us, all right. The Plymouth was an all-steel-panel wagon, like ours.

SIA: You noted in your book, *Rolling Sculpture*, that Earl MacPherson wanted an imitation "woody" like Chevrolet's.

Buehrig: That's right: He wanted a four-door, steel station wagon with "wood" styling, and that was it! Ford was building a two-door, wooden-bodied wagon at that time, and they were losing money on it. It didn't sell very well.

SIA: Given the fact that the Plymouth Suburban was then the best-selling station wagon on the market, why would MacPherson want you to follow the Chevrolet concept? Chevy's wagon sales didn't amount to much in those days.

Buehrig: Well, MacPherson had his prejudices. He had come to Ford from Chevrolet, you know. Incidentally, he was responsible for the development of the MacPherson strut suspension. But that wasn't while he was at Ford.

SIA: What was his role at Ford at the time you were working on the Ranch wagon?

Buehrig: Chief Engineer.

SIA: The Chief Engineer taking a hand in styling? Wasn't that unusual?

Buehrig: Not in those days! John Oswald was with him, too. He was in charge of styling and body engineering.

SIA: How did Oswald feel about MacPherson's idea concerning the design of the wagon?

Buehrig: That's hard to say. You see, MacPherson was over Oswald.

SIA: How did MacPherson react when you developed the wagon along entirely different lines than what he had asked for?

Buehrig (chuckling): We did it while he was vacationing in Florida! Actually, we did two studies, one along the lines that he wanted, with the imitation wood structure, and the other designed the way I thought it ought to be—to look like a steel body.

I had done a station wagon like that when I was with Studebaker. The dealers wanted a wagon and the company didn't have one. Their car wasn't very powerful, so to save weight I designed a fiberglass-bodied wagon for them, using sedan doors. A two-door model. They built one prototype on a Champion chassis and some of the company executives used it on a couple of camping trips. It was an attractive car. Looked quite a bit like the Ford Ranch Wagon eventually did.

SIA: So when MacPherson saw the two concepts as you worked them up, his "fake woody" and your Ranch Wagon, he went for your design?

Buehrig: No, it was [Ford executive vice president] Ernie Breech who made that decision. Ernie was really running the company at that time, and he was a "money

man." He wanted something that would sell. And it did! For several years after that, Ford *owned* the station wagon market!

And by the way, we also worked up a little pickup, something on the order of what later became the Ranchero. But they didn't put it into production at that time."

Indeed, Ford *did* "own" the station wagon market! By 1953, with three station wagons built to Gordon Buehrig's design—the two-door Ranch Wagon, the four-door Country Sedan and the wood-trimmed Country Squire—Ford wagons were outselling those from Chevrolet and Plymouth combined! Chevrolet was still turning out the ungainly "imitation woodys" that Earl MacPherson had favored. And Plymouth, which was having an otherwise dismal year and in any case had no counterpart to Ford's increasingly popular four-door station wagon models, was outstripping Chevrolet by something like 15 percent in the increasingly lucrative wagon market.

But one has to wonder why it took another five years—until 1957—for Ernest R., Breech and the rest of the High Command at Ford to discover that Gordon Buehrig had another potential winner for them in the station-wagon-based pickup that we now know as the Ranchero!

way, faithfully duplicates the original Channel Green color, and the flawless matching enamel on the dashboard has never been touched. Even the original woven fiber headliner is in near-mint condition,

Len has added a number of improvements to his car. Factory-approved extras include a radio, heater (not of the fresh-air variety, however), rear fender skirts, white sidewall tires and full wheel covers. Borrowed from the Special Deluxe model are the dual horns and steering wheel horn ring.

One would really have to be "picky" to find fault with such an attractive, practical car as the Plymouth Suburban. We'll downgrade it just a little in one respect, however: it leaves something to be desired as a car for mountain roads. It takes the turns with aplomb, and even on long, steep downhill grades the brakes are excellent. Furthermore, it will climb almost anything, the problem being that it jolly well takes its time about it. When the acclivity grows steeper than high gear can handle, the driver finds himself faced with a 1.83 second-gear ratio that disabuses him of any thought of hurrying! The 1.60 ratio of the Ford, or the Studebaker Champion's 1.63 would be preferable, in our view. But that's a minor enough matter; and perhaps there's even some advantage to the lower gearing in a car that is intended, after all, for utility rather than for hotshot performance.

We could see the early Plymouth Suburbans—what few there are left of them—becoming a sort of "cult" thing some time in the future. In fact, the more we looked at these pleasant, practical cars, the more we thought that they would make a perfect 1982 offering in terms of size, utility, durability and comfort. Are you listening, Lee Iacocca? ༄

Above: *With tailgate and rear seat down, Suburban offers nearly 7-1/2 feet of cargo-carrying length.* **Below:** *MoPar's famous chair-high seats offer excellent comfort and knee support.* **Bottom:** *Despite the modern all-steel body concept, some antique touches such as old-timey tailgate hinges and split rear window were carried over to Suburban.*

Acknowledgements and Bibliography

Automotive Industries, *various issues:* *Gordon Buehrig*, Rolling Sculpture; *Don Butler*, The Plymouth and De Soto Story; *Jerry Heasley*, The Production Figure Book for U.S. Cars; *Allan Nevins*, Ford: Decline and Rebirth; *Leonard Westrate*, *"1949 Plymouth and Dodge Cars,"* Automotive Industries, *February 1, 1949.*

Our thanks to Jim Benjaminson, Cavalier, North Dakota; Gordon Buehrig, Grosse Point, Michigan: Sherwood Kahlenberg, North Hollywood, California: Mike Lamm, Stockton, California: Vince Manocchi, Azusa, California: Hank Schulken, San Mateo, California: Brooks Stevens, Milwaukee, Wisconsin; Bob Zarnosky, Granada Hills, California.

Special thanks to Len Kolodziejski, San Jose, California: John D. Robertson, Oak Park, Michigan,

1950 Plymouth
P-19 Fastback
Overlooked and Underrated

Driving Impressions

by Tim Howley
photos by David Gooley

OUR 1950 Plymouth P-19 two-door fastback is owned by Elias Valle, who owns an auto body shop in San Diego, California. He is the third owner, and this is one of two of these cars which he owns. The owner brought it to Valle's body shop for restoration and Valle fell in love with it. Eventually the owner parted with the car. Valle then lowered it, and added a lot of accessories. This car has a radio, aftermarket accessory skirts, outside sun visor, outside rear view mirrors, eyebrow shades, bluedot taillights, desert cooler, and wind breakers on the vent windows. Valle belongs to "The Oldies Club," which goes in for low riders. He wanted to have the low rider look but keep the car original. The car has slightly under 80,000 original miles.

The car is fun to drive, gets about 18 miles per gallon on the road, and cruises up to 90 mph with C-76 15 steel belted radial tires. It has full instrumentation, no red warning lights, nice placement of all instruments and controls, plus a turn signal which was optional. There was no cigarette lighter on this model. This car does not have a clock. The car has a gas heater instead of a factory fresh air heater.

This car is a lot faster than its reputa-

tion, but definitely slows down in second gear. Shifting is smoother than with a Ford or Chevrolet. The lever never drops when moved to second gear. Steering is easy but slow, and the car

runs circles around contemporary Fords and Chevrolets in the the tight turns and on twisty mountain roads. The only objection again is that second gear. This is truly a mountain goat, taking longer to climb the High Sierras than the '49ers did. The car corners flatter than a Ford but leans more than a Chevrolet. The braking is very good and the ride is as comfortable as that of the same era Pontiac or Mercury. For a complete comparison of the 1949 Ford, Chevrolet and Plymouth see *SIA* #104, April 1988.

Top: *Plymouth's handling shows more body lean than its competitors, but chassis sticks better.* **Above:** *Correct period accessory sun visor adds to Plymouth's personality and style.*

Originally published in Special Interest Autos #164, Mar.-Apr. 1998

1950 Plymouth

History & Background

K.T. Keller was a remarkable man. President of Chrysler Corporation from 1935 through 1950, he looked backward when everyone else was looking towards the future. Yet he fostered some remarkably dependable and durable automobiles that are excellent collectibles today. His approach was direct and decisive, and he ran the company to appeal to conservative Americans and to his stockholders.

In his famous address at Stanford University in 1947 he said, "Automobiles are looked at and admired. The buyer is proud of his car's symphony of line; its coloring and trim express his taste; he welcomes the applause of his friends and neighbors. But he bought the car to ride in, and for his wife, and children, and friends to ride in.... Though at times one might wonder, even head room is important. Many of you Californians may have outgrown the habit, but there are parts of the country containing millions of people, where both the men and the ladies are in the habit of getting behind the wheel, or in the back seat, *wearing hats*."

This was the basis of Keller's "three-hatbox" styling which dominated the entire Chrysler line from 1949 through 1954. During this period styling plus V-8 power sold Fords. While Chevrolets were not quite as powerful as Fords, their six-cylinder engines had overhead valves. Chrysler products, except for the hemi, were L-head sixes. Keller under-

Big styling change for 1950 Plymouth was in grille area. It went from fussy, busy '49 rendition to this simple, attractive single bar.

stood that a large segment of the American public still wanted conservative transportation at all price levels.

In producing the second series 1949 models, Keller saw the low-priced market as being divided into two wheelbases. Ford did not get this message until l957, Chevrolet not until 1960. So at a time when Ford offered one 114-inch wheelbase and Chevrolet one 115-inch-wheelbase, Plymouth offered two wheelbases—1949–52. The P-17/19/22 rode on a 111-inch wheelbase and the P-18/20/23 came on a 118.5-inch wheelbase.

Initially, the 1949 Plymouth was called the first series which was the same car as the 1948. Second series 1949 Ply-

mouths came in late March as the P-18 and in early April as the P-17. The P-18 was offered in a four-door notchback sedan and two-door notchback club coupe in the Deluxe series. Further up was the P-18 Special Deluxe four-door, two-door, convertible and four-door wooden bodied station wagon. The P-18 competed directly with Ford and Chevrolet at a price of approximately $100 more model for model. But this is a "not exactly" figure, as we shall see later.

Even though these Plymouths looked more contemporary than the 1946–48 models, they were not as sleek as the Fords and Chevrolets. The busy grille looked more prewar than postwar. The taillights were tacked on. The instru-

Tom McCahill Travels 4,000 Miles in a 1949 Plymouth Suburban

The 1949–52 Plymouth Suburban ushered in the station wagon era. Up until that time wagons were wood, squeaked and rattled, were expensive and quickly deteriorated.

The all-steel Suburban clobbered the termite-ridden competition. For years the Ford woody dominated the wagon market. In 1950 Plymouth produced 59 percent more wagons than Ford. However it should be pointed out that Chevrolet, Pontiac and Oldsmobile all offered both woody and all-steel wagons in 1949, then dropped the woodies in 1950 in favor of the all-steel wagons. Standard catalogs state that Chevrolet built 166,995 wagons for 1950. This writer questions this figure, in view of Plymouth and Ford wagon production that year plus Chevrolet wagon production for the remainder of the decade. When Ford introduced the all-steel Ranch Wagon for 1952 it regained top position in wagon sales. Most sources agree that the Plymouth Suburban spelled the end of the woody, primarily because of its much lower price than other wagons, and Plymouth brought about the all-steel station wagon era which eventually

led to the van and minivan era. The car was a real milestone.

In the April 1950 issue of *Mechanix Illustrated*, Tom McCahill reported on a 4,000-mile winter trip from New York City to Florida and back in Plymouth's all-steel station wagon. He raved about the car's chair-height seats, excellent visibility and ability to cruise for hours at 75–80 mph. He was especially impressed with the lack of typical woody noises, commenting, "One thing that struck me as odd, and definitely not station waggy, was the blessed lack of squeaks and rattles. The Suburban was as quiet as a bought-off insurance witness."

He tried to fix that by driving the Suburban for several miles in a few inches of water in the surf at Daytona Beach. Blam! A big wave hit the Suburban and the engine conked out. The wagon started, but just barely. But once he got back on land it took an hour to get the wiring dry enough to fire up the engine again. This demonstrated to him that the waterproof ignition was not quite ocean proof, pointing out that nobody but him would be mad enough to dunk a Plymouth in the ocean. After the dunking he

waited to see if squeaks and corrosion would set in. They did not.

At Daytona Beach he made his usual time trials. Zero to 60 took 24.6 seconds. Ten to 60 in high gear only required 31.9 seconds. After a long buildup he found the car's top speed between 84 and 85 mph. The Plymouth coupes that raced at Daytona and elsewhere did considerably better than that, but then they were more than 200 pounds lighter.

Tom summed up the car by saying, "In two weeks I covered more than 4,000 miles, dunked the Suburban in the Atlantic and tried everything but a head-on collision to break it down. Many of those long miles I drove were at speeds ridiculously fast for a small station wagon. I wanted to give the car a real stamina test—and I'm pretty confident I gave it the works on that score. When I finally turned the Suburban back to Chrysler in New York it was just as sound and quiet as when I took it away.... Naturally, the Suburban isn't any ball of fire in acceleration, but its high-speed cruising and fine roadability are outstanding."

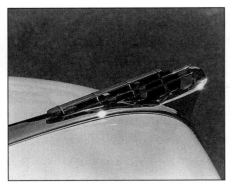

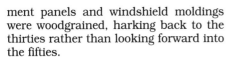

*Above left: Plymouth's traditional sailing ship points the way. **Right:** fifties add-on gizmo out back. **Below right:** Headlamp visors were all the rage back then. **Below:** Trim rings are another dress-up item on driveReport car.*

ment panels and windshield moldings were woodgrained, harking back to the thirties rather than looking forward into the fifties.

More competitive in uniqueness and utility, but not necessarily in price, were the shorter wheelbase P-17s. They came in three body styles that Ford did not offer, one body style that Chevrolet did not offer. At first the P-17 was offered in only a three-window business coupe, not seen since 1932. In May/June, Plymouth introduced a P-17 two-door all-steel station wagon. (See sidebar, page 40.) Then in July they added a fastback two-door sedan which immediately became the most popular of all three body types. P-17 interiors and trim were as severe as Miles Standish's wardrobe. The standard sedan and coupe interiors were woven fabric, with vinyl offered at no extra cost. Striped broadcloth was offered as a modest $5 option. Not offered until later were armrests, rear fender scuff guards, foam seat cushions and wheel covers. In fact, the P-17 was so plain that it did not even

have the Plymouth crest on the hood above the grille. But it did have a wood-grained instrument panel and window moldings. It would seem that the spirit of the Plymouth colony, the *Mayflower* and the Pilgrims is best preserved in the puritanical P-17/19/22 series Plymouths.

While both Ford and Chevrolet offered business coupes, these were five-window club coupes without a back seat. The Ford wagon was a woody. Chevrolet offered both a woody wagon with a minimum of wood and an all-steel wagon with wood appliques. All were far more expensive and less suited to hauling than the Plymouth P-17 station wagon (see *SIA* #72). So popular was this wagon that it lifted

specifications

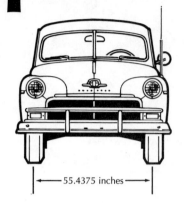

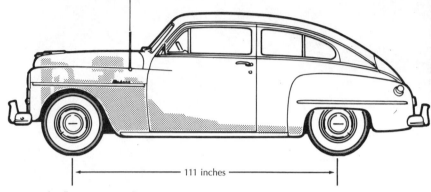

←——— 55.4375 inches ———→

←——— 111 inches ———→

1949 Plymouth P-19

Price $1,492 f.o.b. factory, plus federal excise tax

Optional equipment on this model Radio, directional signals, scuff guards, wheel covers, after-market skirts, outside sun visors

Total 1950 production for this body type 67,584

ENGINE
Type 6-cylinder, in-line, L-head
Bore x stroke 3.25 inches x 4.375 inches
Displacement 217.8 cubic inches
Max. bhp @ rpm 97 @ 3,600
Taxable horsepower 25.3
Max. torque @ rpm 175 foot pounds @ 1,200
Compression ratio 7.0:1
Main bearings 4
Lifters Solid
Induction system Carter 1.5-inch single down-draft carburetor
Electrical system 6-volt; 40-amp generator

TRANSMISSION
Type 3-speed selective, column-mounted control; synchronized second and third gears
Ratios: 1st 2.57:1
2nd 1.83:1
3rd 1.00:1
Reverse 3.48:1

CLUTCH
Type Single dry disc
Diameter 9.25 inches
Actuation Mechanical, foot pedal

DIFFERENTIAL
Type Hypoid
Ratio 3.73 standard, 3.90:1 or 4.10:1 optional
Drive axles Semi-floating

STEERING
Type Worm and roller
Turns lock-to-lock 4.25
Ratio 18.2:1
Turn circle 37 feet 8 inches

BRAKES
Type 4-wheel internal hydraulic,
Drum diameter 10 inches
Total swept area 158 square inches

CHASSIS & BODY
Frame Box-section type
Body construction Rigid all steel
Body style 2-door sedan

SUSPENSION
Front Independent, coil springs

Rear Longitudinal leaf springs, diagonally-mounted shock absorbers
Tires Originally 6.40 x 15
Wheels Pressed steel, 4.5-inch x 15-inch safety rims

WEIGHTS AND MEASURES
Wheelbase 111 inches
Overall length 186.5 inches
Overall width 72 inches
Overall height 65 inches
Front track 55.4375 inches
Rear track 58.4375 inches
Shipping weight 2,946 pounds

CAPACITIES
Crankcase 5 quarts (6 with filter)
Cooling system 15 quarts
Fuel tank 17 gallons

PERFORMANCE
Top speed 84-85 mph
Acceleration: 0-60 mph 24.6 seconds
10-60 mph in high 31.9 seconds
Gas consumption 17 mpg, best; 13-14 at high speed

Source: *Mechanix Illustrated*, April 1950, for a 1949 Plymouth Suburban; the 200-pound-lighter two-door sedan would be some 5 seconds better.

Rare accessory desert cooler unit on driveReport car was popular in the West for trips across the hot open spaces in the fifties before air conditioning became commonplace.

1950 Plymouth

Above: There's also an under-dash heater for cooler climates. **Below:** Wood-grained dash adds touch of elegance to what is essentially a stripped down model. **Bottom:** Trunk space is particularly suited for triangular shaped objects.

Plymouth from about fifth to second place in wagon sales. The Plymouth Suburban did not have the eight-passenger seating capacity or cargo volume of the Plymouth P-18 woody, but at $1,840 it was priced $532 less.

All 1949 Plymouth models were powered by the time-proven 217.8 L-head six-cylinder engine which developed 97 horsepower at 3,600 rpm. Engine improvements over 1948 were a compression boost from 6.6:1 to 7.0:1, a new cylinder head and intake manifold, and an electrically operated automatic choke. Plymouth additionally featured lightweight aluminum pistons with four rings per piston, and chrome plated top piston rings. Compare Plymouth horsepower to the flathead Ford V-8 at 100 horsepower and the ohv Chevrolet six at 90 horsepower. Ford also offered an L-head six at 95 horsepower. Although a 1949 Plymouth could keep pace with a Chevy, a Ford V-8 could outrun it at all speeds. A '49 Ford could go from 0–60 in approximately 15 seconds, Plymouths and Chevrolets took at least five seconds more. Both makes were about 10 mph slower than the Ford V-8 flat out. In the P-17 coupe the Plymouth six could slightly outrun the Chevrolet and almost hold its own against the Ford V-8. The P-17 coupe weighed over 200 pounds less than the P-18 two-door notchback.

Plymouth claimed its '49 model was "The car that likes to be compared." But was it? A 1949 P-18 series Special Deluxe four-door sedan was $1,629, compared to $1,539 for a 1949 Chevrolet Styline Deluxe four-door sedan; $1,559 for a 1949 Ford Custom six four-door, or $1,638 for a Custom V-8 four-door. The P-17 fastback was only $27 less than the P-18 Deluxe two-door. Price-wise, Plymouth got a little more competitive in 1950. For example the base price of a 1950 Plymouth Special Deluxe two-door sedan/club coupe was $1,519 compared to $1,482 for a 1950 Chevrolet Styleline Deluxe two-door sedan or $1,511 for a 1950 Ford six Custom Deluxe two-door sedan. But was it competitive in the P-17/19/22 series? A 1950

The Plymouth 111-Inch Society

This *mythical* club takes the small wheelbase 1949–52 Plymouths very seriously.

Their basic credo is "Long live puritanical, no-nonsense transportation." The society does not recognize 118.5-inch-wheelbase Plymouths or Dodge Wayfarers of the same era, feeling they all destroyed the Spartan purity of the original. At national meets, cars with such options as radios and whitewall tires are not allowed on the field. Cars with armrests, optional upholstery and wheelcovers are allowed but will receive point deductions. No points will be added or deducted for original-type seat covers. The Plymouth 111-Inch Society adheres strictly to the rules. Even though cars will be disqualified if they are not on the field on time, optional clocks are not permitted. Even the dress code forbids casual wear at national meets. Early fifties-style suits are the order of the day. Meet entrants not wearing hats will not be allowed on the field. Their national publication, *The Puritan,* is published six times annually. Unfortunately, our feature car, with all its options and accessories, has been disbarred from national meets.

1950 Plymouth

Above: Factory accessory fender skirts are rare as icebergs in the Sahara. Below: Faithful six-cylinder flathead's design and engineering go back to the early thirties in Plymouths.

Plymouth P-19 two-door sedan was $1,492 compared to $1,403 for a 1950 Chevrolet Styline two-door sedan or $1,424 for a 1950 Ford six Deluxe two-door sedan. A 1950 Plymouth P-19 business coupe was $1,371 compared to $1,329 for a Chevrolet business coupe, $1,333 for a Ford six business coupe. Obviously the P-17's appeal was not price, but compactness, utility and economy.

Knowing that they could not compete with Ford and Chevrolet on the basis of styling, horsepower or price, Plymouth stressed easier clutching, easier steering and parking, more passenger room, easier entry and exit, more luggage room, better shocks and front suspension, floating power engine mountings, better brakes, better visibility, all steel welded construction, safety rim tires, better automatic choke, resistor type spark plugs, ignition key starting and waterproof ignition. A particular Plymouth advantage over the other two was comfort, especially in the longer wheelbase P-18. The Plymouth's chair-height seats are in a class by themselves. They fit right in with Keller's people who wear hats. Arguably, Plymouth engineering and quality overall were superior to either Ford or Chevrolet, and that was what appealed to the Plymouth buyer.

Plymouth second series production for 1949 was 522,385 — 458,930 P-18s and 63,455 P-17s.

Plymouth received a mild and definitely improved facelift for 1950 and was renumbered the P-19 and P-20 series. The fussy grille gave way to a simpler, bolder look with a single center bar. Neat contemporary taillights were nicely faired into reshaped rear fenders. The sedans and three-window coupe received a larger rear window. Smooth bumpers replaced the triple-fluted units of 1949. The lineup of models was the same except for the addition of a Suburban Special Deluxe wagon in the P-19 series. (Some claim this model appeared in mid-year 1949 as the Suburban Savoy, but catalog books do not show this model until 1950.) Mechanical changes were virtually none except for a slight increase in front and rear tread. Plymouth production for 1950 was 610,954 of which 492,051 were P-18s and 118,903 were P-17s.

While Plymouth was standing still, the competition was moving ahead. Chevrolet introduced Powerglide coupled to a larger 235.5-c.i.d., 105-horsepower six. Also new was the Bel Air two-door hardtop. Ford greatly improved the quality of its trouble-ridden 1949 Ford with the "50 Ways New" 1950 model. Ford answered Chevrolet's Bel Air with the

Plymouth P-17 Performance

Some collectors have a lot of respect for 111-inch wheelbase 1949–52 Plymouths, claiming they excelled in performance, ride, comfort, safety and styling. The 1950 three-window Deluxe coupe weighed in at 2,872 pounds compared to 3,040 pounds for the Deluxe club coupe. These slightly lighter Plymouths had a lot of get up and go once you mastered the slower second gear. They could hold or beat a Ford in first gear, lose it in second and gain lost ground in third gear. The standard axle ratio for the P-17/19/22 was 3.73:1, 3.90:1 and 4.01 were optional. The standard axle ratio for the P-17/19/22 wagon and the P-18/20/23 was 3.90:1; 4.10:1 was optional.

A short-wheelbase Plymouth proved to be the fastest of the "little big three" at the 1950 Daytona Speed Week with an 89.75 mile mark. In order of final standing, Otis Martin's 1949 Plymouth was ninth out of 13 cars. Richard and Lee Petty campaigned 111-inch wheelbase 1949 and 1950 Plymouths and won several races.

Johnny Mantz won the Darlington stock car race in 1950 with a P-19 two-door fastback. While his average speed was only 76 mph, tire mileage, gas mileage and just plain durability made him outlast the bigger, faster cars. Three other Plymouth P-17s/19s were in the top 10 in that race.

Tom McCahill also discovered the amazing qualities of the P-17. Writing about a 4,000-mile trip in a 1950 Suburban in the April 1950 issue of *Mechanix Illustrated*, he waxed, "A lot of us, including your Uncle Tom, have underrated Plymouth as a big-time fast-traveling road car.... It is low in snap and immediate punch, but don't sell it short on a 500 mile run — it's a hotshot sleeper from way back." (See sidebar, page 40.)

Above: driveReport car has been slightly lowered in keeping with owner's desires to have an early fifties street cruiser.
Below: Rear styling is the most interesting aspect of the car. It looks slightly foreign, slightly retro and quite different from contemporaries.

gussied up Crestliner two-door sedan.

Dodge also built a short-wheelbase model during this period utilizing the P-17 bodies. This was the Wayfarer D-29/33/41 series. While Dodge did not pick up on the Suburban wagon body, they made a roadster out of the coupe. Dodge Wayfarers were placed on a 115-inch wheelbase.

The short-wheelbase Plymouths and Dodges were around for two more years. They had major changes in grilles and instrument panels for 1951; so did the longer wheelbase lines. Plymouth's Deluxe name was replaced with the name of Concord. The Special Suburban was known as the Concord Savoy. Production of 1951 and 1952 models is lumped together due to the Korean War with virtually no changes for 1952 other than the addition of overdrive.

There is a simple purity in all of these cars that has to be admired, and the performance, particularly in the 111-inch-wheelbase Plymouth, has been greatly underrated for all too many years. ᕕ

Acknowledgments and Bibliography

George H. Dammann, Illustrated History of Plymouth; *F. Donald Butler,* Plymouth/DeSoto; Standard Catalog of Plymouth, *Krause Publications; Richard M. Langworth and Jan P. Norbye,* Complete History of Chrysler; *Tom McCahill,* "Mechanix Illustrated Tests the Plymouth All-Metal Suburban," April 1950; 1949 Plymouth Suburban, SIA# 72, December, 1982; "1949 Ford/Chevrolet/Plymouth Compared," SIA #104, April 1988.

Our special thanks to Elias Valle, San Diego, California, for sharing his 1950 Plymouth with us.

California and Back in a 1950 Plymouth Special Deluxe Sedan

For years my wife's father sold for and then owned a tire retreading company for state and county road building equipment. This means he did a lot of driving out of Minneapolis/St. Paul and owned more cars than Jay Leno, but one at a time. In 1950 he took his family on a trip from Minneapolis to Southern California to Northern California and back to Minneapolis in a brand new blue 1950 Plymouth Special Deluxe four-door sedan. Since neither his wife nor any of his three daughters drove, Hal did all the driving. The trip took three weeks with only 10 days of driving! He joined the Lincoln Highway in Iowa and followed it to Salt Lake City, then turned southwest to Las Vegas, and finally Pasadena to visit his brother. They spent a week in Los Angeles, seeing the sights and meeting the movie stars. Hal had a lot of connections in the theater, going back to the twenties. Then they drove to San Francisco, going up Highway 1, spending two

days visiting another relative in San Mateo. They visited both San Francisco and Oakland, went on to Sacramento and Reno, returning east via the Lincoln Highway, leaving the Lincoln Highway to visit Mt. Rushmore, the Black Hills and the Badlands, then returning to the Twin Cities. While on the road, Hal drove 75 mph everywhere the traffic permitted. He put on more miles than Tom McCahill and reported the same type of experiences. Excellent high-speed comfort, excellent cruising, and no trouble at all except once running out of gas in Iowa. Hal was truly a Chrysler product motorist as envisioned by K.T. Keller. He not only wore a hat all the way to California and back, but owned seven hats, all very expensive. Great Grandpa Hal Sandeen recently celebrated his 100th birthday. His favorite car was his 1956 Lincoln Premiere, but the one he remembers most for cross-country travel was the '50 Plymouth sedan.

1954 PLYMOUTH BELVEDERE SUBURBAN

drive report

INSPIRATION FOR THE NOMAD?

By John G. Tennyson
Photos by the author

BY MOST measures, the 1954 Plymouth was not an especially exciting car. It was not longer, lower, or wider, nor was it bedecked with the chrome or sweeping panoramic windshields of the trendsetters from General Motors.

Rather, the Plymouth was a plain Jane with a somewhat squat, boxy appearance, like other Chrysler products of the early 1950s. Plus, it was a warmed-over 1953.

But the competition from Ford and Chevy was warmed over as well, and sales for the industry were not good in 1954. At Plymouth it was a disaster. Plymouth lost its traditional third place to Buick and Oldsmobile, respectively, which had snappy all-new styling.

Still, the 1954 Plymouth was the same low-priced, dependable and well engineered car, with a lot of value for the buck, which Plymouth had always been.

Consumer Reports — in its February 1954 issue — had high praise for the Plymouth in riding and handling characteristics, as well as overall quality. Plymouth was one of the few cars "at any price" which gave owners "faithful

and economical service together with top-notch handling characteristics...," CU reported.

But the '54 Plymouth was not the same "no-nonsense" car it had always been, for although warmed over in styling, it blossomed with a whole array of new colors, new interior fabrics, and new accessories, which had not previously been available. Plymouth called it "Color Tuned" styling, but it was really not styling at all. Rather, an ingenious use of bright colors and contrasting pastels, as well as a tasteful but more plentiful use of chrome garnishments, made the Plymouth look more modern. It was a stopgap measure used on many 1954 Chrysler products to buy time before the completely redone 1955 "forward look" models would appear.

The 1954 Plymouth Belvedere Suburban station wagon particularly exemplified this "new" style. It was designed and promoted as a station wagon for women. A variety of "Color Tuned" canary yel-

lows, sea-mist greens and coral pinks, with contrasting pastels was offered, with matching interiors in a doeskin and basket weave vinyl material on both seats and door panels. Full front and rear all-wool carpeting was offered in matching colors. The steering wheel was a massive affair, with a large, chrome-laden horn ring, featuring an almost pearl-like white steering rim. The rear seat of the Suburban included handy, covered compartments at each end of the seats for storing maps, flashlights, and perhaps a mirror and com-pact to please madame. Or the buyer could order her own optional lighted, battery-powered vanity mirror for either the driver or passenger-side sun visor.

Other optional equipment included power steering, a HyDrive semi-automatic transmission, which Plymouth claimed could hold the car on hills for short periods without the use of the brake, a fully automatic Powerflite transmission and power brakes, offered in mid-year. Additionally, directional signals, a push-button radio, a foot-operated window washer with standard electric wipers, genuine wire wheels, or

simulated wire wheel covers, and an outside left spotlight with rearview mirror were available.

With Plymouth ads touting the car as "a perfect harmony of color…in rich new fabrics, in glowing color and sparkling chrome…," we have the first indication that the otherwise dour folks at Plymouth were trying to shake their maiden-aunt image.

Plymouth had the dressiest two-door station wagon in the low-priced field, with a chassis measuring no more than 15 feet and weighing less than 3,200 pounds. Lighter and nimbler to park and handle, the Suburban stood in contrast to the somewhat larger "lumber wagons" from Ford and Chevrolet.

Ford, too, had a two-door wagon, but on a larger four-door chassis, weighing some 300 more pounds. Chevy would take the hint the next year by offering a stylish two-door Nomad station wagon, and Pontiac the Safari.

Plymouth only offered this two-door luxury-style wagon for one year — 1954. Later two-door wagons were bare bones, and fancier four-door wagons from Plymouth grew in such size and weight that by 1957 they were almost as big as a Chrysler New Yorker. Apparently, the market for the larger four-door wagon, long dominated by the Ford Country Squire, was more profitable.

But referring to the Plymouth Suburban for 1954, *Consumer Reports* wrote, "No other wagon that CU 5 consultants have driven combines so well the ability to carry moderately heavy or bulky loads with: 1) easy maneuverability and compact dimensions: 2) an easy-to-clean interior; 3) riding comfort of the same order as the sedan model; 4) even better handling and roadability than the sedan model, due to a more equal distribution of weight between front and rear wheels."

The car selected for this driveReport is an original, 79,000-mile car, purchased

Above and right: Smallest and lightest of the low-priced '54 wagons, Plymouth wouldn't be considered a big car even today. Below and below right: Plymouth boasts a proper tailgate built for carrying loads, unlike the hatchback-style tailgates seen on today's wagons. Facing page, top left: Big wheel offers lots of steering leverage. Top right: Wire wheel covers are scarce '54 factory accessory. Center: Wagon's front seat is split 2/3 so passenger can slide over rather than get out to admit rear-seat riders. Bottom: Full instrumentation in an uninspired design.

from its first lady buyer by its present owner, John Ryan, of Roseville, California. Dolled-up in coral pink with contrasting off-white accents, this Suburban sports its original baked enamel finish and pink and white vinyl-weave interior, including salmon pink carpeting.

The Suburban is powered by the trusty L-head "floating power" six-cylinder engine, the same basic motor used by Plymouth since 1933. With a compression ratio of 7.1:1, the car develops an advertised horsepower of 100 at 3,500 rpm. This car is equipped with the standard three-speed, column shift, fully synchronized transmission. Overdrive and two optional automatic transmissions were also available: HyDrive, a semi-automatic requiring clutching when shifting from first to second or to reverse but otherwise "shiftless," and Powerflite, a fully automatic two-speed made available in mid-1954. One interesting feature of HyDrive was the engine oil shared by the transmission, requiring 10 quarts when changing oil, 11 with filter.

At 62 inches in height and with wide-opening doors, the Plymouth Suburban has an ease of entry and exit, typical of, if not better than, cars of the 1950s.

Low-Priced Three
1954 Top-of-the-line Station Wagons

	Plymouth Belvedere Suburban 2-door	Ford Country Squire 4-door	Chevrolet Bel Air Townsman 4-door
Engine	L-6 217 c.i.d. 100-hp	ohv V-8 239 c.i.d. 130 hp	L-6 235.5 c.i.d. 115 hp
Bore and stroke	3.25 x 4.63	3.50 x 3.10	3.56 x 3.94
Passenger capacity	6	8	8
No. seats	2	3	3
Wheelbase	114 inches	115.5 inches	115 inches
Length	189.4 inches	198.1 inches	195.5 inches
Weight	3,186 pounds	3,624 pounds	3,540 pounds
Price	$2,288	$2,339	$2,283
Production	9,241	12,797	8,156

Seats are chair height, and the view from the driver's seat is commanding, with a semi-curved, one-piece windshield, a sloping hood and short front end, and the all-glass-around design of the station wagon. From the driver's perspective, the view of traffic in all directions could not be better, except for shorter people whose view might be obstructed by the monstrous fifties-style steering wheel, almost too big for this modest sized car.

The Suburban is well designed. Little things like electric windshield wipers are much appreciated, if one remembers those old vacuum designed units still in use in 1954 by some competitors, which had the annoying characteristic of stopping in a heavy downpour upon acceleration.

Another interesting feature of the

illustrations by Russell von Sauers, The Graphic Automobile Studio
© copyright 1986, Special Interest Autos

specifications

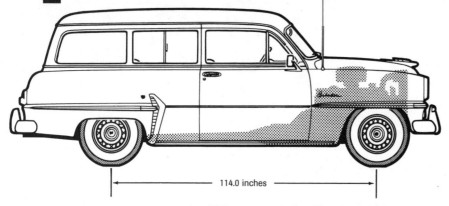

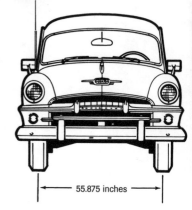

114.0 inches

55.875 inches

1954 Plymouth Belvedere Suburban

Price	$2,288 f.o.b., Suburban with
Standard equipment	Deluxe interior, full wheel covers, deluxe steering wheel, full carpeting front and rear passenger areas, full body side molding, automatic choke, Oilite oil filter, electric windshield wipers, directional signals
Options on dR car	Push-button radio, heater, two-tone paint, wire wheel covers, white sidewall tires, bumper guards, tissue dispenser, exhaust extension deflector, locking gas cap, left and right outside rear view mirrors

ENGINE

Type	6-cylinder
Bore x stroke	3.25 inches x 4.64 inches
Displacement	217.8 cubic inches
Valve configuration	L-head
Max. bhp @ rpm	100 @ 3,600
Max. torque @ rpm	N/A
Compression ratio	7.1:1
Main bearings	4
Induction system	Single bbl. downdraft
Lubrication system	Full pressure rotary oil pump
Cooling system	Centrifugal pump
Exhaust system	Single
Electrical system	6-volt

TRANSMISSION

Type	3-speed synchromesh, steering column mounted shift

DIFFERENTIAL

Type	Hypoid
Drive	Hotchkiss, through rear springs
Ratio	3.73:1

STEERING

Type	Worm and roller
Ratio	21.1:1
Turning circle	Wall to wall, left 41½ feet

BRAKES

Type	4-wheel hydraulic drum, front dual wheel cylinders

CHASSIS & BODY

Frame	Double-channel box-type side rails with 4 cross members
Body construction	Briggs all-steel
Body style	2-door station wagon

SUSPENSION

Front	Independent with coil springs, torsion sway bar eliminator
Rear	Tapered leaf springs (splay mounted)
Tires	6.50 x 15 inch
Wheels	Pressed steel "safety rim"

WEIGHTS AND MEASURES

Wheelbase	114 inches
Overall length	189.5 inches
Overall width	74.25 inches
Overall height	62.125 inches
Front track	55.875 inches
Rear track	58.5 inches
Ground clearance	8 inches (at differential)
Shipping weight	3,186 pounds

INTERIOR DIMENSIONS

Head room, front	38 inches
Head room, rear	36.374 inches
Leg room, front	43.875 inches
Leg room, rear	43.25 inches
Hip room, front	58.5 inches
Hip room, rear	58.5 inches
Shoulder, front	55.5 inches
Shoulder, rear	56 inches
Cargo space vol.	66 cubic feet (tailgate shut)

CAPACITIES

Crankcase	5 quarts (6 w/filter)
Cooling system	13 quarts (14 w/filter)
Fuel tank	16 gallons

Plymouth's faithful flathead six first appeared in 1933 and, with steady development and improvements, lasted through the '59 model year, when it was replaced with the famous "slant six."

Continued on page 57

Color Gallery

Photograph by Bud Juneau

1929 Plymouth

By 1929, the Plymouth marque was off and running. After its debut the previous year, the new Model U was updated with a larger, 175.4-cu.in. in-line four, though the 45hp rating remained the same. Production continued through early 1930 and was succeeded by the Model 30U in April 1930. Total Model U production was 108,345 units.

Photograph by Robert Gross

1928 Plymouth

As with all freshman year Plymouths, this five-passenger Touring car rides on a 109.7-inch wheelbase and is powered by a 45hp, 170.3-cu.in. inline-four that's coupled to a non-synchro 3-speed manual gearbox. I-beam front axle and solid rear axle, all mounted on semi-elliptic springs, comprise the suspension. Optional equipment includes dual side-mount wheels, trunk with luggage rack, dual taillamps and cowl lamps.

Photograph by Robert Gross

Photograph by Bud Juneau

1932 Plymouth PA Convertible
With a newly redesigned body, Plymouth PA moved into third place in sales in 1931. PA production was so successful that it lasted from May 1931 to July 1932. The convertible shown here is one of the late-model versions. Power increased to 64hp from a 196.1-cu.in. four-cylinder engine. Advertised by Plymouth as "Floating Power," the PA was one of the first cars to use rubber engine and transmission mounts.

1935 Plymouth Deluxe
Plymouth made big engineering changes for 1935. Its six-cylinder engine was redesigned for better cooling, and the X-type frame was improved to withstand torsional stress from the 82hp, 201.3-cu.in. straight-six. A tube front axle and new taper leaf springs replaced the independent front suspension of the 1934 models. On the exterior, all Plymouth Deluxe models had chrome headlamps, taillamps and windshield frame, and stainless hood rings. Inside, the Deluxe line had ivory knobs and horn button, and six vertical nickel-plated trim bars on its instrument panel.

Photograph by Don Spiro

1941 Plymouth Woody
Available in either the P11 Deluxe or P12 Super Deluxe line, the wood-bodied station wagons were as stylish as they were utilitarian. The most obvious exterior feature on many 1941 Plymouth Super Deluxe models was a two-tone paint scheme. This even included the "woody" wagons, which had light and dark wood framing and paneling. Power for both models was an 87hp 201.3-cu.in. straight-six.

Photograph by Robert Gross

1937 Plymouth Woody Station Wagon
Built on a truck chassis, the PT50 station wagon was a very rare woody wagon even when it was new. This is one of 60 or so built by J.T. Cantrell in Huntington, New York. With straighter body styling and flatter panels, Cantrell-bodied wagons are very different from those built by U.S. Body & Forging. Power comes from a 201.3-cu.in. straight-six that makes 82hp and is mated to a 3-speed manual gearbox. Instruments include an 80-mph speedometer and fuel, amp, temp and oil gauges.

1950 Plymouth P-19 Fastback
Even at $1,500, the P-19 was still more expensive that a standard Chevrolet or Ford; hence Plymouth's push to advertise its smoother clutch, easier steering and parking and many other welcome features that made driving a base-model car that much easier for 1950. It used a 97hp, 217.8-cu.in. straight-six, and the standard transmission was a column-mounted three-speed. Styling cues feature a single bar front grille, peaked rear fenders and simpler bumpers.

1941 Plymouth P-12 Special
Advertised as "The One For '41," the 1941 Plymouths looked very similar to those offered in 1940. Using the all too familiar 201.3-cu.in. inline-six, power for the 1941 models increased to 87hp. The high-end Special Deluxe models such as this pristine example were spruced up with chrome windshield trim, window vents and striped upholstery material. Nearly half a million Plymouths were sold this year and came close to dethroning Ford in the No. 2 spot for total sales this year.

Photograph by John Tennyson

1954 Belvedere Suburban

With two doors and a station wagon body, the Suburban just may have been the inspiration for the revered Chevrolet Nomad. For 1954, the year prior to the introduction of the highly anticipated V-8 engine and all-new body styling, Plymouth offered a rather plain line that included the Plaza, Savoy and Belvedere. Standard engine for all models was a 100hp, 217.8-cu.in. straight-six, though a 110hp, 230.2-cu.in. version was optional.

Photograph by Jeff Godshall

1955 Plymouth Belvedere

Belvedere was Plymouth's high-priced model for 1955. It had the same styling changes as other models this year including a longer, lower body, and new sheet metal all around. A more lavish interior and extra brightwork distinguished the Belvedere from the others. Standard power was either a 117hp, 230.2 straight-six or the new V-8 that sported 157hp from 241-cubic inches. A larger, 260-cu.in. V-8 that produced 167hp was optional.

1956 Plymouth Belvedere
Tall fins and exaggerated headlight hoods were typical features of all cars from the mid 1950s, and the Belvedere convertible was no exception. Available with a straight-six or a 187hp, 276-cu.in. V-8 as found in this example, it was as peppy as it was attractive. Push-button automatic transmission selector, vacuum-brake servo and Highway Hi-Fi were some of its more distinctive features. With only 6,735 built, the Belvedere convertible was quite a rare car.

1960 Plymouth Valiant
In an attempt to capture the small car market, Plymouth offered the Valiant, its concept of a compact, in 1960. Features included unitized construction, torsion bar suspension and a highly sculpted body, with a long hood and short deck. Standard power was a 170.9-cu.in. "slant" six-cylinder that produced 101hp. "Hyper-Pack" performance option was available for the diminutive engine and included a 10.5:1 compression ratio and a four-barrel carburetor that increased power to 148hp.

Photograph by Rick Lenz

1962 Sport Fury

In 1962, the Fury came standard with a 225-cu.in. slant-six. Optional was a 318-cu.in. V-8 that produced 230 horsepower. The Sport Fury was introduced four months after the rest of the Plymouth lineup and was available as either a two-door hardtop or convertible such as this fine example. Standard engine for the Sport Fury was a 305hp, 360-cu.in. V-8. All told, less than 1,600 Sport Furys were built this year.

Photograph by James Dietzler

1963 Plymouth Savoy

To compete in the NHRA's Super Stock drag racing class, Plymouth introduced the 426-cu.in. Max Wedge engines and made them available in some of its lightest cars such as this Savoy. Available in 415hp and 425hp power levels, the "Super Stock" as it was called, was a rather ferocious beast. As rare as they were, most of these cars were strategically placed in the hands of professional race car drivers to win races, with the idea of bringing the masses into the showrooms to see what other cars the company offered for sale.

1964 Valiant

Mild revisions to the Valiant in 1964 resulted in a new grille, repositioned taillamps and restyled brightwork. The Signet series represented the highest trim level option on these little cars, which were easily identified by lower chrome rocker panel moldings, special badging and standard bucket seats. Base power was a six-cylinder, but a 180hp, 273-cu.in. V-8 was a popular option. Just less than 2,600 Signet convertibles were built.

1965 Barracuda

Designed as a head-to-head competitor with the Ford Mustang, the Barracuda was high on styling and came with a variety of high-performance options. Whereas the Mustang had all new sheet metal, the Barracuda used the already existing Valiant front section with a grafted-on fastback rear section. Standard eight-cylinder power was a 180hp, 273-cu.in. V-8, but the base model came with a 145hp, 225-cu.in. slant-six.

Plymouth Suburban is the fold-down back rest of the front seat. Shared with other Chrysler two-door products, the back of the front seat was divided, not in half, but with two-thirds of the back rest on the driver's side. This was handy for front-seat passengers, who could just slide toward the driver, rather than having to get out of the car, to let someone in or out of the back seat.

The glove compartment is also conveniently located in the lower center of the dash, within easy reach of the driver. Chevy likewise adopted this design in 1955 and later models. Defrost venting for the Plymouth windshield is one wide groove covering almost the entire width of the windshield, rather than smaller slots, as in most cars. This provided more effective defrosting of the glass.

Driving Impressions

Driving the Suburban is, of course, a throwback to the cars of the 1950s. *Consumer Reports* found the Plymouth to handle "outstandingly well" in corners and curves and claimed its riding qualities were …as good as any car at any price." Of course, this was from a 1954 perspective.

Although the Suburban is fairly agile in traffic and provides a good ride on its 114-inch wheelbase, it does lean some on turns, and handling is a little slow by today's standards. Plymouth advertised that with power steering, which our test model does not have, parking could be accomplished with one finger, and steering could be reduced from 31 to 6-3/4 pounds pressure. Unfortunately, other mid-fifties Chrysler products with power steering we have driven have almost no road feel, leaving the distinct impression there is nothing connected to the other end of the steering wheel. But power assist is really not needed on the Plymouth, as even parking can be accomplished with relative ease, perhaps due in part to the leverage of the big steering wheel.

Power from the six-cylinder engine is quite adequate for most situations, although it's a bit sluggish in picking up after corners in high gear. The three-speed column shift is practically foolproof and slips right into gear every time. Clutching, likewise, is simple. The speedometer and gauges are centered in front of the driver, with complete readings for amps, fuel, oil and temperature large enough to see with relative ease.

The rear cargo area is smaller than Ford or Chevy but provides almost six feet of cargo length with the rear seat folded down. The spare tire is concealed in a recessed compartment under the cargo floor with a bolt-down lid, which matches the ribbed floor design. The

Left: Taillamps have built-in provision for backup lights. **Below:** *There's a handy storage bin and assist strap in back seat area.* **Below center:** *Factory rendering of Belvedere Suburban makes it look less attractive than the real thing.*

Above left: There's 66 cubic feet of cargo space with the tailgate closed and lots more when it's open. **Above right:** *With tailgate buttoned up, Plymouth presents a tidy if frumpy appearance.* **Below:** *Spare tire hides conveniently out of the way in underfloor well.*

tailgate window lifts up in the traditional fifties design, and the tailgate itself folds down to provide extra loading floor.

An area which we did not have an opportunity to judge was gas mileage. Mileage for the Plymouth was a little better than Ford or Chevrolet, which had more powerful engines, but not as good as Studebaker, with only a slightly less powerful six. Overall mileage ratings by *Consumer Reports* gave the Plymouth sedan a little better than 16 mpg.

Plymouth did a good job of dressing up a maiden aunt in 1954. Of the 9,241 Belvedere Suburbans made, how many were actually purchased by and for women is only a matter of speculation.

Perhaps the feminine motif never really caught on at Plymouth, as it was not offered in later years. But it makes for a unique and interesting collector car. After all, it's not every day you see a pink Plymouth, with carpeting and basket-weave upholstery to match. 🐾

1956 Plymouth Belvedere
Good Gets Better

by John F. Katz
photos by Vince Wright

NINETEEN fifty-six was the year that fins took flight at Chrysler Corporation. Unfortunately, they didn't do Plymouth much good.

Not that the '56 Plymouth wasn't handsome, or that it didn't pack some significant engineering advances. On the contrary, noted *Motor Trend* Detroit Editor Jim Lodge, "The '56 possesses new performance, new appearance, [and] many buyer attractions that are far beyond even the vastly improved '55."

But that '55 Plymouth, with its sleek new styling, was a tough act to follow (see *SIA* #68). It was the '55 that turned Plymouth around. Buoyed by a boom year for car sales in general, Plymouth's 1955 production soared 85.8 percent over 1954's dismal figures, climbing past Oldsmobile's output and into the industry's number-four position. Plymouth's busy factories built 2,400 cars a day, six days a week.

In those fickle, flamboyant times, however, even successful designs sold for only one season. Nineteen fifty-six brought the inevitable face lift, with new grilles, taillights, and quarter panels for all Chrysler products. It was up to the Chrysler designers, under corporate design director Virgil M. Exner, Sr., to translate those few parts into an entirely new look.

Exner pointed the way with a pair of show cars called Flight-Sweep I and II, a convertible and hardtop coupe, respectively, that made their public debut late in 1955. Designed largely by Maury Baldwin, the Flight-Sweeps used tall tail fins and strategic two-toning to achieve a dynamic wedge profile. "Ex" told *Motor Trend's* Lodge that the Flight-Sweep wedge emulated the fastest things on the land, in the sea, and in the air: championship race cars, unlimited racing boats, and jet aircraft.

For '56, Ex applied "Flight-Sweep" styling to the entire Chrysler line. On the '55 Plymouth, the rear fender had

tapered gently downward to a reverse-canted taillight; the '56 model kept this graceful fender line, but now a sharp fin rose high above it, housing a taller, thin-

Above: *It's not a fifties car without an aircraft-style hood ornament.*
Below: *"Flight Sweep" side trim for Belvedere was new for '56.*

ner red light with a large, round reverse light beneath it. The fin, explained Exner's son, Virgil Exner Jr., "lifted up the rear end to give an aero feel to the whole car, to give the car poise, balance, and a forward direction." Up front, the Plymouth surrendered the pouting grille bar it had worn since 1953 in favor of mesh-filled scoop.

To Plymouth studio manager Hal

Pilkey, the re-styled '56 fit the definition of success: "If you can make the car look fresher, if you can make the car look newer, without spending a lot of money. . . ." Pilkey, Dave Scott, Bud Gitschlag, and the rest of the Plymouth Studio designers had done exactly that.

Advertisements and brochures usually showcased either a red-and-white four-door hardtop or a yellow-and-white convertible. "Here's the jet age on wheels," proclaimed one memorable ad. An illustration juxtaposed a jet fighter with Plymouth's new tail fin, pounding home the fin's resemblance to the jet's vertical stabilizer and blazing exhaust. Plymouth sales literature confirmed that "the distinctive rear fins mark this car as the fashion leader of its class."

Backing up the bold new styling was a new V-8 engine, the first actually assembled by the Plymouth Division. Plymouth had offered a Dodge-built V-8 in '55, a situation which so bottlenecked production at Dodge that in May Plymouth advised its dealers to steer prospects toward the old flathead six. Meanwhile, Plymouth rushed to complete its own "Qualimatic" (quality control through automatic processes) engine facility. *Motor Trend* described the new factory as "the epitome of automation"; Plymouth immodestly called it "the most modern engine plant in the automotive industry."

The "Hy-Fire" engine Plymouth built there superficially resembled the base Dodge V-8; like the Dodge, it was not a true Hemi but a "polyspheric" design, with cast combustion chambers and diagonally opposed valves operated by a single row of rockers. But the Plymouth block stretched longer than the Dodge, providing more space between the bore centers for improved cooling—and future expansion. Its main and rod bearings were bigger, too, and a revised oil gallery delivered the slippery stuff more efficiently.

Originally published in Special Interest Autos #160, Jul.-Aug. 1997

Further, a bigger bore and shorter stroke netted a displacement increase from 260 to 277 cubic inches, and compression jumped from 7.6 to 8.0:1. Larger intake valves leading to re-shaped ports enhanced breathing, while re-contoured combustion chambers allowed a leaner fuel mixture. A lighter valve train with mechanical pushrods replaced the hydraulic lifters favored by Dodge. In standard two-barrel tune — with each venturi feeding one bank of cylinders — the '56 Plymouth V-8 produced 187 bhp at 4,400 rpm and 265 foot pounds of torque at 2,400. An optional "Power Pack" with a four-barrel carb and dual exhausts boosted power and torque to 200 and 272, respectively, at the same rpm. (Plymouth released the dual exhausts as a stand-alone option for the two-barrel engine in January 1956.)

Unfortunately, Plymouth didn't quite get the new engine plant up to speed in time, and for at least part of the model year the division continued to install a Dodge-supplied V-8 in Plaza and Savoy sedans — saving its own engine for wagons and Belvederes. But even the Dodge V-8 was bored out to

Wheel covers were a variation on 1955 design, which stylistically was an all-new Plymouth from bumper to bumper.

270 cubes for '56, and with the new 8.0:1 compression ratio it now produced 180 bhp — 13 more than in '55. Of course, the old "PowerFlow" six remained as standard equipment in most Plymouth models. With compression modestly increased from 7.4 to 7.6:1, the 230-c.i.d. unit now made 125 bhp at 3,600 rpm — up from 117 in '55.

Buyers of both sixes and eights could choose a three-speed manual transmission — with or without overdrive — or a two-speed PowerFlite automatic. New for '56, of course, was a mechanical keypad or "push-button" control for the PowerFlite, replacing 1955's dash-mounted shift lever. The push-button system has been attributed to designer Cliff Voss, but Pilkey offered his own version of its origin: "Someone was driving down Highway 90," he told us, "and noticed a Ford on the side of

59

Above: It takes a sharp eye to distinguish 1956 from 1955 front ends. Below left: "Forward Look" symbol graces rear fenders. Right: If there's a V-8 under the hood you must have a V on the outside to proclaim the fact.

1956 Plymouth

Belvedere. The Plaza and Savoy even kept essentially the same side trim and two-tone patterns they had worn in '55, although Plymouth added a two-door hardtop or "sport coupe" model to the Savoy range. On Belvederes, however, 1955's diagonal slash of chrome and color evolved into a forward-pointing arrow, even more complex but arguably more attractive as well. And of course the Belvedere line now included the requisite four-door hardtop or "sport sedan."

Wagons became a separate series for '56, with the two-door Deluxe Suburban, two- or four-door Custom Suburban, and four-door Sport Suburban corresponding to the Plaza, Savoy, and Belvedere trim levels, respectively. This represented a rethinking of 1955's wagon lineup, where Plymouth had offered a base-trim four-door but no mid-range wagons at all. Wagon buyers obviously liked the 1956 model range better, because Plymouth wagon sales climbed 24 percent over '55.

the road with a push-button shift on it. And we got started like crazy." Ford's system didn't see production until the debut of the '57 Mercury, but Chrysler had push-buttons on the entire line in '56.

Plymouth integrated the push-buttons into a revised version of 1955's "Flight Deck" instrument panel. Beautifully symmetrical, the '55 panel had been roundly criticized for locating the oil pressure and water temperature gauges on the passenger side, where the driver could hardly read them. Plymouth's non-solution for '56 was to move the temp gauge to the left side of the dash, where the ammeter had been in '55; to replace the ammeter and oil gauges with

idiot lights; and to plug the holes left in the right side of the dash with rotary heater and defroster controls.

The Plymouth chassis, on the other hand, remained virtually unchanged from 1955 — softly sprung, with a high roll center, less than ideal for road racing, perhaps, but perfect for tip-toeing over the frost-heaved pavement left behind by a Northeastern winter. As before, six-cylinder Plymouths made do with 10-inch brakes all around, while V-8 sedans carried 11-inch brakes up front. V-8 wagons had 11-inchers all around. All featured dual cylinders in front, a Plymouth exclusive among the low-priced three. Sixes and eights also employed different steering linkages, resulting in a 17 percent faster overall ratio for six-cylinder cars.

Plymouth also carried over the same series names it had used since '54: painfully plain Plaza, medium-range Savoy, and bodaciously beautiful

(Those Suburban wagons, incidentally, were the only Chrysler Corporation wagons to receive new quarter panels for '56. Dodge, DeSoto, and Chrysler wagons saved corporate tooling dollars by wearing '55-vintage fenders topped with bright metal caps. Plymouth, after all, sold more than two and a half times as many wagons as the other three divisions *combined*. Plymouth wagons also pioneered one-piece molded plastic headliners — a running change made in mid-'55.)

Then, on January 7, 1956, Plymouth unleashed the Fury: Conceived as a budget-priced Chrysler 300, this specially trimmed hardtop packed an exclusive, Canadian-built, 303-c.i.d. V-8, high-test hungry 9.25:1 compression, and a single four-barrel carb — producing 240 bhp at 4,800 rpm, and 310 foot pounds of torque at 2,800. With this set-up and a three-speed manual transmission, *Road & Track* recorded 0-60

mph in 9 seconds flat, a 16.6-second quarter-mile, and a top speed of 114.8 mph. Plymouth backed up all that go-fast-ability with stiffer, shorter springs that lowered the ride height by one inch; 11-inch brakes all around with heavy-duty linings, and 7.10 x 15 tires on 5.5-inch rims. More daring souls could approach the Plymouth parts counter and walk away with a second four-barrel, an aluminum intake manifold and a longer-duration cam, which together boosted peak output to 270 bhp.

A factory-prepped Fury posted a new stock-car record of 136.415 mph at the NASCAR Speed Weeks in Daytona Beach. And even the Eurocentric *Road & Track* allowed that the Fury "does in fact have many sports-car-like attributes over and above the performance which is truly 'furious' if not actually sensational. . . . It is without question

one of the best handling domestic sedans we have ever driven. . . . Not many enthusiasts could drive the stick-shift Fury for more than five minutes without getting a thrill."

Meanwhile, *Motor Trend* sampled a Belvedere sedan and found its acceleration "up there with the rest of the boys." So improved was the new V-8 that the four-barrel version delivered 10-15 percent better gas mileage than the two-barrel Plymouth tested the previous year. And despite its soft suspension, the '56 Belvedere would "stick to the road long after you'd expect most cars to drift or actually slide around at the rear." The Plymouth, the editors concluded, "stacks up solidly as a top-notch family car. . . . In fact, the Plymouth appears to be firmly re-trenched in the low-price field."

It was all in Plymouth's favor: dynam-

ic styling, a hot new engine, a high-performance flagship, and good press too. And yet it wasn't enough. The total automobile market shrank 26.9 percent in 1956, but Plymouth sales plummeted more than 37 percent. At least the division managed to hold on to fourth place.

Fortunately, big changes were on their way. Exner hadn't been able to influence the '55-56 Plymouth as much as he would have liked, because the basic engineering of the '55 body was already established when he took over production-car design in early 1953. The 1957 model would be the first Plymouth designed from the ground up under his supervision, and the first to incorporate stabilizing fins as an integral component of a longer, lower design. A new torsion-bar chassis would deliver handling previously unheard-of in a big American sedan. And, however briefly, Plymouth

Compared to later years, fins on '56 models are quite subdued, yet they changed the car's appearance dramatically from the 1955 edition.

The Plymouth Family for '56

	Price (6/V-8)	Weight*(6/V-8)	Production
Plaza			
business coupe	$1,726/1,829	3,030/3,170	3,728
two-door sedan	$1,825/1,928	3,100/3,250	43,022
four-door sedan	$1,868/1,971	3,145/3,275	60,197
Deluxe Suburban			
two-door wagon	$2,138/2,241	3,285/3,460	23,866
Savoy			
two-door sedan	$1,924/2,027	3,125/3,255	57,927
four-door sedan	$1,967/2,070	3,160/3,295	151,762
sport coupe	$2,071/2,174	3,155/3,275	16,473
Custom Suburban			
two-door wagon	$2,209/2,312	3,355/3,500	9,489
four-door wagon	$2,255/2,358	3,375/3,565	33,333
Belvedere			
two-door sedan	$2,008/2,111	3,125/3,285	19,057
four-door sedan	$2,051/2,154	3,170/3,325	84,218
sport coupe	$2,155/2,258	3,165/3,320	24,723
sport sedan	$2,223/2,326	3,270/3,415	17,515
convertible	$ — /2,419	— /3,435	6,735
Sport Suburban			
four-door wagon	$2,425/2,528	3,420/3,605	15,104
Fury			
sport coupe	$ — /2,807	— /3,650	4,485

*shipping weight in pounds

specifications

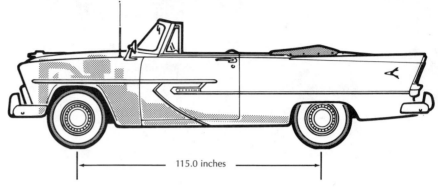

58.4 inches

115.0 inches

1956 Plymouth Belvedere convertible

Base price	$2,419
Standard equipment includes	V-8 engine, PowerFlite transmission, oil-bath air cleaner automatic choke, dual horns, electric wipers, unique Belvedere trim, "Aztec" cloth upholstery
Options on dR car	Dual exhaust, Easy-Glide power seat, radio, heater, full wheel discs, white sidewall tires, dual outside mirrors, two-tone paint, reverse lights, directional signals, windshield washer

ENGINE

Type	V-8
Bore x stroke	3.75 inches x 3.13 inches
Displacement	276.1 cubic inches
Compression ratio	8.0:1
Bhp (gross) @ rpm	187 @ 4,400
Torque (gross) @ rpm	265 @ 2,400
Taxable horsepower	45.0
Valve gear	Ohv
Valve lifters	Mechanical
Main bearings	5
Induction system	1 Ball & Ball BBD 2407S 2-barrel downdraft
Fuel system	Mechanical pump
Lubrication system	Pressure, with metered jet spray to piston pins and metered flow to cylinder walls and timing chain
Cooling system	Pressure-vent
Exhaust system	Dual
Electrical system	12-volt

TRANSMISSION

Type	PowerFlite 2-speed automatic with torque converter
Ratios: Low	1.72:1
Drive	1.00:1
Reverse	2.39:1
Max torque converter	2.7:1 @ 1,690 rpm

DIFFERENTIAL

Type	Hypoid, semi-floating
Ratio	3.54:1

STEERING

Type	Worm and three-tooth roller
Turns lock-to-lock	5
Ratio, gear	18.2:1
Ratio, overall	27.1:1
Turning circle	40.5 feet (curb/curb)

BRAKES

Type	4-wheel hydraulic
Drum diameter	11 inches, front; 10 inches, rear
Effective area	166 square inches
Parking brake	Mechanical, 7-inch drum on transmission output shaft

CHASSIS & BODY

Construction	Separate body and frame
Frame	Welded box-section side rails with central X-member and 4 cross members
Body	Welded steel stampings
Body style	6-seat convertible coupe

SUSPENSION

Front	Independent, upper and lower control arms, coil springs, linkless anti-roll bar
Rear	Live axle with semi-elliptic leaf springs
Shock absorbers	Front, Oriflow direct-acting; rear, Oriflow direct-acting
Tires	Originally 6.70 x 15, now Goodrich Silvertown 7.10 x 15 4-ply
Wheels	Stamped steel disc, 15 x 4.5K

WEIGHTS AND MEASURES

Wheelbase	115 inches
Overall length	204.8 inches
Overall width	74.6 inches
Overall height	60.1 inches
Front track	58.4 inches
Rear track	58.5 inches
Min. road clearance	5.6 inches
Shipping weight	3,435 pounds (without options)

CAPACITIES

Crankcase	5 quarts (less filter)
Cooling system	21 quarts (with heater)
Fuel tank	17 gallons
Transmission	20 pints
Rear axle	3.25 pints

CALCULATED DATA

Bhp/c.i.d.	0.68
Lb./bhp	18.4
Lb./c.i.d.	12.4
P.S.I. (brakes)	20.7

This page: Traditional sailing ship travels up front on grille. *Facing page, top:* Cornering is typical of US mid-fifties cars; lots of body roll and understeer. *Below:* Front fender shape is quite graceful; speaker grille reminds you what car you're in.

1956 Plymouth

would regain the number-three spot in industry sales.

Driving Impressions

The story of our driveReport car actually begins with a '56 Dodge Custom Royal which, if its interior color had been right, would have been Leon Wolf's first new car. "I originally ordered a Dodge," recalled Leon, a retired clothing manufacturer from central Pennsylvania. "It would have been tri-colored with black, aqua and white; and I wanted the black and white upholstery." But it was late in the season, Dodge had run out of black and white upholstery, and Wolf would not accept green as a substitute. "And then the dealer found this black-and-yellow Plymouth for me." It was a Belvedere convertible, black-and-yellow inside and out, and Leon liked it well enough to buy it.

He traded it in '59 for a new Dodge convertible. "But the very first one you own is the one you always want to go back to, all through your life."

In 1978, Leon found a white-and-yellow '56 Belvedere convertible in *Hemmings Motor News*. Although located in Louisiana, it still belonged to the same family that had owned it new in Cape Cod. It was rough but running and relatively rust free. Leon bought it and drove it home. The driver's side door

Plymouth GT

A very special '56 Belvedere sedan drove into the record books as the first gas turbine-powered automobile to cross the North American continent. The second of Plymouth's gas turbine prototypes, it journeyed from New York to Los Angeles with just two breakdowns: First, an overheated bearing failed in the reduction gear, and later an intake casting cracked from fatigue. Chrysler put a brave face on the results, announcing that "the gas turbine suffered fewer failures than newly designed piston engines have in the past when submitted to the same test." The engineers had limited their cruising speed to 45 mph, which delivered 13-14 mpg.

The Chrysler turbine was of the two-shaft type, meaning it incorporated two independently rotating turbine wheels: one to drive the compressor and accessories and another to actually power the wheels. Operating speeds ranged from a 20,000 rpm idle (measured at the compressor) up to a "redline" of 50,000 rpm; somewhere between the two, horsepower peaked at 120. Chrysler claimed that the roughly three-foot-by-three-foot-by-two-foot unit

weighed 200 pounds less than a piston engine of similar output. A simple forward-reverse gearbox was all the transmission it required since, as Chrysler pointed out, a two-shaft turbine acts as its own torque converter.

The designers neatly integrated the specialized turbine instrumentation into the stock '55-56 dash. A huge tach displaced the speedometer, which moved right to the space normally occupied by the radio speaker. Gauges for compressor outlet pressure, fuel level, oil pressure at the turbine, and oil pressure at the oil pump occupied the stock accessory gauge locations; while a big, rectangular temperature gauge (measured at the turbine inlet) replaced the radio.

Outside, turbine-powered Plymouth sported a special "Turbine" logo on its deck lid, "Turbine Special" lettering on the side trim where it usually said "Belvedere," and a foot-wide exhaust duct integrated into the center of the rear bumper. Just in case anyone missed those subtle hints, the words "Chrysler Turbine Special" stretched from the front door to the fuel filler.

1956 Plymouth

wouldn't open, the hood wouldn't stay closed, and the leaky rear end spattered oil all over the bottom of the car. The body was still full of Massachusetts sand. Reinhold's Restoration brought it back to like-new condition, painted the colors of Leon's first new car. It won its first AACA Senior in 1993.

The camera tends to shorten and flatten '55-56 Plymouths, whereas in three-dimensional reality, these cars stretch long and low, with a delicate grace and an integrated sense of style that suggests an Italian sports car as much as a full-size sample of American iron.

The forced symmetry of the "Flight Deck" dash, on the other hand, recalls an English roadster. The heater and defroster controls occupy the passenger-side location vacated by the oil and temperature gauges at the end of '55. It's hardly an ideal spot for anything, but the reach isn't as long as it looks. The '56 model provides gauges only for speed, temperature, and fuel; with simple white numerals on circular black faces, they'd all read easily if only the horn ring weren't in the way.

The framework for the convertible top looks impressively sturdy, yet it leaves plenty of head room. Leg room isn't quite as generous. The "Easy Glide" power seat settles 1.125 inches downward as it travels to its extreme rear position, but even there, the brake pedal rises uncomfortably high and close. The steering lies at

Above: *187-horse V-8 delivers satisfying performance under all regular driving demands.* **Below left:** *Push buttons replaced Plymouth's "magic wand" selector of 1955.* **Right:** *All gauges and controls are round. Dash design is symmetrical.*

an almost Italian angle, so that while the bottom edge nearly brushes my belt buckle, the top tilts away to a more comfortable distance. The chair-high seat is firmly and pleasantly stuffed, if just a little too upright for my taste.

Getting in the back is relatively painless, and once there you might want to stay a while. Passengers sink low to the floor, but enjoy reasonable under-thigh support and a comfortably angled backrest. The people who designed the rear

Chrysler Engineering Features for '56

Chrysler Corporation introduced a number of engineering advances to all of its car lines in 1956. The most conspicuous, probably, was the push-button automatic transmission. Packard also had push-button shifting in '56; Mercury offered it in '57–58, Edsel in '58 and Rambler in '58–62. But only Chrysler's remained in production halfway through the sixties.

The Chrysler system succeeded because of its simplicity. To begin, it was purely mechanical, relying on electricity only to light the buttons. Each button moved a flat, vertical plate or "indexing slide." The forward edge of each slide was cut differently, like so many keys, so that each one would push a horizontally pivoted rocker bar into a unique position. The pivoting bar then pushed or pulled a cable which rotated the controlling valve in the transmission. The entire mechanism was hardly more complicated than a column-mounted shift linkage—and arguably more convenient.

Along with the new push-button transmission, Chrysler debuted a new vacuum brake servo, which substituted a sizable bellows exposed to the atmosphere for the usual diaphragm-in-a-chamber setup. Chrysler claimed better feedback, and

Motor Trend noted shorter pedal travel. A reserve tank assured vacuum-assisted braking even when the engine stalled.

Like Ford and even American Motors, Chrysler followed GM's lead and introduced four-door hardtops in all five divisions. But while GM's pioneering pillarless four-doors surrendered rear-seat room for their rakish roof lines, Chrysler's four-door hardtops maintained the same roof contours and rear-door openings as the corporation's four-door sedans. This solution, however, created its own problem. On MoPar sedans, a fixed rear quarter window kept the rear door glass small enough to roll all the way down into the door. But the designers didn't want the fixed window cluttering the hardtop's clean lines. So they devised something they called a "K-door," with a *two-piece* movable window.

"That one I did," remembered Hal Pilkey. "It brought the window way back over the wheel well for access to the back seat." As passengers turned the window crank, a small quarter window pivoted forward, while the main window tipped backward; the two windows slid past each other as they disappeared completely into a stepped slot in the top of the door. A sliding clip

held the two pieces of glass together at the top. When raised, a mechanism pressed the windows against each other to assure a waterproof seal.

Highway Hi-Fi appeared this year, too. Jointly engineered with CBS Columbia, this was a phonograph that fit under the dash, providing pre-recorded road music in those pre-eight-track days. Chrysler claimed that the specially designed tone arm wouldn't skip under "normal" driving conditions. Meanwhile, Columbia monopolized the supply of 7-inch, 16-rpm discs, which played 45-60 minutes per side. Chrysler even packed six discs with every Highway Hi-Fi that rolled off the assembly line; standard-equipment titles included *The Pajama Game,* Paul Weston's *Quiet Jazz,* and *Davy Crockett.*

Safety also received some attention from Highland Park. Like Ford, Chrysler introduced a new door latch that hooked into a U-shaped strike plate, so that it wouldn't pull apart in a crash. Chrysler also debuted its first 12-volt batteries, introduced longer-reach spark plugs to burn a leaner mixture in V-8s, and developed new production techniques that reduced distortion in curved windshields.

seats of GM's convertibles should have been forced to sit in a Plymouth first.

The engine springs to life with a twist of the key (not with a push on the "neutral" button, as on some later, higher-priced MoPars). It idles almost silently as we open up the top: Just release a single chromed lever above the center of the windshield, and then twist the handsome, plated switch to the left of the steering column and the canvas retracts into its storage space behind the seats.

With the top safely stowed, I punched "Drive" and opened the carb. The Belvedere doesn't exactly scream off the line, but once rolling it gathers speed quickly, smoothly, and with so little fuss I was astonished to see how rapidly the speedometer wrapped around from 0-60—and then how soon it reached 75 from there. Leon said he "never had too much trouble getting up to 100" in his original car, and I have no trouble believing him.

With the top down the windshield looks

Above and below: *Vinyl interior has comfortable chair-high seats up front and offers easy access to rear. Abstract pattern and horizontal embossing looks like fifties home furniture design.* **Below right:** *Exceptionally good trunk space for a convertible.*

low and shallow, like the minimal windscreen of a foreign roadster. Yet despite this and the high seats, we cruised at 65 mph without any uncomfortable buffeting. We didn't even have to raise our voices much to talk to each other. The engine barely whispers an electric whir, and the suspension and tires do their jobs with a minimum of road noise. The non-assisted brakes provide firm feedback and seem pretty effective for their time.

Motor Trend groused that its '56 Plymouth test car "wandered at high speeds," and likened its ride to "a foot-thick layer of sponge rubber." But Leon's Belvedere seems to track straight and stable, requiring less course-correction than I've come to expect in a fifties-vintage automobile. Its ride is soft, but controlled and level; the manual steering turns easily, feeding back just enough information to inspire confidence. Of course, a 90-degree change in direction requires some wheel-winding, but again not as much as I expected.

By the standards of its time, in fact, the Plymouth feels tight and responsive. Like most cars of its era, however, it quickly reaches the limit of its handling. Charging into an off-ramp, the chassis remains poised, even as the Fury-size tires Leon has fitted howl a warning. But push it just a little harder, and suddenly a combination of extreme body roll and grinding understeer threaten

the meager grip of the outside front tire. In this respect the Plymouth is no worse than any other mid-fifties sedan—just more disappointing, because its taut, solid road feel promises so much more.

Road-race handling, however, was never Plymouth's goal. Instead, the Belvedere excels in overall refinement: smooth power, a quiet ride, a consistent impression of solid, quality construc-

Selling Plymouths: The Continuing Saga

Just as the '56 models appeared in late '55, Chrysler president Lester L. "Tex" Colbert announced a major change in the way that Plymouths would be sold—ending the 25-year-old arrangement in which Chrysler, De-Soto, and Dodge franchises all sold Plymouth as a second line. Among other reasons, Colbert noted that "the multiplicity of body styles, color combinations, and accessory options demanded by today's buying public" made it impractical for a dealer to stock parts for more than one make. Colbert expected to introduce stand-alone Plymouth stores in selected cities first, then later in more rural regions. "The point is being reached," continued Colbert, "...when deeper market penetration for each of the company's car lines can best be achieved in many areas through divisional-line dealerships."

tion. In these categories, the '56 Belvedere leaves Ford and Chevrolet behind and approaches the medium-price field.

Interestingly, I've come away from other Plymouths, from other eras, with exactly the same impression. Could Plymouth be one of America's most underrated nameplates? ଚ

Acknowledgments and Bibliography

Books: Jim Benjaminson, Plymouth 1946-1959; *Don Butler,* The Plymouth and DeSoto Story; *John A. Gunnell (editor),* Standard Catalog of American Cars 1946-1975.

Periodicals: Jeffrey I. Godshall, "1955 Plymouth: MoPar's Runaway Success," SIA #68; Jim Lodge, "The '56 Chrysler Line" and "Spotlight on Detroit," Motor Trend, November 1955; and "'56 Plymouth Road Test," Motor Trend, February 1956; Walt Woron, "'55 Plymouth V8," Motor Trend, February 1955; "New Motion," Motor Trend, October 1955; "Chrysler Gas Turbine," Automobile Engineer, July 1956; "Plymouth Fury," Road & Track, November 1956.

Thanks to Virgil M. Exner, Jr.; to Chrysler Corporation designers Bill Brownlie, Jeff Godshall, and Hal Pilkey; Pat Foster; Kim M. Miller of the AACA Library and Research Center; Henry Siegle; and of course, special thanks to owner Leon Wolf.

By Terry Boyce, *Associate Editor*

Plymouth launched the Fury on January 10, 1956, at Chicago and Daytona Beach. Phil Walters, ex-general manager of Briggs Cunningham's Le Mans team, set two NASCAR records on the Beach that day in a stock pre-production Fury. Simultaneously, the Chicago Auto Show spotlight gave America its first glimpse of the Daytona Fury's twin. Plymouth wanted it understood right away that the Fury was a real show *and* go machine.

The Fury arrived in the wake of the Chrysler 300, the car that had spread performance fever all over Chrysler Corp. The 300's AAA and NASCAR triumphs during 1955 confirmed Mopar management's decision to go ahead with "a little 300" in every division lineup. The Fury's debut at Daytona and Chicago rounded out Chrysler Corp.'s total performance cadre for 1956. The Fury and the 300-B bowed on the same day, with the hot Dodge D-500 and the De Soto Adventurer already in production.

Putting genuinely furious stomp into the Fury had been a job for Chrysler's Corp.'s performance engineers. They decided not to use Plymouth's 277-c.i.d. "poly" V-8, rejecting it as too small. They decided, too, not to dump in one of the other division's "hemis," but instead to go to Canada and use the 303-c.i.d. V-8 from the Canadian Chrysler Windsor and Dodge Royal models. This engine used the same polyspherical combustion chamber as the U.S. Plymouth V-8 and was identical externally. Chrysler's performance engineering team found that by simply throwing in all the trick goodies of that era—domed pistons, 9.25:1 compression, big, solid-lifter cam, stronger valve springs, Carter WCFB special 4-barrel carb, and free-flow twin exhausts—that the Canadian 303 could be turned into a 240-bhp bomb. Those were horses plenty enough to make the 3,650-pound Fury hotly competitive in the mid-1950s' horsepower race, so Plymouth began to import the Canadian 303 in quantity.

Meanwhile, chassis engineers beefed the power train, suspension, and brakes to take the extra performance. Stronger U-joints and a sturdier prop shaft linked a 10-inch clutch and heavy-duty (H-D) 3-speed manual transmission (or an optional beefed bush-button PowerFlite) to a 3.73 (or 3.54) 4-pinion differential.

Heavy-duty springs went in all around, the front coils being 45%

driveReport

A month after 124.01-mph debut record, Fury ran in FX class at Daytona Speed Week. Strange quirk of fate kept pilot Phil Walters from FX honors.

In fast cornering, test Fury leans hard on outside tires, feels as if rear might let go, but it just hangs there. 1956 Fury uses front coils, went to torsion-bar front suspension for '57.

CHRYSLER CORP.

Bob Cahill (foreground) hands Chrysler 300 manifold to Donaldson as Walters looks on.

Headlights taped to give better streamlining, record-setting Fury poses with (l-r) driver Phil Walters, W.E. Zierer and Bob Cahill of Chrysler, NASCAR prexy Bill France, and mechanics Donaldson and Scales.

Fury came out as a mid-year model. As part of its debut, a pre-production coupe went to Daytona Beach, where NASCAR officials saw it set class records for the flying and standing mile: 124.01 and 82.54 mph.

Since Fury hadn't been in production 90 days required to run in stock class at Speed Week, factory put on Chrysler 300 two 4s, ran in FX.

Fury used Canadian-built 303, while biggest U.S. Plymouth V-8 was 277. Drivetrain, suspension, brakes were much beefier than in other models.

The Fury's low roof, relatively high floor, and bulky seat make entry and exit awkward for rear passengers. Front seatbacks tilt inward slightly so only one can be pushed forward at a time.

Virgil Exner, Chrysler's styling chief, and Henry King of Plymouth, collaborated on Fury.

PETERSEN PUBLISHING CO.

With radio and glovebox in center, heater, wipers, and lighter stand in front of passenger. We found gauges poorly placed, hard to see.

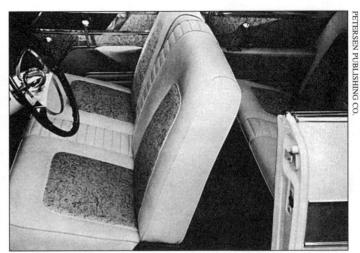

Gold metallic threads in upholstery cloth tend to tarnish and break. All 1956 Furys came in one exterior color and this single interior decor.

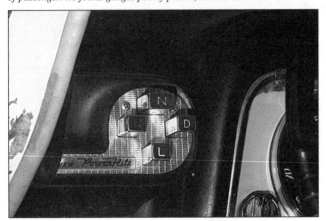

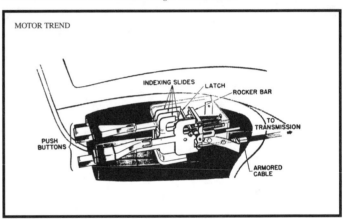

MOTOR TREND

Heavy-duty PowerFlite was optional, used pushbuttons linked to transmission via cable. Buttons determined length of cable, which determined gear.

stiffer than in conventional Plymouths (torsion bars were still a year away). Furys stood an inch lower to the ground due to those H-D springs. A high-rate front stabilizer bar, H-D Oriflow shocks, 11-inch Dodge brakes with police linings, and 7.10 x 15 tires completed the Fury's very impressive handling package.

Promoting the Fury fell to Jim Wangers, the man who eight years later made GTO a household word. Wangers and factory performance engineer Bob Cahill thought it might give the Fury a good initial boost to set some speed records on intro day. With the 303 V-8, it meant running in NASCAR's hotly contested Class 5 (259-305 c.i.d.). A 1955 De Soto, driven by *Motor Trend*'s Detroit editor, Don MacDonald, held both Flying and Standing Mile records for that class.

Hired to pilot the Fury in these pre-Speed Weeks runs was Phil Walters, also known as Ted Tappet, a man who'd helped bring Briggs Cunningham's Chrysler-powered sports cars within a trice of winning Le Mans. One of Cunningham's mechanics, Jack Donaldson, who also happened to be a close friend of Walters' (they now own a VW agency together in New York), came along to work on the Fury engine. Bob Cahill acted as project manager and direct link with the factory.

After the first pre-production Daytona Fury had been put together, it was driven from Detroit to New York to make sure it was properly broken in. Phil Walters recalls, "We had much fun enroute, dusting off Cadillacs, Fordillacs, and assorted hot rods. Then from New York, he drove the car down to Daytona Beach, and just before the runs, Donaldson did a valve job "...just to be sure."

On the morning of January 10, Walters squared off the Fury on Daytona's smooth sand. First up was the Flying Mile, Walters handily clipped off a 124.611-mph run, then backed it up with a 123.414-mph return. This gave an average of 124.01, topping the 1955 De Soto mark by some 12mph.

Next up: the Standing Start Mile. Here, the Fury ran out faultlessly

for a 2-way average of 82.54 mph. Bill France Sr. himself tech inspected and certified the Fury and its records.

With the annual Daytona Speed Week only a month away, Cahill and Wangers decided to enter the Fury in that, too. Trouble was, NASCAR's rules barred the Fury from stock-class competition because it hadn't been in production for the required 90 days. Thus, it would have to run in the anything-goes Factory Experimental (FX) class. Plymouth mulled it over, and decided to give it a whirl.

The Plymouth team hustled back to Detroit to get ready. Time was woefully short, so the Fury didn't get nearly all the modifications allowed in FX. Working feverishly, Cahill, Donaldson, and several other Plymouth engineers managed to insert a wilder cam, gain a little compression, and fit a Chrysler 300-B dual-4-barrel manifold and two Carter WCFB carbs.

The 2-4 manifold, designed for the big hemi, proved too narrow to span the 303's block valley, so Chrysler engineers fabricated half-inch steel spacers, matching them carefully to the intake ports. As time ran out, there were still problems—water outlets to be altered and linkages to hook up. Cahill, who's now Chrysler's performance planning manager, told *SIA*, "It was just a cobble job, in fact."

On February 22, the day of the Speed Week runs, the Fury boys figured they'd gotten most of the bugs out, but they worked right up to the last minute. Walters again did the driving, and the Fury turned a scorching 143.596 mph on its first, southbound run. That was five mph above the record. Swinging around for the northbound run, Walters didn't think the mild headwind would keep him from a 140-plus average.

As the Fury neared the north trap, its power dropped suddenly, the engine sputtered, and it felt to Walters as if he'd run out of gas. The gauge, though, showed plenty in the tank. That northbound run netted a disappointing 129.917, giving a respectable but under-the-record 136.415 average for the day.

What had happened? Baffled by the sudden power loss, the

Sending unit for standard Stewart-Warner tachometer fits between cap and body of distributor.

Dick Bosio, an insurance broker from Escalon, California, uses his Fury for daily commuting, drives 36 miles between home and office. At 76,000 miles, car is original except for front upholstery.

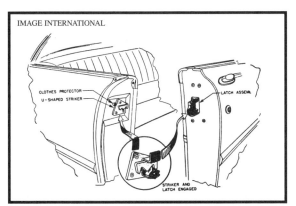

Rollover tests by Chrysler showed effectiveness of safety door latches introduced in all 1956 lines. Latch can't pull away from striker plate.

Since hood has no creases or beauty lines, hood ornament helps driver sight car in lane. Factory reports that 4,485 1956 Furys were built.

Waffled, anodized, golden aluminum side trim acts as shield for gas filler. This trim has held up amazingly well against the ravages of time.

Large, flat-floored trunk accommodates much luggage. Twin exhausts were standard, had plated tips. Fins house taillights and parking lamps.

Plymouth crew checked everything. The car was running all right again, and they couldn't find anything wrong. Says Cahill: "We knew it had to be more than the wind differential. Other cars weren't getting that much difference in time. It just happened that I took off the gas cap, and when I did, it went *schooooop*. So then we knew what had happened. The gasket on the cap had slipped and sealed off the vent hole. When Phil got going really fast, this created a vacuum in the tank—it wouldn't feed fuel." Later, back in Detroit, Cahill tossed the faulty cap into his desk drawer, and he has it there even today. For the want of a nail...," he says.

While Cahill and his crew were searching for the Fury's problem, the only other FX entry stormed up for its runs through the traps. This was the Bill Stroppe-prepped '56 Merc coupe running a Hilborn-injected, overbored Lincoln V-8. It averaged 147.26 mph, setting a new record. But the Fury still came out looking pretty good, especially with its two pre-Speed Week records intact.

(In 1957, a Fury returned to Daytona. This was a '57 hardtop, and it was an all-out FX car. Its injected 392 Chrysler hemi blew off everything at the beach that year.)

The Fury became Plymouth's top offering for 1956. Its styling had been a refinement of the regular '56 line, and the '56, of course, was a facelifted 1955.

The entire 1955 Chrysler Corp. lineup—all four divisions—became the first in which Virgil Exner enjoyed a relatively free hand. He called the shots as Chrysler Corp.'s director of design (he was later to become vice president of design), and the '55s, all of them totally new, presented a great challenge to him.

To review Exner's career briefly: He was born in 1909 in Buchanan, Michigan, grew up there, and attended Notre Dame in South Bend for two years. "And then I went to work in an advertising art studio in South Bend Advertising Artists. These people had the Studebaker account at the time. I was a car buff from about age 11 on, so I got involved in automotive work doing illustrations and catalogue design for Studebaker.

"In 1934, I came to Detroit and got a job at GM Art & Colour under Harley Earl, and I was there for four years, ending up as head of the Pontiac studio. Then from 1938 to 1949, I was back in South Bend with Studebaker, and I was responsible for all the cars designed during that time, including the postwar jobs.

"I left Studebaker in '49 and came to Chrysler. When I got there, Chrysler had no styling head—this was an extremely loose group and was controlled by Chrysler Engineering. Mr. K. T. Keller [president of Chrysler Corp.] was a pretty strong figure, as you might know, and he was quite a dictator in styling matters and had been for some years, along with Engineering.

"My first big assignment there—the first cars I had major responsibility for—were the 1955 De Soto and Chrysler. In early 1952, I was called into the Plymouth studio by Mr. Keller and Tex Colbert, and they had been doing some minor facelift work on the 1953-54

Plymouth for a proposed '55 model. Well, this car—this body shell—was completely used up, in my opinion. So when I was asked what I could do, well, I stuck my foot and neck out and said, 'I don't think there's anything you can do with this car, Mr. Keller. You need a whole new skin on it.' This was quite a shock to him—he wasn't used to having people tell him things that bluntly, but anyway it worked. A day or two later I was called in to do the job, and the 1955 Dodge followed immediately."

Work began on the 1955 Plymouth's styling on May 15, 1952, the job being shared by Exner and Henry King, Plymouth's studio head. On November 28, proposals in the form of full-sized clays for all Chrysler Corp. divisions were wheeled out into the sunlight for inspection and approval by Management. The 1955 Imperial, Chrysler, and De Soto designs were approved with minor revisions, but the Dodge and Plymouth designs were rejected. Exner admitted he wasn't happy with the grille, and he outlined changes on the spot. Management gave him the go-ahead, so Exner and King worked all the next week making drastic changes to the '55's front sheet metal. Give-and-take continued until May 18, 1953, when Chrysler's top brass finally approved the Plymouth and Dodge. The 1955 Plymouth bowed on November, 17, 1954, 30 months after work began.

For the 1956 Fury, Henry King shied away from the wild 3-color paint schemes of the time, opting instead for the broad, gold-anodized aluminum side sweeps against basic eggshell white. Gold appliqués were then all the rage, although on most cars the gold soon faded. But on Furys, the side sweep has held up very well; better than on their turbine-spoke wheel covers and grille center. De Sotos used the same golden wheel covers but with "DeS" centered in the spinner. The Fury's spinner was plain.

Inside, the Fury got a handsome eggshell-and-black upholstery material, with gold metallic threads running through it. These threads haven't worn well, and it's a rare Fury today that has much of its original upholstery left.

We had one devil of a time finding a stock '56 Fury to drive and photograph for this report. When we finally did, it turned up virtually in *SIA*'s backyard. Dick Bosio, an Escalon, California, insurance broker, uses his 76,000-mile Fury to commute 36 miles a day to and from work. It's a good old car, he says.

I took my *SIA* tape recorder along on this driveReport, and the playback sounds something like this: "The first thing that hits me as I climb into the Fury is an anticipated wave of nostalgia—anticipated because a decade ago I learned to drive in my dad's '56 Plymouth Plaza 6. Dad's Plaza came from the other end of the option spectrum, but I recognize it even here. It was white, too, and even though the Fury's dash is dressed up, it still has those familiar gauge faces—the same dials used, it seems, in all 1955-56 Chrysler Corp. cars.

"The Fury has idiot lights for oil and amps, yet I believe they're an improvement over the '55 Plymouth, which stuck real oil and amp gauges way over in front of the passenger. For '56, heater and wiper controls have been put in those gauge holes, and they're a long reach past the center-mounted glovebox.

"Another mild goof is the position of the ignition key. The Fury's standard 6,000-rpm tach fits where the key used to be. This puts the key up behind the steering wheel. Even for long-armed me, it's a bit awkward.

"Once I get hold of the key and twist it, the 303 roars to life instantly. There's no PARK position, so for parking I have to rely on the T-handle emergency brake. I simply push Button D on the PowerFlite console and I'm off. 1956 was the first year for pushbuttons—'55s had a lever that poked menacingly out of the dash. I don't believe it takes more time for the pushbutton to select a gear than it did to move the '55 lever, but since I'm not doing anything else, the wait seems longer. This pushbutton system, by the way, operates a single push-pull cable to the transmission. Pushing a button moves the cable to a position corresponding to the range selected. It's all mechanical, with no solenoids or electrical hookups as in the Edsel and Packard pushbutton systems.

"Out on the highway, cruising at 60, two things bother me. First, there's a lot of wind noise, even though this Fury has wind deflectors. Second, the special squared-off horn ring cuts directly into my line of sight to the speedo and tach. This electronic tach, by the way, supplied

WHAT IS A POLYSPHERICAL HEAD?

It's an unusual combustion chamber arrangement based on a theory worked out by pioneer engine designer Harry Ricardo. Simply stated, it's that volumetric and thermal efficiency are improved by *not* placing intake and exhaust valves parallel to one another.

In the Plymouth head, this meant moving the intake valve longitudinally but keeping it laterally inclined in relation to the cylinder axis, as per the hemi (see SIA No. 8, p. 12). The poly's exhaust valve is located parallel to, but offset from, the cylinder axis. Between the two valves and outboard of the combustion chamber is the sparkplug. What it all boils down to is that Plymouth's poly head configuration is only slightly less efficient than the hemi's, but it's considerably less expensive to manufacture. One big reason for the cost saving is that the poly uses a single rocker shaft per head, while the hemi used two shafts. The poly heads are also smaller and lighter and require less machining.

specifications

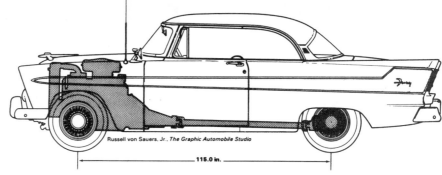

6.25 in.

58.8 in.

1956 Plymouth Fury hardtop

Russell von Sauers, Jr., *The Graphic Automobile Studio*

115.0 in.

1956 Plymouth Fury Special 8 sport coupe

Price when new	$2,599 f.o.b. Detroit (1956)
Current valuation*	Xlnt, $860; good, $575; fair, $150
Options	H-D PowerFlite; power steering, brakes, windows, seat; Search-Tune radio

ENGINE

Type	Ohv V-8, cast en bloc, water-cooled, full pressure lubrication
Bore x stroke	3.81 inches x 3.31 inches
Displacement	303.0 cubic inches
Compression ratio	9.25:1
Horsepower @ rpm	240 @ 4,800
Torque @ rpm	1310 @ 2,800
Induction system	Single 4-bbl. Carter carburetor, mechanical fuel pump
Exhaust system	Dual exhausts, twin reverse-flow mufflers
Electrical system	12-volt battery/coil

TRANSMISSION

Type	Heavy-duty PowerFlite 2-speed automatic, pushbuttons on dash
Ratios: 1st	1.72:1
2nd	1.00:1
Reverse	2.39:1

DIFFERENTIAL

Type	Open driveshaft, hypoid, spiral-bevel gears
Ratio	3.73:1
Drive axles	Semi-floating

STEERING

Type	Full-time, integral power steering, worm & roller box
Ratio	20.1:1
Turns lock-to-lock	3.75
Turn circle	40.5 feet

BRAKES

Type	Heavy-duty 4-wheel hydraulic drums, internal expanding
Drum diameter	11.0 inches
Total lining area	173.5 square inches

CHASSIS & BODY

Frame	Channel-section steel
Body construction	All steel
Body style	2-dr., 4-pass. hardtop coupe

SUSPENSION

Front	Independent, unequal A-arms, coil springs, tubular hydraulic shocks, anti-roll bar
Rear	Semi-elliptic H-D longitudinal leaf springs, tubular hydraulic shocks, anti-roll bar
Tires	7.10 x 15, 4-ply whitewall
Wheels	Pressed steel, drop-center safety rims, lug-bolted to brake drum

WEIGHTS AND MEASURES

Wheelbase	115.0 inches
Overall length	204.8 inches
Overall height	58.8 inches
Overall width	74.6 inches
Front track	58.8 inches
Rear track	58.9 inches
Ground clearance	6.25 inches
Curb weight	3,650 pounds

CAPACITIES

Crankcase	5 quarts
Cooling system	21.0 quarts
Fuel tank	17 gallons

FUEL CONSUMPTION

Best	11-13 mpg
Average	9-11 mpg

PERFORMANCE (from **Motor Trend,** 6/56)

0-30 mph	3.7 sec.
0-60 mph	10.2 sec.
Standing 1/4 mile	17.5 and 79.5 mph
Top speed	111.0 mph (up to 143.6 mph at Daytona with modifications)

*Courtesy **Antique Automobile Appraisal**, Prof. P.B. Hertz

---

by Stewart-Warner, didn't win any honors—several road testers of 1956 mentioned that it was sluggish and couldn't be trusted.

"The Fury makes lots of gutsy engine noise, especially when I tromp it. The 303 winds willingly and smoothly up to 60 very quickly, and then it seems to flatten out. But all I have to do is push the L button to hold it in LOW safely up to 60 or so. Kickdown is automatic, and it comes in mightily in the 30-40-mph range.

"One driver back in 1956 said he could take the Fury through corners a full 15 mph faster than other 1956 Plymouths. This Fury, though, doesn't inspire my confidence that much. I have to keep in mind, however, that the suspension does have 76,000 miles on it. Going into a sharp turn, the Fury heels quite a bit. Then, just as I've decided I've taken it too fast, the car almost magically flattens out, putting me out of the turn on an even, stable keel. As ever, the coaxial, full-time power steering lacks road feel, but that's something you get used to.

"Those 11-inch Dodge binders still pull the Fury down straight and

quick, and the vacuum boost isn't too touchy. This car rides nicely, taking bumps smoothly and gently—perhaps too gently for an H-D suspension job. I would have expected more jostling."

It's a modern, comfortable car that can run with the best of them, even today. Primary drawbacks as I see them are the fragile upholstery (Dick Bosio put clear vinyl seatcovers over the rear bench but was too late to save the front one) and the fact that in areas with salted winter roads, '56 Plymouths soon rusted out beyond redemption. total production of '56 Furys was 4,485, according to Chrysler Corp., yet it took us 13 months to locate just one that was anything near original shape. 👓

Our thanks to Dick Bosio, Escalon, California; John Bunnell and bob Cahill of Chrysler Corp.; Virgil M. Exner, Birmingham, Michigan; Phil Walters, Woodbury, New York; Donald Frolich, Cupertino, California; and Bob Dupin, Louisville, Kentucky.

1959 Chevrolet, Ford, and Plymouth

by Tim Howley
photos by Rick Lenz

NINETEEN Fifty-Nine! What a year! Alaska and Hawaii were admitted to the union. Castro's guerrilla forces overthrew the Batista government in Cuba. Soviet Premier Nikita Khrushchev visited the United States. And Senator John F. Kennedy began his long campaign for the US Presidency. In the world of automobiles, Ford and Chevrolet slugged it out again for first place, with Ford winning, while both makes enjoyed sales increases of approximately 50 percent. Things didn't go so well at Chrysler compared to their banner year

of 1957. All of their cars gained a somewhat unjustified reputation for shoddy workmanship, and in 1959 their market share dropped down to the 12-13 percent range.

This was the last year that the Big Three fielded only big cars.

And all three of these makes were just

different enough that the buyer had some real choices. Now, 36 years later in the sunny hills north of San Diego, *SIA* has assembled all three makes of '59 convertibles for a nostalgic evaluation, and has rolled back the clock to the time when you could still buy a sundae for 35 cents or catch the first run of Doris Day and Rock Hudson in *Pillow Talk* for about $1.50.

We assembled three '59 convertibles at Deer Park, which has been the site of several of our driveReports in the past. Deer Park, a winery and auto museum a few miles north of Escondido, California, has over 100 convertibles. Two of the convertibles in this report belong to Deer Park. The other hails from Bloomington, California, near San Bernardino.

1959 Chevrolet

Once GM styling got a sneak look over the fence at the 1957 Chrysler offerings, it was back to the drawing boards on a crash basis. The result was an entirely new 1959 General Motors lineup from Cadillac on down to Chevrolet. Now, for the first time, Chevrolet had the bigger B body which was shared with Pontiac, Oldsmobile and Buick. (Some sources say that even the '59 Cadillac had the B body.) Chevrolet decided to turn the Chrysler fins on their sides, creating the famous bat wings.

While the Chevrolet chassis was not completely new, there were significant changes to accommodate the wider bodies and wider track. The track was not as wide as the Pontiac's, but 1.5 inches wider in the front and .5-inch wider in the rear than the 1958 Chevrolet. The '59 chassis had a 119-inch wheelbase, 1.5 inches longer than the 1958. The length went from 209 inches to 210.9 inches. This chassis, combined with the body, brought the height down 1.3 inches from 1958, while allowing even more head room, leg room, hip and shoulder room than the 1958, even in the Impala two-door hardtop. Maybe it wasn't the best Chevrolet ever, but it was a vast improvement over the craziness of '58. (See *SIA #140*, April 1994.)

Realizing early-on that air-suspension was dead, Chevrolet made important 1959 suspension changes to offer better handling with standard four-coil suspension. The front suspension was refined slightly, but not changed. In the rear, a new anti-sway bar and anti-twist arm were added. The purpose of this was to keep the rear axle in position better on fast turns or on bumpy roads. The overall steering ratio was higher with manual steering, but not power steering; turns-lock-to-lock were the same.

Brakes got a big boost for '59. While retaining the same 11-inch drum diameter, the drums were widened an inch to increase the total brake swept area from 157 inches to 199.5 inches. Both drums and wheels were redesigned for better cooling to give Chevrolet what *Motor Trend* described as "just about the best brakes in the Big Three."

Except for minor changes in the six-cylinder engine for improved fuel economy, specifications for the eight-cylinder engines remained unchanged. No new V-8 engines were added at the beginning of the year. But mid-year a 335-horsepower 348 replaced the 315-horsepower engine. There was a change in spark advance, better cooling around spark plugs and an optional dual exhaust system was offered. This was insignificant

People may complain that new cars all look like flying jelly beans, but that wasn't the case in 1959, when a quick glance could tell the many differences between Ford, Chevrolet and Plymouth styles.

Three approaches to a car's identity. Impala model was only a year old in '59, yet the crossed flags and leaping animal were already a familiar sight. Ford's coat of arms had been around since the early fifties and has a traditional look. Plymouth went full space age in '59 with rocket-like fender accents.

compared to the increased weight which dragged down performance and fuel economy for all Chevy eight-cylinder engines.

A number of improvements were made in the optional Turboglide transmission. In fact, some improvements had been made during the 1958 model year. However, the basic weaknesses of the transmission continued, and no real satisfactory solution was found until Chevrolet replaced it with TurboHydraMatic in 1962.

Once again the lineup of series and body styles changed. The Delray was out and the Biscayne became the bottom end. For the first time since its introduction as a series in 1953, the Bel Air was no longer top-of-the-line. It was replaced by the new Impala line consisting of both six- and eight-cylinder versions of a two-door hardtop, a very distinctive new four-door hardtop with wraparound rear window, a four-door sedan and a convertible. The wagons remained a separate series. An exciting new addition was the El Camino pickup in answer to Ford's Ranchero. Like the Ranchero, it was marketed through the Chevrolet Truck Division.

1959 Ford

Admitting very early on that the 1958 Ford was a mistake, Ford completely restyled both the greenhouse and the outer body panels for '59. The styling strategy for the '58 Ford was to "lunch" off the Thunderbird. It wasn't one of Ford's better ideas. The '59 Ford was a refreshing change. This model year was the ultimate expression of Ford styling head George Walker's "crisp" look, and Walker in later years told the press it was his favorite model. The head of Ford Division styling at the time was Joe Oros, and much of the actual execution of the '59 was done under John Foster. The Galaxie models were a mid-year addition created by adding a Thunderbird-style roofline with the nearly flat backlight. This was one Thunderbird imitation that came off extremely well, and Ford stayed with the Galaxie look for years.

In 1959, all Ford body styles were offered on one wheelbase, 118 inches, the 116-inch wheelbase for the Custom and Custom 300 series being dropped. The Custom series itself was dropped, but the Custom 300 series was continued on the larger wheelbase with a two- and four-door sedan and a business sedan without a back seat. The number of Fairlane models was paired from four down to two, a two- and four-door sedan. The Fairlane 500 series was continued with a two- and four-door hardtop and a two- and four-door sedan. However, early in the year, the Skyliner

retractable hardtop and Sunliner convertible were moved up into the Galaxie series. This new series, which arrived in the very early spring, also included a two- and four-door hardtop and a two- and four-door sedan. The only addition in the wagon series was the four-door Ranch Wagon, and now all Ford wagons came on a 118-inch-wheelbase chassis rather than 116 inches.

Ford's 1959 advertising boasted wider bodies, a thinner roofline, more luggage space and all-new exterior sheet metal. Ford frames now extended out to nearly maximum body width, allowing passengers more leg and foot room and affording a slightly lower center of gravity than the '57-'58s. Suspension changes were minimal, but in keeping with Chevrolet's optional *Posi-traction* limited-slip differential, Ford announced one of their own design for 1959 called *Equa-Lock*.

Cruise-O-Matic, introduced a year earlier, now was adjusted to take better advantage of low-speed torque, and was coupled with slightly higher rear-end ratios. One noticeable improvement was its ability to pull out of mud, loose gravel or snow, without spinning the wheels, and it also provided better engine braking on downgrades. The two-speed Fordomatic, which had been around since 1951, received its first major redesign. The new Fordomatic was over 20 percent lighter and had 105 fewer moving parts. The results were an improvement in economy and low-speed performance.

The engine lineup was the same as in 1958 except the engines were detuned and the horsepower slightly lowered in the 292 and 332 to allow the cars to run on regular gasoline. The 292 was now rated at 200 horsepower as opposed to 205 in 1958, and the 332 was rated at 225 horsepower, down from 240. The 265-horsepower version of the 332 was no longer available. The Thunderbird 352, however, remained an option, still developing 300 horsepower.

Instrument panels were completely redesigned for easier reading, and along with the new instrumentation came a rainbow of new interior colors and fabrics. Coming or going, '59 Fords were sharp-looking cars, and they sported the biggest round taillamp design of any Ford ever. Tom McCahill called them "Jello mold" taillamps.

1959 Plymouth

1959 Plymouths were essentially much-warmed-over '58-'59 models. Tailfins were bigger. The grille was now an eggcrate. The hood was flatter and the headlamps had huge eyebrows, possibly inspired by DeSoto-Plymouth's wisecracking salesman, Groucho Marx. The more expensive Plymouths used anodized-silver side trim panels. The Savoy replaced the Plaza at the low end with a club sedan, four-door sedan and

*Dashboard designs also show wide variance. Chevrolet's, **top left**, looks to be the most readable. Ford's, **above left**, is simple to the point of nearly Spartan, while Plymouth, **right**, uses the Buck Rogers approach.*

business coupe. The Belvedere was downgraded a notch with a club sedan, four-door sedan, hardtop sport coupe, four-door hardtop and a convertible. The Fury became the slightly above the middle range model with a four-door sedan and hardtop coupe and a four-door hardtop. The Sport Fury was the top of the line, offered only in a hardtop and convertible. This year Plymouth offered seven models of Suburban station wagons, one more model than Ford, but still three less than Chevrolet.

By comparison, the choice of engines was quite simple. The standard Savoy, Belvedere and Suburban engine was a 132-horsepower six of 230.2 cubic inches. The most popular engine was the 230-horsepower version of the 318, standard on the Fury. The Sport Fury came with a 260-horsepower version of this engine standard. The "Golden Commando" 361 developing 305 horsepower was available on any Plymouth and was frequently opted for on the Sport Fury.

Complementing Plymouth's lineup of shining V-8s was TorsionAire front suspension. All Chrysler products got TorsionAire in '57, the Plymouth system was just much simpler than the others. In an era when the whole industry was just plain sloppy in the suspension department, Chrysler had a real breakthrough. While conventional coil front springs in those years just wobbled away, the torsion bar wound up tight against its anchor point with a twisting motion. The result was lack of road shock in the passenger compartment and incredibly positive control without all the characteristic understeer of Fords and Chevys of the era. In addition, Chrysler products had a wide, lateral spring base, higher spring rates, lower center of gravity and improved rear tracking. TorsionAire was a front suspension system only. Rear suspension was parallel leaf springs.

What type of car was tested?

CHEVROLET: Impala series convertible, 119-inch-wheelbase. Standard 283-c.i.d., ohv V-8 with two-barrel carburetor, 8.5:1 compression ratio developing 185 horsepower. A Powerglide transmission combined with a 3.36:1 rear-end ratio. Power steering, radio and heater.

FORD: Galaxie 500 convertible, 118-inch wheelbase. 292-c.i.d., ohv V-8 with two barrel carburetor, 8.8:1 compression ratio, developing 200 horsepower. Ford-omatic transmission combined with a 3.29:1 rear end ratio. Radio and heater.

PLYMOUTH: Sport Fury convertible, 118-inch wheelbase. 317.6-c.i.d., ohv V-8 with four-barrel carburetor, 9.0:1 com-

Motor Trend's Test of the 1959 Big Three

In their February 1959 issue, *Motor Trend* evaluated a 1959 Chevrolet Impala with a 280-horsepower, 348-c.i.d. V-8; a 1959 Ford Fairlane 500 with a 300-horsepower, 352-c.i.d. V-8; and a 1959 Plymouth Fury with a 305-horsepower, 361-c.i.d. V-8. The cars were brand new, the test conditions at the Riverside Speedway were totally controlled, all three cars were four-doors, and the engines were as closely matched as possible.

Our three cars were all convertibles with the base engines offered in these models. The Ford and Chevrolet are Deer Park cars and both are in good but not perfect condition. The Plymouth Sport Fury belongs to Gary Grossich of Bloomington, California, near San Bernardino. While the car is mostly original, the interior is all new. He drives the car regularly and is constantly upgrading it; consequently, it was in the best condition of the three cars, which may have influenced our driving impressions, to a degree.

Here's how *Motor Trend* in '59 summed up the best points of all three cars:

CHEVROLET: "This is probably the smoothest, most quiet, softest riding car in its price class. Handling and steering are not up to the high performance of the engine, but it is certainly a comfortable family touring car with ample passenger and luggage space. Personal opinions are varied concerning horizontal fin treatment, but if 'all new styling' is important to the buyer, then that is another point in the car's favor.

FORD: "The outstanding feature of the Ford is the solid feel of the body. Doors close like bank vaults and give a feeling of extreme rigidity and safety. For those who like a little feel to their power steering, the Ford is the best choice, although the wheel requires more turns and a bit more effort than the Plymouth's."

PLYMOUTH: "Outstanding points for Plymouth's Fury are its performance and handling. Here is a car that is fun to drive out in the flat, on curving roads, or through the mountains, yet it provides comfort and usable luggage space for family touring. Styling is a matter of opinion, but this sporty design, not too much different from the 1958 models, should hold up well for several years without becoming outdated by major facelifts by competitors."

Specifications: 1959 Chevrolet Impala/1959 Ford Galaxie/1959 Plymouth Fury

	1959 Chevrolet Impala	1959 Ford Galaxie	1959 Plymouth Fury
Base price when new	$2,967	$2,957	$3,125
Standard equipment	Full wheel covers, pull-up rear seat arm rest, Impala body and trim package	Full wheel covers, Galaxie body and trim package	Sport Fury trim package, full wheel covers, simulated tire on the trunk, swivel seats, dash padding
Extras on this car	Radio, Powerglide, power steering	Radio, Fordomatic	Radio, heater, TurboFlite, power steering, power brakes, power windows, power seats, remote left-hand outside mirror, right hand outside mirror
Engine	V-8	V-8	V-8
Bore x stroke	3.875 x 3.0 inches	3.75 x 3.30 inches	3.906 x 3.312 inches
Displacement	283 cubic inches	292 cubic inches	317.6
Compression ratio	8.5:1	8.8:1	9.0:1
Horsepower @ rpm	185 @ 4,600 rpm	200 @ 4,400 rpm	260 @ 4,400
Max. torque @ rpm	275 foot pounds @ 2,400	297 foot pounds @ 2,400	N/A
Induction system	2-bbl carburetor	2-bbl carburetor	4-bbl carburetor
Exhaust system	Cast-iron manifolds, single exhausts	Cast-iron manifolds, single exhausts	Cast-iron manifolds, single exhausts
Electrical system	12-volt battery/coil	12-volt battery/coil	12-volt battery/coil
Transmission	Powerglide 2-speed automatic, column shift, max. torque conv. 2.1	Fordomatic 2-speed automatic torque converter	TorqueFlite 3-speed automatic planetary torque converter, dual range
Ratios	1st: 1.82; 2nd: 1.00; Reverse: 1.82	1st: 2.40; 2nd: 1.47; 3rd: 1.00	1st: 2.45; 2nd: 1.43; 3rd: 1.00
Differential	Hypoid	Hypoid	Hypoid
Ratio	3.36:1	3.29:1	3.36:1
Drive axles	Semi-floating	Hotchkiss drive w/leaf springs	Hotchkiss drive w/leaf springs
Steering	Saginaw internal recirculating ball type, power assisted	Recirculating ball type, power assisted	Recirculating ball type, power assisted
Turns, lock-to-lock	5.2	4.75	3.5
Ratio	24:1	25.2:1	20:1
Turning circle	40.2 feet	40.6 feet	42 feet
Brakes	Bendix 4-wheel hydraulically operated, cast-iron drums, power assist	Bendix 4-wheel hydraulically operated, cast-iron drums, power assist	Bendix 4-wheel hydraulically operated, cast-iron drums, power assist
Drum diameter	11 inches	11 inches	11 inches
Total swept area	199.5 square inches	180.2 square inches	184 square inches
Frame	Box and channel section welded steel, tubular center membrane, X-configuration (no side rails), 2 crossmembers	Ladder-type boxed side rails with 4 crossmembers	Channel section steel
Body construction	All steel, bolted to frame at 12 points	All steel, bolted to frame	All steel, bolted to frame
Body style	2-door, 4-5 passenger convertible	2-door, 4-5 passenger convertible	2-door, 4-5 passenger convertible
Front suspension	Independent unequal length upper and lower control arms, coil springs, tubular hydraulic shock absorbers, torsional front sway bar	Independent ball-joint with tubular shocks located inside the coil	TorsionAire torsion bar, with tubular shocks
Rear suspension	Rigid axle, coil springs, 3 locational members, tubular hydraulic shock absorbers	Semi-elliptical leaf springs with tubular shocks	Semi-elliptical leaf springs with tubular shocks
Wheels	5.0 x 14-inch stamped steel, 5 bolt	5.0 x 14-inch stamped steel, 5 bolt	5.0 x 14-inch stamped steel, 5 bolt
Tires	Tubeless, 7.50 14-inch 4-ply	Tubeless, 7.50 14-inch 4-ply	Tubeless, 7.50 14-inch 4-ply
Wheelbase	119 inches	118 inches	118 inches
Overall length	210.9 inches	208.1 inches	214.5 inches
Overall width	79.9 inches	76.6 inches	79.4 inches
Overall height	55 inches	56 inches	53.5 inches
Front track	60.3 inches	59 inches	60.9 inches
Rear track	59.3 inches	56.4 inches	59.6 inches
Ground clearance	6 inches	6 inches	6 inches
Shipping weight	3,650 pounds	3,628 pounds	3,670 pounds
Crankcase capacity	4 quarts	5 quarts	5 quarts
Cooling system capacity	18 quarts	18 quarts	18 quarts
Fuel tank	20 gallons	20 gallons	20 gallons

pression ratio, developing 260 horse-power. TorqueFlite transmission combined with a 3.36:l rear-end ratio. Power steering, power brakes, radio and heater, power windows, power seat, Mirror-Matic left-hand remote mirror, right-hand mirror, deluxe bumper guards.

We note that Plymouth offered two convertibles in 1959, the Belvedere and the Sport Fury. A 1959 Chevrolet Impala with our base V-8 listed for $2,967. A 1959 Ford Galaxie convertible with our base V-8 listed for $2,957. The closest Plymouth convertible was the Belvedere with the 230-horsepower Fury engine, the engine we tested. That car listed at $2,814. The Fury listed for $3,125, considerably more than the Ford and Chevy. For that price you got a lot fancier package than the top-of-the-line offered by either Ford or Chevrolet. You got deluxe exterior trim, a fake tire on the rear deck and deluxe interior with swivel seats and dash padding all standard equipment. Plus this particular car was loaded with power seats, power windows, power steering, power brakes and a host of goodies. All of the side trim on the Sport Fury is unique to that model and is interchangeable with no other Plymouth of that year.

Which car has the best overall quality?
Hard to comment. Chrysler products were severely criticized for poor quality in the late fifties, but 1959 models were much better than 1957s and 1958s. In fact, quality control was dealt with during the 1958 model year. This author owned both a 1959 Ford wagon and a 1959 Bel Air sedan when they were new, and considered them both fine cars. All three makes gave the buyers a lot of quality for the price. Of the three cars, we prefer the 1959 Ford styling. The 1959 Chevrolet styling is somewhat bizarre, but we like it. 1959 Plymouth styling takes some getting used to, but overall it is quite pleasing.

Driving Position and Instrument Panel.
CHEVROLET: Driver is positioned for excellent visibility, looking out of a wraparound windshield with very little distortion. Wheel does not block vision of a normal-sized driver. Visibility of all instruments is excellent, with a centrally located speedometer flanked by four other dials. The numerals are a nice crisp white against a black field. Instruments are particularly easy to read at night. Quadrant-type gear selector is mounted on the steering column and has no illumination at night, which is mildly annoying.
Foot-operated parking brake is released by pulling a lever under the dash. Left fresh air vent is actuated by a knob under the dash, but the passenger must operate a similar control on the right. Not as convenient for the driver as the

Engine sizes correlate to their brake horsepower. Chevy has 283 cubes/185 horse, Ford's 292 pumps 200 ponies, and Plymouth's 318 shoves out 260 horses.

Ford. The Chevrolet hood releases from the exterior; so anybody can easily steal your battery.

FORD: Even in 1959 Ford was making progress in the area of ergonomics, or the relationship of the driver to the windshield, the wheel and the controls. It just feels good sitting behind the deep-dish steering wheel of the '59 Ford. There's a little more windshield distortion than the Chevrolet has, but not enough to be annoying. All the controls are within easy reach of the driver, but the white speedometer numerals on a silver field are difficult to read. Quadrant-type transmission selector is mounted on the steering column, but the indicators are in the instrument panel and are lighted at night; they are much easier to read than Chevrolet's. A left-handed starter key position is a bit annoying. This year Ford went to a foot-operated parking brake, which is released not by pulling up, but by pushing down on the lever.
We particularly liked the simplicity and convenience of the Ford air vent levers directly in front of the driver to the left and right of the steering column. The Ford hood releases from below the instrument panel to protect your battery from theft. In addition, Ford hoods of 1957-59 were forward-hinged for some-

what better engine accessibility than other makes. This was done, however, not for owner convenience but for production line cost savings.

PLYMOUTH: It would appear that Plymouth has the most windshield glass of the three, and also the least distortion. However, if you're small you may find that the rear-view mirror mounted on the top of the instrument panel blocks your vision. The left-handed push-buttons are bizarre. From top to bottom they are Drive, Neutral, Reverse, Second and First, which means that Drive and Neutral are switched from the normal detent positions, and there is *no* Park. To hold the car you must use the hand brake, which is the old-fashioned handle you pull out, not a foot brake with a hand release as on Ford and Chevrolet. Buttons also control all functions of heater, ventilator and defroster, but the actual heat control is by a ball-tipped lever sliding vertically in a dash slot next to the button "console." This is the most gadgety of all three cars, and it takes some real getting used to, but all of the controls are extremely well laid out and gauges are quite easy to read. There is only one vent on the Plymouth for both the driver and passenger, but the ducts can be controlled. Like the Chevrolet, the Plymouth hood releases from the exterior.

*All three comparison convertibles have multicolored vinyl or vinyl/cloth interiors. Chevy, **above,** has rear seat radio speaker. Ford, **below,** uses three tones of vinyl but only Plymouth, **facing page,** goes all-out with swiveling seats.*

What are they like to drive?

CHEVY: Respectable but not astonishing acceleration with the base V-8 combined with Chevy's tried and true Powerglide. Comfortable and quiet at all speeds up to about 70 mph. Engine and transmission noise are very low, and road rumble is well insulated from the passengers. (These comments apply to the closed cars. Convertibles are a special case. You put up with the wind to have a collector car that costs several times as much as a sedan.) Wide curves present no problems. Power steering makes turning easy at all speeds. There is, however, plenty of body lean on the tight curves at almost any speed above 20 mph. This car is definitely not a mountain goat. Understeer can get annoying, and the front wheels don't seem to want to go in the direction they are pointed. But try as we did, we could not get the rear end to break loose. This was no doubt due to the Chevy's excellent rear suspension. We also suspect that the wider track played no small role in improved handling. One and a half

inches wider in the front and a half inch wider in the rear than the '58 may not look like a lot on paper, but it sure translates to great benefits on the highway, although not the byway. This car is no great hill climber. The 348 is definitely the recommended engine if you're heading for the mountains.

In 1959 *Motor Trend* tested an Impala two-door hardtop with the 280-horsepower 348 and Turboglide, but the rear-axle ratio went down to 3.08:l. Their 0-60 time from a standing start was nine seconds, and their quarter mile time was 16.3 seconds and 83.1 mph.

As for brakes, what a difference a year and 42.5 square inches of total brake lining area made. Here's how *Motor Trend* summed up the '59 brakes: "Grooved linings, increased heat dissipation area and air path slots in the wheels do a great deal to reduce brake fade. Nine panic stops from 60 mph still left a fair margin of stopping power, although maximum pedal pressure was required for the tenth effort." (Our own driveReport Impala did not have power brakes.)

FORD: The 292 is a good all-around engine but probably not quite up to the weight of the Galaxie convertible. Even though the engine is rated at higher horsepower than the Chevrolet, we did not notice any improvement in performance. The transmission on this car was the improved 1959 Fordomatic; we would have much preferred Cruise-O-Matic. Steering on this car was not power, and this really posed no problem. In fact, the car turned so easily we thought it had power steering until we looked under the hood. Wind noise at highway speeds was a real problem with all '59 Fords due to windshield and greenhouse design. Windwings also contributed to the annoyance. But road noise is pretty well insulated from the body.

As much as we like those '59 Fords, they do not handle nearly as well as the Plymouth on curving roads, and are really not even up to the Chevrolet. It loves to lean, and the tires love to squeal. And if you try taking the sharp curves too fast, the front wheels will just slide sideways and the rear end can easily get out of control. Understeer is even more extreme than the Chevrolet's. When pushed hard in turns, even at fairly low speeds, the rear end will tend to break loose. It is regrettable that Ford did not have a trailing arm at this time. *Motor Trend* noted in their 1959 three-car comparison, "Ford was just unable to come even close to the maneuverability of Plymouth or Chevrolet under as near-exact conditions as it is possible to create."

The Ford that *Motor Trend* tested in '59 for their three-car comparison was a strange combination of the 352-c.i.d. engine and Fordomatic transmission. Their 0-60 time was 10.5 seconds. The quarter-mile was done in 18 seconds at 76.5 mph.

Ford does not match up to Chevrolet in braking, either. Brake fade is noticable after three or four near panic stops, and the Ford brakes do not quickly recover either. The brakes are certainly adequate for normal stopping, but in mountain conditions the brakes will require a lot of help from downshifting. One problem is that the heavy convertible has the same 180.2 square inches of lining as the passenger cars; the wagons and retractable convertible have 191.4 square inches of brake lining. (Our driveReport Ford did not have power brakes.)

PLYMOUTH: The Plymouth Sport Fury had the biggest of the three engines tested and consequently packed the most punch. The Plymouth steers the easiest of the three (the Ford did not have power steering) and is responsive without a lot of wheel cranking at 3.5 turns lock-to-lock. But Chrysler's form of power steering leaves you with very little road feel, especially at high speeds. Wind noise at speed is greater than the Chevy but not as great as the Ford; again, this would apply to closed cars, not the convertibles tested. On the highway this car was the best of the three to drive due to the excellent all-around visibility and the best reserve of power at cruising speeds. In the mountain roads it handles like a much more modern car than it is. There is some body lean, but the car wants to go in the direction you put it without the front wheels sliding or the rear end breaking loose. The fast steering is also a big help. This car will hang on the turns at any speed up to the limit of safety. The reason, of course, is Chrysler's outstanding TorsionAire front suspension which had the other two beat by a winding country mile.

Now combine this with the 318, which was a great little engine in any Plymouth V-8 of this period, and you have one fabulous automobile. Optional on all Plymouth V-8 models was the Golden Commando package of a 361-c.i.d. V-8 with four-barrel carburetor and ten to one compression ratio to develop 305 horsepower. (The Golden Commando package had been offered in '58 with a 350-c.i.d. engine.) With this engine *Motor Trend* did 0-60 in 7.7 seconds and achieved a quarter-mile in 16.4 seconds at 83.3 mph.

Under normal driving conditions the Plymouth's brakes were adequate. But considering that this car just begs to be driven hard, they are probably not quite up to the power. After three or four panic stops, the brakes quickly fade, then recover fairly fast.

Plymouth in those years had double wheel cylinders in the front, and on models equipped with power brakes the cannister or bellows (they had two different types) is directly over the fluid resovoir, making it extremely difficult to refill.

But forget about the marginal braking, the gimmicky instrumentation and especially the pushbutton drive; the '59 Plymouth is hands-down the best of the big three, at least in our opinion. It has the look, feel and riding qualities of a much more expensive automobile. It is still a standout after 36 years. ᔕᕣ

Acknowledgments and Bibliography

Big Three Road Test, Motor Trend, February 1959; The Complete History of Chrysler, 1924-1985, *Richard M. Langworth, Jan P. Norbye, Auto Editors of Consumer Guide; 1958-59 Chevrolet Impala comparisonReport*, SIA #140, March/April 1994; 1959 Ford Country Squire driveReport, SIA #127, January/February, 1992; Ford's Buyer's Digest of New Car Facts for '59, *Ford Motor Company*; Standard Catalog of American Cars, 1946-1975, *by the Editors of Old Cars Publications.*

Special thanks to Bob Knapp and the staff at Deer Park, Escondido, California, and to Gary Grossich, Bloomington, California.

You can tell them apart out back, too. Chevy's famous gullwing rear is unique to the '59s. Ford takes their V theme to extremes in '59, and Plymouth's fins are just a hint of bigger things to come in 1960.

"NOBODY'S KID BROTHER"

1960 PLYMOUTH VALIANT

by Arch Brown
photos by Bud Juneau

FOR more than 20 years, the Chrysler Corporation had toyed with the idea of building a small car. Between 1949 and 1952 they even built a bobtail version of the Plymouth, known initially as the P-17 series. But although the P-17 was six inches shorter than the larger P-18 series, in two-door sedan form it was actually six pounds heavier than the 1949 Ford. So it could hardly be classed as "small."

The small-car project was eventually aborted, but in 1953 Plymouth cut the wheelbase of its standard cars from 118.5 to 114 inches. The cars looked stubby; the public was unimpressed, and by 1954 the hapless Plymouth had tumbled from third place to fifth in the sales race. So despite the remarkable sales record of Germany's diminutive Volkswagen, and the gains being posted by American Motors' compact Rambler, Chrysler was cautious about becoming involved in the small-car game.

By May of 1957, however, it had become common knowledge that both Ford and Chevrolet were preparing to introduce compact cars of their own. That information prompted Chrysler president "Tex" Colbert to give the green light to a highly secret research project, code-named "A907." Ultimately, 32 hand-built prototypes were developed, along with 57 engines. Some 750,000 miles were logged

Originally published in Special Interest Autos #144, Nov.-Dec. 1994

in a rigorous testing program.

The result of all this effort was the Valiant, introduced at the start of the 1960 model year, hard on the heels of Ford's Falcon and Chevrolet's Corvair.

Note, by the way, that in its first year of production, Chrysler's compact did not bear the Plymouth name. The car was a corporate endeavor, built by the Dodge Division and marketed almost entirely through Plymouth dealers. But it was neither a Dodge nor a Plymouth — nor, for that matter, a Chrysler. It was simply the Valiant. "Nobody's Kid Brother!" declared the ads.

For many years Plymouths had been sold through three separate dealer networks, side-by-side with Dodges, DeSotos and Chryslers. Possibly the original intent had been to market the Valiant the same way, but the corporation was undergoing a major realignment at that time. The DeSoto was dying; by the end of November 1960 it would disappear from the marketplace. Dodge, meanwhile, was introducing the Dart (in its original, full-sized form), and out of the corporate realignment two dealer networks were emerging, one handling Chrysler and Plymouth while the other concentrated on the Dodge.

Chrysler, of course, had always demonstrated a tendency to march to its own drummer, and certainly this was the case with respect to the Valiant. Ford's Falcon was determinedly conventional in every respect, resembling a scaled-down version of the company's full-sized models. The Corvair, meanwhile, borrowed many of its engineering concepts, including its four-wheel independent suspension and the flat-opposed, air-cooled engine, from the phenomenally successful Volkswagen.

The Valiant, on the other hand, while conventional enough with respect to its front engine/rear drive layout, offered a number of mechanical innovations. And it featured highly unusual, not to say controversial, styling, the work of Virgil Exner.

The contemporary automotive press was universally enthusiastic about the new Valiant. *Motor Trend* termed it "an excellent buy," and called attention to its "smooth ride." *Sports Car Illustrated* called it "attractive in detail and intelligent in design," describing its handling as "generally very good," which is high praise coming from that particular source. *Popular Science* said its "handling can't be faulted," describing the steering as "light and quick," and noting that "The car stays flat and upright, without body roll or sway, even when cornered fast and furiously." And Tom McCahill, writing in *Mechanix Illustrated*, declared that "The 1960 Valiant has more horsepower, more performance, more looks, more size and more price than its two closest rivals, Corvair and Falcon. Pricewise, however, a $100

*Above: First-generation Valiants were the most Euro-looking of the Big Three compacts, embodying many of the styling themes and touches Exner had been developing for years.
Below: Originally, Valiant was a separate nameplate with no Plymouth surname.*

bill will just about cover the spread of the three.... The Valiant gets my vote as the best buy of the three new compact cars and the one I'd most like to own."

Apart from the continental flavor of its styling, which *Popular Science* described as "flashy, with a European tang," the most distinctive feature of the Valiant was its "Slant Six" engine (see sidebar, page 85). American motorists were accustomed to six-cylinder engines that stood straight up, and some people poked fun at what they called the "Weary Six." But this new, over-square engine provided the Valiant with superior performance, some 19 percent faster in the zero-to-sixty run than either the Falcon or the Corvair. And in the long run it proved to be the most durable of the lot as well, which more than made

up for the fact that it wasn't quite as stingy with fuel as the competition.

Another important "first" for the Valiant, this one destined to set the pattern for the entire industry, was its use of an alternator, in lieu of the traditional generator. The new device offered a number of advantages. For one thing, it was about nine and a half pounds lighter than the generator, partly because of the aluminum used extensively in its construction. But more important, the alternator, which generates alternating, rather than direct current, keeps right on charging, even at idle, something the generator could not do. This, of course, enabled the driver to play his radio, run the heater fan, and even turn on the dome light while poking through heavy traffic — an engraved

*Top left: Hood release snaps out from center of grille. **Above:** Cat's-eye taillamps are unique to Valiant. **Right:** Deep body sculpting gives compact a big-car appearance.*

1960 Valiant Prices, Weights And Production

	Price	Weight	Production
V-100 Series:			
Sedan, 4-door, 6-passenger	$2,033	2,635 lb.	52,788
Suburban, 6-passenger	$2,345	2,815 lb.	12,018
Suburban, 9-passenger	$2,468	2,845 lb.	1,928
Total production, V-100 series:			66,734
V-200 Series:			
Sedan, 4-door, 6-passenger	$2,110	2,655 lb.	106,515
Suburban, 6-passenger	$2,423	2,855 lb.	16,368
Suburban, 9-passenger	$2,546	2,860 lb.	4,675
Total production, V-200 series:			127,558
Grand total, 1960 (model year) Valiant production:			194,292

invitation to trouble, had the car been equipped with a conventional generator.

This is not to suggest, by the way, that the Valiant was designed to operate on alternating current. As *Popular Science* explained, "six silicon diodes rectify the alternating current into standard 12-volt direct current."

There was more. Like the full-sized Chrysler products of that era, the Valiant employed "Torsion-Aire" front suspension, which does good things for its handling. And ever since its introduction on some of the 1956 Chryslers, the TorqueFlite transmission had been recognized as an outstanding automatic, probably the best in the industry at that time. For use in the Valiant, Chrysler engineers developed a smaller version of the TorqueFlite, called the "904," but familiarly known in later years as the "TorqueFlite Six." Every bit as satisfactory in operation as the full-sized version, the smaller unit — which added $172 to the price of the car — was very much lighter, thanks to the use of aluminum castings for both the transmission case and the torque converter

housing.

Other weight-saving measures included the use of precision casting techniques for the engine block. The distributor, water pump and oil pump housings were all aluminum castings, along with a number of smaller engine components. By mid-year there was even an optional aluminum block, but evidently its availability was limited.

Body and frame formed an all-steel, welded unit, incorporating more than 5,300 spot welds and seam welds. This type of construction could have led to some unpleasant vibrations, but thanks to some fine engineering work, it did not. *Popular Science* explained: "The engine mountings are 'tuned' to the rest of the car structure. This was accomplished by determining the rate at which the structure vibrates most severely when jiggled — 'excited' is the term engineers use — by the suspension. Then the engine mounts were designed so that the entire engine vibrates exactly out of phase with the structure. When the car structure bounces up, the engine pushes it down, and vice versa."

The Valiant came in two trim lines, known as the V-100 and V-200. In addition to some additional exterior brightwork, the latter series offered a two and a half inch foam cushion under the front seat, flashy vinyl and nylon upholstery in a choice of three colors, and carpeted floors. The V-200 was priced, in sedan form, $77 higher than the plain-Jane version — money well spent, evidently, in the eyes of most buyers, who opted two-to-one for the fancier car.

Just five colors were offered: green, blue, red, black and white. Two body styles were built in each trim level, that first year: a sedan and a "suburban," or station wagon, each offering the convenience of four doors that opened to 88 degrees. The wagon came in six- or nine-passenger form, the latter featuring a rear-facing third seat. Truthfully, however, that third seat was a lot more suitable for two passengers than for three.

Despite its many outstanding characteristics, the Valiant was not faultless. At that time, all of the cars from the Chrysler Corporation were suffering from problems of quality control. Evidently this was particularly true of units built — as the Valiant was — at the old Dodge Main plant in Hamtramck, where labor problems were described as "a scandal." Construction was solid enough, and for the most part, mechanical components performed well, but fit and finish were not as good as the competition.

Tom McCahill, writing in *Mechanix Illustrated*, called attention to a handling peculiarity, noting that "the characteristics when you make a hard right turn are quite different from those when you make a hard left turn.

"When I first drilled this Valiant over the Daytona International Speedway sports car course," Uncle Tom contin-

ued, "I found it the best-handling American car I've ever driven through a tight turn — while bending to the *right* (emphasis his). When I hit a tight curve going to the *left*, I experienced a very deep plowing effect.... This is something the average driver might never notice, even on several trips from coast to coast. But on a tough mountain road, if he descends too fast, he'll definitely feel the difference.

"This condition isn't dangerous but it is interesting and it shows what balance can do."

Of course, when McCahill road-tested an automobile, he was noted for pushing it to the absolute limit. We didn't, and don't, do that to these treasured collector cars, but we did put the Valiant through a number of fairly vigorous right and left turns, without becoming aware of any problem with the steering. In fact, we rate its handling as superior, particularly for a car of this type.

Driving Impressions

As a young man, Cliff Fales, of Rancho Cordova, California, owned a 1960 Valiant, his first brand new car. So when, in 1974, he found just such an automobile in a classified ad, he checked it out. As it happened, he responded too late; somebody had beat him to it and purchased the Valiant at an incredibly modest price. Cliff, who evidently doesn't give up easily, contacted the purchaser and offered double the price the man had paid, which still amounted to a reasonable figure. And so, after several years of standing out in the original owner's yard, the Valiant found a new home in Cliff's garage.

The car was sound, solid and complete, with a little over 60,000 miles on its clock, but it needed a lot of help. It

Left: Full wheel openings and horizontal fender line hark back to early sports cars like Mercer Raceabout. Top: Wheel covers are slightly reminiscent of Cord hubcaps. Above: The famous "birdbath" trunk lid, carried over from Exner-designed Imperials.

Valiant Versus The Competition

Here's how 1960's "Big Three" compacts stacked up against one another (all cars equipped with standard engines and three-speed manual transmissions):

	Valiant V-200	Corvair 700	Ford Falcon
Base price, 4-door sedan	$2,110	$2,103	$2,040*
Shipping weight (lbs.)	2,655	2,315	2,288
Wheelbase	106.5 in.	108 in.	109.5 in.
Overall length	184.0 in.	180.0 in.	181.2 in.
Overall width	70.4 in.	66.9 in.	70.0 in.
Overall height	53.3 in.	51.3 in.	54.5 in.
Track, front/rear	56.0 in./55.5 in.	54.0 in./54.0 in.	55.0 in./54.5 in.
Engine	In-line 6	Opposed 6	In-line 6
Bore	3.406 in.	3.375 in.	3.50 in.
Stroke	3.125 in.	2.60 in.	2.50 in.
Stroke/bore ratio	0.917:1	0.770:1	0.714:1
Displacement (cu. in.)	170.8	139.6	144.3
Compression ratio	8.50:1	8.00:1	8.70:1
Horsepower @ rpm	101/4,400	80/4,400	90/4,200
Torque @ rpm	155/2,400	125/2,400	138/2,000
Taxable horsepower	27.74	27.30	29.40
Cooling system	Water	Air	Water
Automatic transmission	3-speed	2-speed	2-speed
Extra charge for a/t	$172	$146	$159
Axle ratio (automatic)	3.23:1	3.55:1	3.10:1
Steering	Worm/ball nut	Recirc. ball	Recirc. ball nut
Turning diameter	37 feet 1⅛ in.	39 feet 6 in.	38 feet 9½ in.
Turns, lock-to-lock	4.45	5	4.64
Braking area (sq. in.)	129.1	120.8	114.3
Drum diameter	9 in.	9 in.	9 in.
Tire size	6.50/13	6.50/13	6.00/13
Horsepower per c.i.d.	.591	.573	.624
Weight (lb.) per hp	26.3	28.9	25.4
Weight per c.i.d.	15.5	16.6	15.9
Lb./sq. in. (brakes)	20.6	19.2	20.0
Acceleration: 0-45 mph**	10.0 seconds	11.5 seconds	12.2 seconds
0-60 mph	17.2 seconds	21.2 seconds	21.0 seconds
30-50 mph	6.2 seconds	8.2 seconds	9.0 seconds
45-60 mph	7.0 seconds	8.5 seconds	8.8 seconds
50-80 mph	22.4 seconds	24.0 seconds	29.8 seconds
Standing 1/4 mile	20.5/66.1 mph	22.2/61.3 mph	22.8/62.0 mph
Top speed (est.)	95-105 mph	88 mph	85 mph
Stopping distance	182.0 feet	182.6 feet	189.0 feet

* Including trim package
** Test cars equipped with standard engine, three-speed manual transmission

Above: Torsion bar suspension combines taut handling with a very good ride. **Below left:** Push-button tranny selector was also carried over from previous MoPar machines. **Below right:** Door panels are simple and modern. **Bottom:** Simply one of the best engines, ever, the indestructible Slant Six. **Facing page:** Instrument grouping and controls are nicely balanced and easy to read.

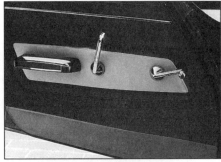

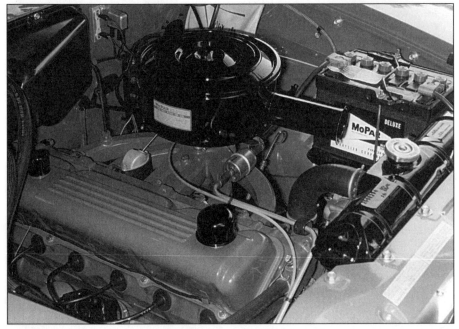

had been a one-family, Sacramento area car, and had evidently logged very few miles on the highway. Furthermore, the owner had used non-detergent oil; so there was a tremendous build-up of sludge in the engine. Cliff pulled the engine, rebuilt it completely, and installed a new water pump. He also rebuilt the TorqueFlite transmission, replaced all suspension and steering parts, and overhauled the brakes.

Turning his attention to the cosmetic problems, Fales took the car apart as completely as its unitized construction permitted, in order to paint it properly. That part of the operation, along with some minor body work, was delegated to Brian Moore Restorations, a local firm. The original Valiant Red color, a bright hue shaded just slightly toward vermilion, was retained. Cliff Fales himself, a man of many skills, did the upholstery work.

While all this was going on, Cliff had a number of original decals replicated, and somehow he was able to locate new-old-stock replacements for the instrument panel, steering wheel, headlamp rims and radiator grille. So the Valiant literally looks now just as it did when it was delivered to its first owner. Or perhaps a little better, for prior to the paint job Cliff smoothed down all the rough edges, which had remained after some rather sloppy welding done at the factory.

The job was completed by late 1988, and Cliff entered it in the Modesto Concours, where it placed first in class. Since that time it has taken several more first-place trophies, at Modesto, Chico and Sacramento.

One of the first things one notices upon taking the wheel of the Valiant is how easy it is to climb aboard. Doors open wide, and I found plenty of room to slide my size twelves between the seat and the doorpost. Seating is a little low for my taste, and front leg room wasn't quite what I had hoped for. But in addition to the usual fore-and-aft track, permitting about a four-inch adjustment of the seat, there are two sets of bolt holes by means of which the seat can be fastened to the floor. Cliff Fales uses the forward set of holes, which means that by simply undoing four small bolts, an extra inch of front leg room can be

That Indestructible Slant Six

By the time development of the Valiant got under way, in 1957, it was apparent that the six-cylinder, L-head engine, a Chrysler tradition from the beginning, would have to be replaced. Sturdy and dependable as it was, the flathead was no model of efficiency, and — as General Motors engineers had already learned — it was not compatible with the higher compression ratios that were clearly the trend of the times. The corporation's eight-cylinder models had already adopted overhead valves; now it was time for the sixes to follow suit.

It was also evident, by that time, that design trends in the years just ahead would call for lower hood lines. And therein lay the dilemma, for overhead-valve, in-line engines were distinctly taller than either the modern V-8s or the old-time, in-line flatheads. How, then, to combine these two objectives: overhead valves in a six-cylinder engine that was no taller than a V-8?

The solution proved to be as simple as it was ingenious. Chrysler engineers canted their new six-cylinder engine 30 degrees to the right. At the same time, incidentally, the manual transmission on cars so equipped was inclined 30 degrees to the left, thus helping to balance the weight while providing a more convenient location for the shift lever, and permitting the use of a lower tunnel down the center of the passenger compartment.

But the lower hood line wasn't the only advantage gained by tipping the engine. Not even the most important one, in fact. For the tilt permitted the use of a long-branch intake manifold, likened by one contemporary writer to "a bunch of bananas." This provided the engine with superior breathing capacity — Dodge Division engineers went so far as to call it a "semi-ram" effect — which provided better performance, greater fuel economy, and, it was claimed, longer engine life as well. High turbulence, wedge-shaped combustion chambers further increased the powerplant's efficiency, and six low-restriction, gradually curved exhaust pipes effectively removed the burned gases. Altogether, the Slant Six was a remarkably efficient design.

There were other advantages to the new engine, as well. An extra rigid crankshaft was cradled in larger bearings than Chrysler's 318-, 361- and 383-c.i.d. V-8s. The mains were, in fact, the same size as those of the Imperial's huge 413-c.i.d. powerplant. Even the crankpin journals were

bigger than those of the 318. The result of all this was an amazingly durable engine. Pete McNicholl, writing in *Slant 6 News* (Spring 1993) declares, "In my opinion, the Slant 6 is the best mass-produced inline 6-cylinder engine ever produced in this country." Thousands of owners would undoubtedly agree. There is even a "200,000 Miler's Club" for Slant Six owners, one of whose members is Ralph Dunwoodie, a long-time advisor to this publication and a friend of the present writer. Ralph's 1966 Valiant has logged nearly 400,000 miles to date, with just one engine overhaul.

The "Slant Six" came in two sizes. As fitted to the compact Valiant, it had a bore and stroke of 3.406 by 3.125 inches, yielding a displacement of 170.8 cubic inches (though it was advertised at 170). Horsepower was posted at 101. For the six-cylinder Plymouths and Dodges, on the other hand, the stroke was lengthened by one inch, raising the displacement to 225.5 cubes (advertised at 225) and the standard horsepower to 145.

Of course, there are always those who crave more performance than the standard engine provides. By 1961, for an extra $46, the 145-horsepower unit would become available for any Valiant, and three years later there would be a full line of 180-horsepower Valiant V-8s as well. But in the meanwhile, there was a competition-bred, dealer-installed option called the "Hyper-Pak."

Hyper is right! For $403.30 (plus about $125 labor), the buyer got a four-barrel carburetor; an extended intake manifold making full use of the ram-induction principle; a freer-flowing, dual exhaust system; milled heads and domed pistons, increasing the compression ratio from 8.50:1 to 10.0:1; a scorching camshaft, designed to raise the peak torque point from 2,800 to 4,200 rpm; high-performance valve springs, push rods and clutch assembly; and a recurve kit for the distributor. Thus equipped, the little 170 engine was rated, probably conservatively, at 148 horsepower.

At least by 1961 the Hyper-Pak was available in combination with the larger, 225-c.i.d. engine as well, raising its advertised horsepower from 145 to 196. To borrow a phrase from Tom McCahill, this setup must surely have been "as hot as a horseradish gargle." *Car Life*, road-testing a Hyper-Paked 1961 Dodge Lancer, the Valiant's nearly identical twin, reported a zero-to-sixty time of 8.6 seconds, compared to 16.1 seconds in a *Motor Trend* test

of a Valiant powered by the standard 101-horsepower engine, and something like 14 mph was added to the top speed!

Of course, this sort of performance comes at a price. In addition to adding nearly 20 percent to the sticker price of the car, it is said to have cut about five miles per gallon off its fuel mileage. Even more important, to many buyers, was the fact that either Slant Six, when equipped with the Hyper-Pak, ceased to be the smooth, docile, tractable engine that made it an instant favorite with just about everyone who drove it. *Car Life*, which strongly recommended the 225 engine in standard tune, explained, "The...engine, after having been hyper-packed, is neither smooth nor unobtrusive. The radical valve-timing of the substitute camshaft takes care of smoothness with dispatch, while the fact that the four-barrel carburetor of the package is so huge that no room remains under the hood for an air cleaner takes care of the unobtrusiveness...."

But then, the Hyper-Pak wasn't designed for everyday street use. Pete McNicholl explained that "the Hyper-Pak was intended to put Valiant into the limelight. This it did at Daytona in February 1960 when the first seven places in the Compact race went to Hyper-Pak Valiants." McNicholl then went on to say, "The Lee Petty-prepared Valiants that ran at Daytona were able to attain speeds close to 130 mph."

Few buyers opted for the Hyper-Pak, which remained available only through 1961. Most people didn't need the extra speed; and the sacrifice in smoothness, not to mention the cost, made it a dubious value for the money.

But the basic Slant Six, especially in its 225-cubic-inch form, remained for many years as a Chrysler Corporation mainstay. As late as 1983 it was available to buyers of Plymouth Fury, Dodge Diplomat and Chrysler Cordoba passenger cars, and it remained in production through 1987 for use in domestic Dodge trucks, after which it was replaced by a 3.9-liter V-6. Slant Six production in Mexico, again for use in trucks, continued through October 1991, and reportedly the venerable workhorse is still built on a low-volume basis for marine and industrial use. The tough old Slant Six was a "natural" for a diesel conversion, and prototypes were built, but the project was abandoned during 1983 when demand for diesel-powered passenger cars suddenly evaporated.

specifications

illustrations by Russell von Sauers, The Graphic Automobile Studio

© copyright 1994, Special Interest Autos

← 56.0 inches →

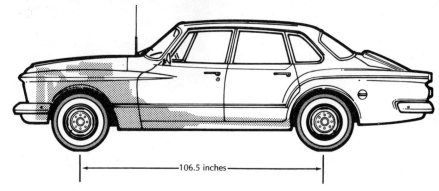

← 106.5 inches →

1960 Valiant V-200

Original price	$2,110 f.o.b. factory, federal taxes included
Options on dR car	TorqueFlite transmission, heater/defroster, radio, tinted windshield, white sidewall tires, driver's side mirror, glove box light, deluxe steering wheel with horn ring, carpeting, backup lights, rear bumper guards, wheel trim rings, windshield washers, bright side window moldings, undercoating

ENGINE

Type	6-cylinder in-line, inclined 30 degrees to the right
Bore x stroke	3.406 inches x 3.125 inches
Displacement	170.8 cubic inches
Compression ratio	8.5:1
Horsepower @ rpm	101 @ 4,400
Torque @ rpm	155 @ 2,400
Taxable horsepower	27.74
Valve lifters	Mechanical
Main bearings	4
Valve configuration	Ohv
Carburetor	Carter one-inch single-bbl downdraft
Lubrication system	Pressure
Electrical system	12-volt battery/coil

TRANSMISSION

Type	TorqueFlite 3-speed automatic, with torque converter
Ratios: 1st	2.45:1
2nd	1.45:1
3rd	1.00:1
Reverse	2.20:1
Max. ratio at stall	2.25:1

REAR AXLE

Type	Hypoid
Ratio	3.23:1
Drive axles	Semi-floating

STEERING

Type	Saginaw worm and ball nut
Turns lock-to-lock	4.45
Ratios	20.0:1 gear; 23.8:1 overall
Turning diameter	37 feet 1.625 inches

BRAKES

Type	4-wheel hydraulic, drum type
Drum diameter	9 inches
Effective area	129.1 square inches

CHASSIS & BODY

Construction	All steel, unitized body and frame
Body type	4-door sedan

SUSPENSION

Front	Independent, ball joints; lateral, non-parallel control arms, torsion bars
Rear	Rigid axle, 55-inch x 2.5-inch 4-leaf semi-elliptic springs
Shock absorbers	1-inch direct-acting
Tires	6.50/13
Wheels	Steel disc, drop-center safety rims

WEIGHTS AND MEASURES

Wheelbase	106.5 inches
Overall length	184 inches
Overall width	70.4 inches

Overall height	55.6 inches (unloaded)
Front track	56.0 inches
Rear track	55.5 inches
Min. road clearance	5.4 inches
Shipping weight	2,655 pounds

INTERIOR DIMENSIONS

Leg room, f/r	42.8 inches/39.8 inches
Head room, f/r	3.79 inches/37.4 inches
Hip room, f/r	56.8 inches/56.9 inches
Seat height, f/r	11.4 inches/13.4 inches
Luggage volume	29.4 cubic feet

CAPACITIES

Crankcase	5 quarts (including filter)
Cooling system	14 quarts (with heater)
Fuel tank	13 gallons
Transmission	13 pints
Rear axle	2 pints

CALCULATED DATA

Horsepower per c.i.d.	.591
Weight per hp	26.3 pounds
Weight per c.i.d.	15.5 pounds
P.S.I (brakes)	20.6

PERFORMANCE

Maximum speed	95-105 mph (est.)
Acceleration: 0-30 mph	5.5 seconds
0-45 mph	9.5 seconds
0-60 mph	16.1 seconds

(from a 1961 *Motor Trend* road test of a Plymouth Valiant hardtop equipped with 170-c.i.d. engine and TorqueFlite transmission)

Right: Spare hides under trunk floor. *Facing page, top:* For a relatively small car, there's loads of leg room. *Center left:* Rear seat room is generous, too. *Center right:* Plywood trunk floor on driveReport car has original jacking cautions. *Below:* Trunk has a totally flat floor but fuel filler pipe intrudes. *Bottom:* There's no mistaking the style of the Valiant from any angle.

gained. At an equivalent sacrifice on the part of rear seat passengers, of course, but still, over-all leg room isn't bad for a small car.

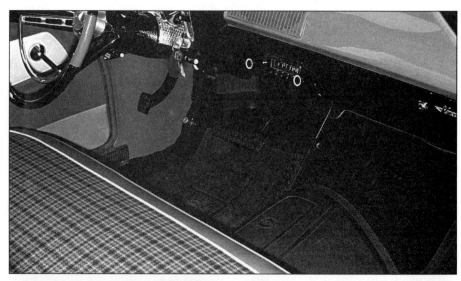

Acceleration is nothing to get excited about, but it's considerably quicker than either Corvair or Falcon. I found it to be at least adequate. The pushbutton-controlled TorqueFlite transmission shifts crisply from gear to gear, and ratios seem to be ideally spaced. (The standard Valiant transmission, a three-speed manual unit, employs a floor-mounted lever, which should add to the joy of driving the car. The only trouble with it, apart from the non-synchro first gear, has to do with the second gear ratio of 1.83:1. That's great, if you're given to second-gear starts, but for most purposes it is simply too slow. The 1.43:1 ratio employed by the eight-cylinder Plymouth would seem to me to have made a lot more sense.)

I once owned a PowerFlite-equipped '58 Plymouth. The transmission was one of that car's better features, but it's a good thing the parking brake worked well, for no provision was made for locking the transmission. The Valiant's TorqueFlite, in contrast, has a 100 percent effective parking sprag, operated by means of a small lever, located next to the pushbuttons.

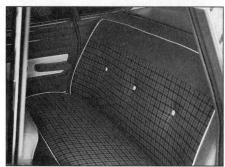

Steering is surprisingly light, and only a little slow at four and a half turns, lock-to-lock. Power steering was available, at $73 extra, but in my view the Valiant doesn't need it. Also on the option list, at $41, were power brakes, but again, the extra expense would have been unnecessary. The binders take only moderate pressure, and they seem to do their job well. *Motor Trend* found the Valiant's stopping distance to be comparable to that of the Corvair, and a little shorter than the Falcon.

On the road, this Valiant feels much newer than it is, thanks no doubt to all those new-old-stock steering and suspension components that Cliff Fales installed. It holds its course with no tendency to wander, and it corners flatter than most cars of its era. The ride is a little on the firm side, which is the way I happen to like it.

There are a number of appealing small features, such as the color-coded steering wheel grips, and the spare tire buried under a piece of plywood, beneath the floor of the comparatively roomy trunk. On the other hand, the battery is fair game for the potential thief, who would need only to lift up on the Valiant emblem in the middle of the grille in order to release the hood. And loss of oil pressure is signaled by means of an idiot light, rather than a proper gauge.

But these are minor matters. Taken all-in-all, Chrysler's first small car is an impressive little automobile, well engineered, comfortable, lively, and fun to drive. ୧ଛ

Savoir Faire

Plymouth's '63 Super Stock Savoy really knew how to do it!

By James Dietzler
Photography by the author

Overriding the deep staccato beat of eight cylinders firing off at the 1,500 rpm idle is the distinctly cyclical cacophony of a solid-lifter mechanical camshaft timing the valve events to perfection and providing a rhythmic music that brings the driver quickly to the realization that this is not a street machine to take lightly.

From first approach, this early '60s Plymouth appears ordinary; though painted in an eye-catching Ruby Red hue, there isn't anything outwardly special looking about it. In its day, this Savoy would have looked equally at home in the local minister's driveway or parked at the local drive-in hoping to scare up a quick street race. Lacking flashy trim or external "here's what's in me" ornamentation, the conservative styling of this '63 Savoy hides its true intent. A closer inspection just hints at what's hidden under its plain hood. Barely visible at the right angle are the exhaust cutouts on the factory three-inch tubular head pipes.

A quick pump of the accelerator and twist of the dash-mounted ignition key confirms

my suspicions, and an unstoppable ear-to-ear grin soon stretches facial muscles to the limit. This is no ordinary car from Chrysler's top-ranked (sales) division of that year. When the spark hits the air/fuel mixture fed by the pair of Carter four-barrel carburetors atop the massive cross-ram intake manifold, 426 cubic inches of Super Stock Mopar power rumble into fiery life. There's no need to use the hand choke that's unique to the Super Stock optioned cars. Even when it's stone cold, the owner informs me, a few pumps of the gas pedal and a little

feathering once it fires off until the heat builds up is all that's needed to get it going.

In basic box-stock form this is a ton-and-a-half of 426 Stage II Super Stock-powered Savoy, a barely disguised street-legal race car that could shred the quarter mile in less than 13 seconds, with nothing more than a set of slicks and its exhaust cutouts uncorked. Weighing in at 3,200 pounds, Plymouth's Savoy was the base-level offering of the B-body line. When that 426-cu.in. chunk of Super Stock power, more commonly referred to as the Max Wedge because of its maximum-performance wedge-shaped combustion chambers, is beneath its hood, this normally nondescript grocery-getter became an absolute beast of the street, something I was about to find out.

After sliding the Park lever to the left of the pushbutton shifter up, and pushing the button for Drive in, we're off to sample what this scarce Savoy has to offer. This interlocking finger-type Park lever was a relatively new feature for the TorqueFlite, which up until 1962 had no Park position.

 Originally published in Special Interest Autos #182, Mar.-Apr. 2001

Park lever introduced in '62 line.

Sedate looks belie startling performance of Super Stock Plymouth.

Taking advantage of light afternoon traffic in the rural farmland of northwestern New Jersey, its virtues and deficiencies soon show through with startling alacrity. Just keeping its 415 horsepower and 470-lb.ft. of torque in check at stops is a leg-muscle-cramping challenge. With both feet jammed hard on the brake pedal, the single-pot manual drum brakes barely keep the Savoy from edging into traffic at stop signs. Relax just a bit on the brakes, even at idle, and it's moving. At traffic lights and stop signs, it's actually safer to shift into neutral and wait for your turn before engaging drive again, a method its owner Chris Sauer often uses.

Getting to a stop in the first place is just as much, if not more, of a workout. With a total swept surface of 195.2 square inches, the 10-inch diameter manual drum brakes offer little progressive feel and need a heavy foot applied far earlier than any modern car on the road. Instead of braking in tandem with the traffic ahead of you, you've got to look far ahead, anticipating everyone else, and hope that you've judged it right and will come to a halt with room to spare! Dismal by modern standards, they were about par for the course in their day. Actually, in 1963, the Bendix duo-servo self-adjusting design was still pretty new for Plymouth, introduced in the 1962 models, before the Bendix duo-servo type, there was no self-adjusting ratchet pawl and lever mechanism, and the parking brake was still applied to the driveshaft and not the rear wheels. Still, it's surprising that little thought was given to enhancing stopping abilities when this body and powertrain combination was thought up; as a matter of fact, with the Bendix system, drum diameter decreased.

Keeping the dash-mounted pushbutton shifter in Drive and carefully rolling into the throttle, the 727 TorqueFlite automatic's valving takes First only out to the 2,000 rpm mark, but with all of its torque and rather tall 3.91 rear gearing, that's far enough. A solid engagement of Second allows for a deep stab with the right foot, and as the tires send up a shriek of protest, Third engages scant seconds later at the 4,000 rpm mark. That's the conservative side of this beast, and it must be said that a few alterations have been made for the sake of driveability. The original torque converter was meant for foot-to-the-floor drag racing-style starts; in everyday driving, it would cause the car to stall after getting about 25 feet down the road, so a Dynamic 3,200 stall-speed converter was installed, along with a less radical Mopar Performance "Purple" single-pattern camshaft.

Having made a short trip to a long, inactive road leading to a defunct quarry, I'm encouraged by its owner to give it a "real" go. So I give the "L" button a poke. It sinks into the dash with a satisfyingly mechanical snick, much like the buttons on early television remotes. In Low, the Wedge is really surging against the brakes at idle. Remembering to take a deep breath and keeping a wary peripheral eye on the period Stahl tach mounted atop the dash, I roll into the gas pedal lightly, then fully. A second or two of squealing wheelspin, then the 426 is roaring up to the 5,000 rpm mark, really pulling strong from 3,500 rpm on, thanks to that short-runner crossram manifold's design with the valvetrain emitting a whirring, clattering overture that seems to float over the thundering roar of the big V-8. Already it's drifting across the road, the half turn of nothingness in the dead center position of the steering wheel making staying on the straight and narrow a real effort. With Second pushed home at five grand, the period Mickey Thompson Indy profile tires mounted on the stock 14 x 5.5-inch steel rims again give a shriek of protest before digging in for good. Too quickly 5,000 rpm comes around again, sounding like there's at least another 1,500 rpm to take advantage of, but in goes the button for Drive. By now, the speedometer is bouncing wildly near the top of its range, the Savoy is hunting and following every groove and depression in the road and I'm hard pressed not to use both sides of the road just to keep it on the pavement. Once it hits 3,500 rpm in Drive I back off the gas and opt for the brakes for safety and sanity's sake, as I've seen enough of the Savoy's potential in this setting.

Despite some initial derisive and disbelieving comments from the competition, racers soon found out that this aluminum-cased, beefed-up version of the TorqueFlite made for quicker ETs and faster mph times than stick-shifted manual gearboxes, whether of three- or four-speed variety. One downside to the pushbutton shifter though, was the location of the Reverse and Neutral buttons. As former Crescent Dodge racer Bob "The Arab" Harrop explained to me a few years ago, on a number of occasions, mostly during night races, drivers going for the Neutral position after completing a pass would inadvertently hit Reverse while still traveling near the triple-digit speed range. You don't need to stretch your imagination too far to envision the result. After several wound up on their roofs at high speed, Chrysler issued the racers a quick fix—a blocking bar to mount over the reverse button!

You'd think a car with this much torque and horsepower would be a handful in regular traffic, but cruising about down low in the rev range the Savoy is surprisingly docile. The idle isn't as lumpy as one would imagine, thanks

1963 styling forsook '60-'62 lines for more conventional appearance.

Slanted indicator light '63-only feature.

Clean, simple instruments and controls.

most likely to that smoother cam profile, and pedal effort isn't so easy as to allow one to accidentally give the accelerator an overly enthusiastic blip that might send one crashing into the car ahead. Despite the wide C-pillar, rearward visibility is quite good. Cornering abilities are about par for the course in a big-engined early Sixties intermediate. Body roll is pronounced, and with the stiff Super Stock spring package and its additional 1/2-spring on the right rear, its ride qualities can hardly be described as smooth. With the big 426 up front, understeer is as pronounced as one would expect it to be; wider tires would do it justice, but because of the 14-inch-diameter rims, not many tire size options exist. There's absolutely no consideration of trying to find this car's limit in hard cornering, as images of the back-end power oversteering its way past the front end quickly come to mind.

Despite the fact that steering is accomplished with a manual box, at speed the required steering effort is light; and at normal speeds in traffic the Savoy exhibits a bit of wanderlust, especially noticeable on crowned roads. The dead spot in the center does nothing to calm one's nerves when its skinny tires start tracking depressions in the road. Parallel parking action in this beast is a different story entirely. With a thin-rimmed two-spoke steering wheel, one must grab a tight hold and really crank on the wheel to point it where it's supposed to go.

When it comes to interior refinement, one could best discuss the subject using the phrase "lack of." The Savoy was the base-level Plymouth, and those optioned with the Super Stock engines were truly nothing more than a no-frills fleet special put together for the individual buyer, one who intended to use it for racing, either at sanctioned dragstrips or on the street. Thin rubber mats front and rear cover the floorpans; there's no carpeting here, or radio, or A/C, or even seatbelts originally for that matter. And the heater? It's an option! The plastic chrome-rimmed gauges set in a finely corrugated silver insert surrounded by a textured black outer rim, though in plain view and easy to read, were minimal. Instead of a gauge for oil pressure, there's only an idiot light, something that took me aback given the nature of the engine. The speedometer is of the dial type with a large face and plain white letters on a black background; there's no tachometer and the water temperature and fuel gauge share a round dial opening smaller than the speedometer. To its left is a voltmeter and below it sits a clock face bereft of any works.

The split folding bench seat was even cushioned with a cheaper foam that's less supportive than any of the line's more upscale siblings. This particular interior trim level was actually referred to as "Low Grade" and is of Alabaster and Black cloth and vinyl variety. The seats offer absolutely no side support, and

Unsilenced air cleaners hide much of 426. Hoses and wires routed on fenders.

Cast iron ram's horn headers.

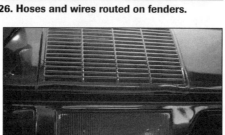
Scenery a blur as owner hits drive at 5,000 rpm.

Factory trim plate covers radio opening.

"Low Grade" interior included arm rests.

without seatbelts (our Savoy owner Chris Sauer installed a driver's side lap belt for safety's sake), staying put during anything approximating hard cornering must have been a matter of how strongly one could hold onto the steering wheel. Up front, the only concessions to refinement are the armrests on the door panels, which make barely adequate grab handles. In the rear, there's nothing to help keep passengers from getting tossed about. The car is quite roomy though—inside it's nearly cavernous, while out back, one could stuff the trunk with a month's worth of groceries and still have room to spare.

The design, styling, and market approach of the '63 Plymouth line were a bit unusual in that, unlike Chrysler, Dodge and Plymouth had to make do with the shortened 116-inch wheelbase chassis for what was actually a substandard full-size line. This effectively kept the Plymouth and Dodge out of the full-size-car competition; instead their biggest products went up against each other and Ford's intermediate Fairlane, while Chevrolet offered a compact and a full-size, but no intermediate. Yet Plymouth sales increased by forty-one percent that year, even with the substandard-size car line, an increase that is most likely attributable to the marketing difficulties that Chrysler had with its 1960-62 product lines. Though the radical fins of the late '50s were largely gone, Plymouth dropped from 3rd in overall U.S. sales in '58 and '59 to 4th in '60, 7th in '61, and 8th by '62.

Internal turmoil might be the best

WHAT TO PAY

Low	Average	High
$9,000	$22,000	$35,000

phrase to describe the goings-on within Chrysler in the late '50s and early '60s that led to the strange marketing approach they took with their lines of the time. The term of Chrysler president William Newberg, who replaced the retiring Tex Colbert in 1960, lasted but a scant few months due to allegations of conflict of interest because of Newberg's holdings in related companies. Colbert was brought back, but bad blood between him and Newberg led to Colbert's resignation, with Lynn Townsend finally succeeding him as president in 1961. Though the downsizing of the Dodge and Plymouth chassis had been at Newberg's insistence, what Townsend found in the styling department led him to order immediate changes. For Chrysler, the result was a decent 1962 sales year; for Plymouth and Dodge with the downsized line, sales plummeted.

Virgil Exner, who had suffered a heart attack that kept him somewhat out of the design of the '62 models, did manage to see some of his influence remain in the 1963 designs; the Savoy's front-end treatment is one example of his input. However, Townsend, though an Exner supporter and under pressure from the Chrysler board, fired him in November of 1961 with the caveat that he work as a consultant to his successor Elwood

Engle. The 1963 models, much like the previous '62s, were redone at Townsend's insistence, with the only vestige of Exner's direct involvement being the front-end with its unique slanted oval indicator lights and flat grille. However, the oddball styling of the '60-62 was gone. In its place was a more conservative side profile with a nicely sculpted downward sloping fender line than ran all the way to the taillights, and a more formal C-pillar treatment.

Townsend, it should be noted, can also be credited with pushing for a street and race performance series of cars, as the Chrysler divisions hadn't presented a serious threat to the competition for several years. The genesis of the Max Wedge Super Stock program was the '62 Plymouth and Dodge line equipped with the R-B block 413-cu.in. V-8. Just how dominant the Savoy/Max Wedge combination was going to be became clear to all when Tom Grove, in a Plymouth named the Melrose Missile, set a new NHRA stock-car record of 11.93 at 118.57 mph in the early summer months of '62. Over at Dodge, a group of engineers, who since the late '50s had called themselves the RamChargers, started putting red and white and blue Darts in the winner's circle. Four NHRA class records were taken by 413 power that year.

The following year, with the 413 bored to 426 cubic inches, a change done to take advantage of the NHRA and NASCAR seven-liter engine displacement limit, a Midwest racer named Roger Lindamood grabbed some shoe polish, scrawled "I am a Plymouth. Color me gone!" on the side

Savoy Super Stocker not meant for high-speed cornering.

Split bench allows easy entry to rear seats.

Roomy but Spartan interior.

Factory exhaust cutouts easily opened.

Huge trunk epitome of go-fast grocery getter.

PLYMOUTH SAVOY 426 VS. THE COMPETITION

Here's how our driveReport car compares against three other comparably sized and powered models from the leading manufacturers of 1963.

	Plymouth Savoy 426 SS	Chevrolet Impala Z-11	Ford Galaxie 427	Pontiac SD Catalina
Base price	$2,387.40+ $615	$2,774+ $1,237.40	$3,268+ $1,099*	$2,859+ $1,240**
Shipping weight	3,419	3,360	3,500 (est.)	3,600
Body	2-door hardtop	2-door hardtop	2-door hardtop	2-door hardtop
Chassis	Unitized steel	Body on frame	Body on frame	Body on frame
Frame	Integral	Welded box-section steel	Welded box-section steel	Welded box-section steel
Wheelbase	116-in.	119-in.	119-in.	119-in.
Overall length	205-in.	209.6-in.	209.9-in.	211.9-in.
Overall width	75.6-in.	n/a	n/a	78.6-in.
Overall height	53.9-in.	n/a	n/a	55.9-in.
Track (front/rear)	59.4/57.5-in.	60.3/59.3-in.	61/60-in.	64/64-in.
Displacement	426-cu.in.	427-cu.in.	427-cu.in.	421-cu.in.
Horsepower	415@5,600	430@5,600	425@6,000	410@5,600
Torque	470@ 4,400	430 @ 4,000	480@3,700	435@4,400
Compression ratio		11:1	11:1	11.5:1 13:1
Carburetion	2 x 4 bbl.	2 x 4 bbl.	2 x 4 bbl.	2 x 4 bbl.
Suspension				
Front	Independent Torsion bar upper and lower control arms, hydraulic shocks	Independent coil-springs upper and lower control arms, hydraulic shocks, anti-roll bar	Independent coil-springs, upper and lower control arms, hydraulic shocks, anti-roll bar	Independent coil-springs upper and lower control arms, hydraulic shocks, anti-roll bar
Rear	Live axle, semi-elliptic leaf springs, hydraulic shocks	Four-link live axle, coil springs hydraulic shocks	Live axle, semi-elliptic leaf springs, hydraulic shocks, torque control arms	Live axle, coil springs, hydraulic shocks, torque control arms
Transmission	3-speed TorqueFlite	2-speed Powerglide	4-speed manual	3- or 4 –spd. (opt.) manual
Steering	Recirculating ball	Recirculating ball	Recirculating ball	Recirculating ball
Turns lock-to-lock		5.3	5.25	5.25 4.25
Turning circle	40 ft., 8 in.	39 ft., 6 in.	41 ft.	42 ft, 8 in.
Brakes	11-in. drums	11-in. drums	11-in. drums	11-in. drums
Tire size	7.0 x 14	7.50 x 14	7.10 x 15	7.10 x 15

* Wholesale price of 427/lightweight conversion package
** Price of 1962 2 x 4 bbl. Super Duty engine package, .

of his '63 Savoy and went out to Detroit Dragway, stomped the competition and began making himself a racing legend. Then there was Jack Werst of Chrysler's warranty department and the infamous "Mr. 5 and 50" Plymouth. Though this was around the time that the manufacturers began to heed the 1957 AMA factory-supported racing ban, in retrospect, it's pretty amusing to see the ways in which it was sidestepped or out-and-out ignored. Plymouth's Super Stocker in '63 alone was responsible for eight NHRA records. In NASCAR competition, though Ford won the championship, with 23 victories, Plymouth showed well with 19— 14 of those attributable to Richard Petty.

Dodge and Plymouth made sure that cars like this Savoy could be bought with the high-performance 426 Max Wedge engine by just about any kid with a driver's license and some six-hundred dollars to spare for the option, while its

illustrations by Russell von Sauers, The Graphic Automobile Studio

© copyright 2001, Special Interest Autos

specifications

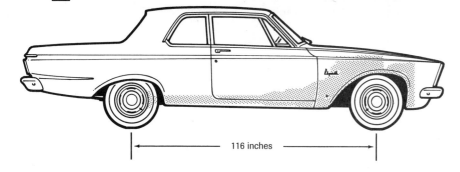

116 inches

59.4 inches

1963 Plymouth Savoy 426 Super Stock

Base price	$2,387.40
Price as optioned	$3,217.50
Std. equipment inc.	Ohv 318-cu.in. V-8, 3-speed transmission, oil filter, turn signals, electric windshield wipers, locking glovebox, dual sun visors, front armrests
Options on dR car	426-cu.in. Super Stock V-8 engine with heavy-duty suspension, automatic transmission, and heater

ENGINE

Type	Cast-iron overhead-valve V-8
Bore x stroke	4.25 inches x 3.75 inches
Displacement	426 cubic inches
Compression ratio	11:1
Bhp @ rpm	415 @ 5,600
Torque @ rpm	470 @ 4,400
Valve gear	Overhead valve
Valve lifters	Solid
Main bearings	5
Induction/fuel system	2 Carter 3447 4-barrel manual-choke carburetors, shrouded aluminum Cross-ram intake manifold, Carter 6-8 psi mechanical fuel pump
Lubrication system	Full pressure, swinging pickup oil pump
Cooling system	Centrifugal pump
Exhaust system	Tubular cast-iron "Ram's Horn" headers, dual 3-in. pipes with "Laker" cutouts, dual mufflers and 2-inch tailpipes
Electrical system	12-volt

TRANSMISSION

Type	727 TorqueFlite 3-speed planetary automatic
Shifter	Dash-mounted pushbutton
Ratios	1st: 2.45:1; 2nd: 1.45:1; 3rd: 1.00:1; Reverse: 2.20:1
Torque converter Max. overall breakaway ratio	5.39:1

REAR AXLE

Type	Live axle, 8.75-inch housing with Sure-Grip differential and adjustable pinion snubber
Ratio	3.91:1

STEERING

Type	Manual
Turns lock-to-lock	5.3
Ratio	25:1
Turning circle	40 feet, 8 inches

BRAKES

Type	Manual internal expanding drum
Size, front	10 inches
Rear	10 inches
Lining area	195.2 square inches
Parking brake	Cable-activated rear drums

CHASSIS & BODY

Body	Unitized steel
Body style	2-door, 6-passenger sedan
Layout	Front engine, rear drive

SUSPENSION

Front	Torsion bar
Rear	Super Stock semi-elliptic leaf with 1/2 spring added on right side
Shock absorbers	Oriflow double-action hydraulic
Wheels	7 x 14 inch steel
Tires	7 x 14 inch Tyrex Cord bias ply

WEIGHTS AND MEASURES

Wheelbase	116 inches
Overall length	205 inches
Overall width	75.6 inches
Overall height	53.9 inches
Front track	59.4 inches
Rear track	57.5 inches
Weight w/out options	3,200 pounds

CAPACITIES

Crankcase	5 quarts + 1 for oil filter
Cooling system	17 quarts (with heater)
Fuel tank	20 gallons
Transmission	18 pints
Rear axle	4 pints

CALCULATED DATA

Bore/stroke ratio	.882:1
Hp/c.i.d.	.997
Lb./ft./c.i.d.	1.103
Lb. per sq. in. (brakes)	17.51

PRODUCTION

Total Savoy 2-dr sedan	20,281
Total Savoy 2-dr sedan with 426 Super Stock option	N/A (2,130 426 Super Stock Dodge and Plymouth cars were sold in 1963)

competition was a bit more conservative. For the most part, to purchase an equally powerful Ford, Chevy or Pontiac, you already needed to be a "name" at the drag strips. Chevy's Z11 427 Impalas, Ford's Galaxie 427s and Pontiac's Super Duty 421 Catalinas didn't roll off the lots in the hands of just anyone who wanted one. No, these were high-performance cars with lightweight body packages that were destined for racers. Street versions weren't as readily available as they were for the Chrysler line. Plymouth, and for that matter Chrysler and Dodge, wanted its most powerful cars to not only be seen on the racetracks, but to be known and feared whenever one pulled up at a stop-

light. For the A-list racers, a 13.5:1 compression ratio, 425-hp version of the Max Wedge was offered along with a lightweight front-end body-panel package and trunk-mounted battery.

Today, few on the roads during an average everyday trip have a clue as to the nature of this beast. Instead, it draws quizzical, bemused looks when a person in his mid-thirties is behind its wheel. "Now why would a guy like that want an old lady's car," they seem to wonder, thinking most likely that an early '70s muscle car or mid-eighties performance import would be more fitting. That sort of look changes to one of a bug-eyed, jaw-dropped stare when this sedate-appear-

ing sedan roars away, showing its tastefully sectioned taillights and chrome bumper to the modern steel cocoon of soft ride, smooth, easy handling and staid but lively performance it just dusted off.

That is unless, of course, said onlooker is among the many fans of 1960 Mopar performance products. And when that's the case, the Savoy would be given a real hard look, because it isn't often that people restore base-level Savoys. The Super Stockers are literally worshipped by the enthusiasts devoted to early-'60s Mopar performance cars. After sampling the raw, brutal power of this Savoy, it isn't hard to understand why. 🔊

93

NORTH AMERICAN HYBRID

by Arch Brown
photos by Bud Juneau

IT was during the Fall of 1959 that production got under way in Detroit on the Valiant, Chrysler Corporation's first compact car. Almost simultaneously, at its Windsor, Ontario, plant, Chrysler Canada began to build a Valiant of its own, virtually identical to the stateside edition.

Initially, on both sides of the border, the Valiant was billed as a distinct marque, rather than a junior edition Plymouth. "Nobody's Kid Brother!" proclaimed the ads. That practice would change when the 1961 models were introduced — but only in the United States. Stateside, at that point, the car became known as the Plymouth Valiant, while the Canadian version still carried the unhyphenated Valiant name.

There was good reason for the difference. In those days the Chrysler Corporation had two dealer bodies in Canada, one featuring the Plymouth while the other sold the Dodge. And from the time of its introduction, both handled the Valiant. This practice was continued, even after the US Dodge dealers introduced the Lancer, a near-twin to the Valiant. First offered for the 1961 season, the Lancer lasted for just two sea-

sons on the American market, but it was neither built nor sold in Canada.

On either side of the border, the Valiant represented what was arguably the most advanced automobile in its field. In a trend-setting move, Chrysler supplied the Valiant with an alternator, in lieu of the customary generator. And as to the 170-cubic-inch, 101-horsepower "slant six" engine, it proved to be by far the best-performing, and probably the most durable powerplant offered by any compact car. By tilting the engine 30 degrees to the right, Chrysler was able to substantially lower the car's hood line. Even more important, the slant provided enough room on the left side to permit the use of long-ram intake manifold passages. As *Motor Trend* noted, "This ram manifold was a brand new concept when the slant six was designed in 1959."

The magazine went on to explain,

"The theory is that separate long passages to each port will let the long column of air/fuel mixture build up momentum when it flows into the cylinder on the suction stroke. Then, when the piston's near the bottom of the stroke and suction reduces, the mixture will continue to ram itself into the cylinder. It's been conclusively shown that long intake passages give more power and torque than short ones. The new ram manifold helped this Chrysler engine produce more horsepower and torque per cubic inch than other sixes of its day. And it's significant that Pontiac used the same type of manifold with the slanted four-cylinder Tempest engine in 1961. When GM copies, there has to be a good reason."

In a road test of one of the early Valiants, conducted by *Car Life* magazine, top speed was found to be 95 miles an hour, while *Motor Trend* recorded a zero-to-sixty time of 16.1 seconds. A dealer-installed "Hyper-Pak," consisting of a four-barrel carburetor, free-flowing exhaust system, hot cam and 10.5:1 compression ratio, raised the horsepower to a rousing 148, but the kit was not available in Canada. It was never partic-

1964 CANADIAN VALIANT

ularly popular in the United States, for that matter, perhaps because of its cost: $403.30 plus labor — enough to bring the installed price to slightly over $500.

Powering the full-sized six-cylinder Plymouths and Dodges was another Slant Six engine. Thanks to a one-inch-longer stroke, this one displaced 225 cubic inches, providing it with 145 horsepower. By the Spring of 1961, this powerplant had become optionally available for the American Valiants and Lancers, priced at a reasonable $47. Tom McCahill, road-testing a 145-horsepower Lancer for *Mechanix Illustrated*, took the car from rest to 60 mph in just 13.5 seconds, and posted a top speed slightly in excess of 100 miles an hour. But not until mid-1962 could Canadians opt for anything more potent than the standard 170-c.i.d. engine.

Commencing in 1961, Chrysler tooled up for a die-cast aluminum version of the 225 slant six. As *Motor Trend* noted, "The thing saved 76 pounds and gave entirely satisfactory service. But production was eventually dropped because not enough buyers were willing to pay extra for the light block."

A much more popular Valiant option was a new, light-weight version of Chrysler's justly famed, pushbutton-controlled TorqueFlite automatic transmission. Combining a three-speed planetary gearset with a torque converter, this unit was noted for smoothness, performance and durability.

Yet another feature, unique to the cars of the Chrysler Corporation, was "Torsion-Aire" suspension, employing torsion bars in front and semi-elliptic springs at the rear. The result, in addition to superior handling qualities, was a comfortable ride that belied the Valiant's short (106.5-inch) wheelbase and light (2,600-pound) weight.

The Lancer was never a hot ticket on the sales floor, though 1961's sales of just under 75,000 units probably kept a number of dealers alive at a time when Dodge had dropped to ninth rank in the industry. So, for 1963 Dodge prepared a new, somewhat larger compact, the Dart.

The styling of the Lancer and the first-generation Valiant had rather a European look. These cars were modern, exotic, different, and controversial. The same could not be said of the second-generation MoPar compacts, introduced in early October 1962. Styling was entirely conventional, and very attractive. The design was basically the work of Virgil Exner, though finishing touches were applied by his successor, Elwood Engel, following Exner's departure in late 1961.

As far as the US versions were concerned, this time there were significant differences between the Dodge and Plymouth compacts. Most notably, the Dart's 111-inch wheelbase was five inches longer than that of the Valiant, and overall length was greater by 9.7

1964 Canadian Valiant

*Top: Styling is half Dart, half Valiant and works very well. **Above:** CAA badge could be mistaken for US's AAA. **Below:** Emblem and name weren't changed for Canadian customers.*

inches. About three inches of the difference was found in the length of the hood, and rear leg room was increased by one inch. The trunk was longer, providing greater luggage capacity in addition to creating a more balanced appearance.

Chrysler Canada, still marketing a single compact through two dealer bodies, borrowed from both American models. Basically, the 1963 Canadian Valiant was a Dodge Dart, fitted with a Valiant front clip. Except for the station wagons, which were built on the 106-inch wheelbase of the American Valiant, the 111-inch Dart chassis was employed. The resultant hybrid was 3.1 inches shorter overall than the Dart (in body styles other than the wagons), but 6.6 inches longer than the Valiant. It weighed about 45 pounds more than the stateside Valiant, but 80 pounds less than the Dart. Some of the side trim was unique to the Canadian car, but the dashboard was identical to that of the American Valiant.

Only minor changes were undertaken on either side of the border, for 1964's MoPar compacts. Grilles on the American Dart and Valiant were attractively restyled, with the latter version being fitted to the Canadian Valiant as well. Then at mid-year, on both sides of the border, the sporty fastback Barracuda was introduced, utilizing the 106-inch wheelbase of the American Valiant. Once again there was a difference in nomenclature. In the States — at least at first — it was the Plymouth Valiant Barracuda, while north of the border the car was known simply as the Valiant Barracuda.

Another late entry, introduced during the Spring of 1964, was a 273-cubic-inch V-8, supplied (for an extra $108) to buyers of the American Valiants and Darts. Basically an under-bored version of the 318, it utilized thin-wall block and head castings, resulting in a weight reduction of about 55 pounds. It was a lively powerplant, rated at 180 horsepower, but for whatever reason, it was unavailable in Canada until 1965.

Three trim levels were offered, paralleling the US practice. The bare-bones V-100 series was available as a two- or four-door sedan, or as a station wagon. Somewhat more sumptuously trimmed was the V-200 line, consisting initially of a four-door sedan, two-door hardtop (a model not yet available in the corresponding Dodge Dart line), and a station wagon. A convertible was introduced for 1964, rounding out this series. And at the top of the line was the V-200 Signet, available in two-door hardtop or convertible form and featuring bucket seats, vinyl upholstery, a padded dash and deluxe wheel covers.

The Valiant proved to be Canada's fourth-best-selling automobile during 1964, behind Pontiac, Chevrolet and Ford (in that order); so for 1965 the line was expanded to 15 distinct models. The 100 and Custom 100 Series used the 106-inch chassis of the American Valiant, while the 200 and Custom 200 lines employed the Dart's 111-inch wheelbase.

Success notwithstanding, Chrysler Canada appears to have been plagued by uncertainty. In a sudden reversal, the company reverted to a single Valiant line for 1966, using the 111-inch chassis. Instead of 15 models, only eight were offered — which at least had the merit of simplifying the dealers' inventory problems.

And as if the situation weren't already confused enough, at mid-year, Valiant production was terminated by Chrysler Canada. Commencing with the 1967 models, Valiants were imported from the United States, and were handled exclusively by Plymouth dealers. At the same time, Canadian Dodge dealers were supplied with American-built Dodge Darts. The distinctiveness of the 1963-66 Canadian-built Valiants was gone.

Why were the Canadian Valiants different to begin with? Jack Poehler, editor of *Slant Six News,* explains, "Canadians, always fearful of being figuratively 'swallowed up' by their overwhelming neighbor to the south, have tried to assert their independence, at least in some small way. Even today, Canadian car buyers tend to be more conservative in their choices and into the mid-1970s a much higher percentage of six-cylinder

Stock US Valiant wheel covers are used, but rear fenders sport Dart trim to accent wheel openings.

How's It Go, Eh?

Performance (from a March 1967 *Car Life* road test of a Plymouth Barracuda hardtop coupe, powered by the 225-c.i.d. engine and fitted with the TorqueFlite transmission and 3.23:1 axle ratio):

Top Speed	97 mph
Acceleration: 0-30 mph	4.3 seconds
0-40 mph	6.6 seconds
0-50 mph	9.8 seconds
0-60 mph	13.6 seconds
0-70 mph	19.6 seconds
0-80 mph	27.9 seconds
0-90 mph	39.4 seconds
Standing 1/4 mile	19.4 seconds/69.8 mph
Fuel consumption, normal conditions	16-20 mpg
Fuel consumption, test conditions	16.3 mpg

Performance (from a February 1963 *Motor Trend* road test of a Dodge Dart GT hardtop coupe, powered by the 225-c.i.d. engine and fitted with the TorqueFlite transmission and 3.55:1 axle ratio):

Top speed	91 mph
Acceleration: 0-30 mph	4.2 seconds
0-45 mph	8.4 seconds
0-60 mph	14.3 seconds
Standing 1/4 mile	20.7 seconds/71.5 mph
Stopping distances: From 30 mph	37 feet, 6 inches
From 60 mph	145 feet, 0 inches

specifications

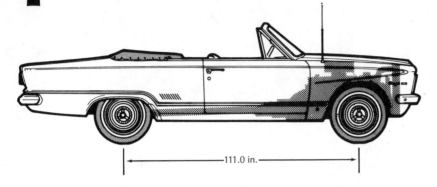

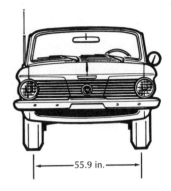

111.0 in.

55.9 in.

1964 Canadian Valiant

Original price	$3,047 (Canadian), f.o.b. Windsor, Ontario, with standard equipment
Options on dR car	225-c.i.d. engine, TorqueFlite transmission, radio, heater, back-up lights, windshield washers, variable-speed wipers, power top, white sidewall tires, spinner wheel covers, left outside mirror, brake warning light, block heater

ENGINE

Type	Ohv "slant six"
Bore x stroke	3.4 x 4.125 inches
Displacement	225.5 cubic inches
Compression ratio	8.5:1
Bhp @ rpm	145 @ 4,000
Torque @ rpm	215 @ 2,400
Taxable horsepower	27.7
Valve lifters	Mechanical
Main bearings	4
Fuel system	Carter single venturi downdraft carburetor, mechanical pump
Exhaust system	Single
Lubrication system	Pressure
Electrical system	12-volt battery/coil
Cooling system	Centrifugal pump

TRANSMISSION

Type	TorqueFlite 3-speed automatic planetary with torque converter; pushbutton control

Ratios:	1st	2.45:1
	2nd	1.45:1
	3rd	1.00:1
	Reverse	2.20:1
Max ratio at stall		2.20

DIFFERENTIAL

Type	Hypoid
Ratio	2.93:1
Drive axles	Semi-floating

STEERING

Type	Worm and ball nut
Turns, lock to lock	4.75
Ratios	24.0 gear; 28.7 overall
Turning diameter	39 feet, 6 inches

BRAKES

Type	4-wheel hydraulic, drum type
Drum diameter	9 inches
Total braking area	153.5 square inches

CHASSIS & BODY

Frame type	Steel, fully boxed, 4 crossmembers
Body style	2-door, 2-passenger sport coupe

SUSPENSION

Front	Independent, lateral, non-parallel control arms with torsion bars
Rear	Rigid axle, 5-leaf semi-elliptic springs
Shock absorbers	Direct-acting tubular type
Tires	6.50 x 13 two-ply
Wheels	Pressed steel, drop-center safety rims

WEIGHTS AND MEASURES

Wheelbase	111 inches
Overall length	192.8 inches
Overall width	69.8 inches
Overall height	53.5 inches (loaded)
Front track	55.9 inches
Rear track	55.6 inches
Ground clearance	5.5 inches
Shipping weight	2,630 pounds (approx.)

CAPACITIES

Crankcase	4 quarts (less filter)
Automatic transmission	17.0 pints
Rear axle	2 pints
Cooling system	12.0 quarts (with heater)
Fuel tank	18 gallons

CALCULATED DATA

Bhp per c.i.d.	.643
Weight per hp	18.1 pounds
Weight per c.i.d.	11.7 pounds
P.S.I. (brakes)	17.1 pounds
Production, this series/ body style	344

This page: Clean, simple styling characterizes Valiant front end treatment. *Facing page:* Only difference out back is Signet model i.d. in backup lamp cove. There's quite decent trunk space.

1964 Canadian Valiant

cars were sold there than in the US....."

Poehler continues, "The main reason for the demise of the uniquely Canadian models can be traced to the 1965 Canadian/American Auto Pact which eliminated the (in effect) 25 percent tariff on cars imported into Canada. It also did away with supercilious 60 percent local content laws. Now cars could flow freely between the two countries. The main benefit was that Canadians could now purchase cars at prices equal to those in the US, and car prices dropped sharply in Canada." (See sidebar, this page.)

Driving Impressions

It was at the 1992 St. Mary's Concours d'Elegance, in Moraga, California, that we found our driveReport Valiant. We happened to be approaching it from the rear, and at first glance we took it to be a Dodge Dart. This awakened feelings of nostalgia, for between 1964 and 1972 a Dart sedan served as our daily driver. That Dart had been one of the most all-around satisfactory automobiles we ever owned, so of course we had to take another look at the ragtop. And for a moment we wondered just what it was that we were looking at.

We tracked down owner Jim Sinclair and asked about this unusual Valiant. He told us that he had purchased the car in 1989 from the daughter of the original owner, a Canadian who had bought it in Winnipeg. This gentleman, a German immigrant, had been planning to move to Santa Clara, California, in order to be near his daughter, and somebody told him that everyone in California drove convertibles. Hence, his selection of a body style not often seen in Winnipeg. (In fact, so rare is this particular model — the Signet convertible, Canadian style — that only 344 of them were built during 1964.)

Jim Sinclair builds, sells and installs garage doors, but as a side line he appraises classic and special interest automobiles. It was in the latter role that he was called upon to appraise the Canadian Valiant. The car hadn't been run in at least a year, due to the owner's final illness, and it was filthy. The tires were bald and the engine was badly in need of a tune-up. But the odometer reading of 63,000 was evidently valid. The ragtop was complete, and had obviously been well cared for, at least until recently. The paint needed only minor touch-up, the original top was in presentable shape, and even the carpeting

1964 Price Comparison
Canadian Valiant versus US Dodge Dart

	Canadian $		US $
V-100 Valiant		**Dart 170**	
Sedan, 2-door	$2,433	Sedan, 2-door	$1,976
Sedan, 4-door	$2,481	Sedan, 4-door	$2,041
Station wagon	$2,807	Station wagon	$2,303
V-200 Valiant		**Dart 270**	
Sedan, 2-door	N/A	Sedan, 2-door	$2,082
Sedan, 4-door	$2,595	Sedan, 4-door	$2,148
2-door hardtop	$2,623	2-door hardtop	N/A
Convertible	$2,892	Convertible	$2,377
Station wagon	$2,912	Station wagon	$2,402
V-200 Signet		**Dart GT**	
2-door hardtop	$2,792	2-door hardtop	$2,306
Convertible	$3,047	Convertible	$2,524

Notes:

1. Since the Canadian Valiant was, apart from its trim, a clone of the American Dodge Dart rather than of the US Plymouth Valiant, the Dart is used here for purposes of comparison.

2. Prices shown are f.o.b. factory, including applicable Federal or Dominion taxes; optional equipment not included.

3. Note that the Canadian V-200 was available as a two-door hardtop, but not as a two-door sedan, while the opposite was true of the American Dodge Dart.

1964 Canadian Valiant

Understressed and over-engineered 225 slant six was famous for durability, longevity and bulletproof reliability.

was in excellent condition.

The lady — that is to say, the original owner's daughter — had no interest in the Valiant, and wanted to dispose of it immediately. So when Jim gave her the appraisal, she asked if he would be interested in buying it at that price. And so the car changed hands.

Jim Sinclair has no interest in restoring the car to high-point condition. It's a "driver," used by the Sinclair family for tours with the Contemporary Historical Vehicle Association and occasional evening jaunts. Jim reports that the top is raised only rarely. He has shown the Valiant from time to time, the St. Mary's concours being its most recent outing, but always with the stipulation "Display Only." The reader can well imagine, however, that

"The Australian Hemi 6"
by Jack Poehler

[In addition to its Canadian operation, during the 1960s Chrysler was doing some interesting things "down under." Here's one example. Condensed from *Slant Six News,* with permission of the author.]

In the 1960s, six-cylinder engines were anathema in the US, with the horsepower race in full swing and all manufacturers going to bigger and bigger V-8 engines. Chrysler's slant six was not exactly a prime candidate for a true "hot" production engine. With its long stroke and four-main-bearing design, high rpm's would require too much reworking on an engine designed for durability and reliability.

In Australia, on the other hand, cars have always been smaller, as have engines. There, four-cylinder powerplants were regarded as six-cylinder ones were here, and sixes were the most accepted.

In the mid 1960s, US Chrysler began to develop an all-new, short-stroke, six-cylinder "hemi" head engine, and even a prototype four-cylinder hemi. Towards the end of the decade, Chrysler Australia had begun to move away from its "stodgy, old folks" image, and in 1969...a highly hopped-up slant six started them on the road to performance cars.

Since there was no demand for a new six-cylinder here with V-8s in their heyday, and Chrysler Australia needed a new engine to update its image, the hemi project was given to them. Also, Australia had passed some of the silly "local content" laws. The slant six was totally of US design and for most of their run in Oz were imported as blocks and pieces and assembled there.

A new Chrysler engine plant at Lonsdale (near Adelaide) went on line in 1970, mainly for the production of the hemi. Chrysler Australia sold 565,000 Valiants in their 19-year run, and in 11 years (1970-81) 300,000 hemis were put together at Lonsdale.

[It has been estimated] that at an Aus-

tralian Chrysler car show you will find about 20 percent of the cars powered by small-block V-8s, five percent by big-block V-8s (all imported), five percent by slant sixes, and 70 percent by hemis.

The new engine, featuring hemispherical combustion chambers, was a straight-up six-cylinder and is a direct bolt-in replacement for the slant six. With the short stroke it was no taller than the slant, but was three inches longer. It featured seven main bearings instead of four, and even in its biggest version was 60 pounds lighter than the slant six. The hemi came in three sizes, 215, 245 and 265 cubic inches.

In the Spring of 1971, Chrysler Australia moved full-bore into the performance era. A sleeker new Valiant...came out. Also debuting was the Charger, their first real sporty two-door sedan. The Charger, built on a new, shorter, 105-inch chassis, was a fastback coupe whose styling can be described as a cross between a 1968 US Charger and a Duster.

The 265 hemi also debuted at the same time, and was eventually offered in five different versions: A one-barrel stock rated at 203 horsepower, a two-barrel with split exhaust at 218 horsepower, and three true high-performance versions. The last three were all fed by three Weber two-throat carbs with exhaust headers and were rated at 248, 270, and 302 horsepower, respectively.

The hemi engines all had a 3.68-inch stroke (as opposed to the 225 slant six's 4.13-inch). The 215 had a 3.52-inch bore, the 245 a 3.76-inch bore, and the 265 a 3.91-inch bore, compared to the 225's 3.40-inch. Hemis also got larger valves. While the slant six had 1.63-inch intakes and 1.36-inch exhausts, the 215 and 245 hemis had

1.84-inch intakes and 1.50-inch exhausts. The 265s got bigger valves yet: 1.96-inch intakes and 1.60-inch exhausts. The hemis, surprisingly for a performance type engine, had hydraulic lifters, and a slightly longer duration cam with higher lift and much stiffer valve springs.

Compression ratios ranged from the 215's 8.0:1 to the 245 and 265's (with one, two, or four barrels) 9.5:1.

The purpose of this article is not to give complete and detailed insight into the hemi engine, but rather to serve as an overview. While the engine was well accepted by the Australian car-buying public, it was not without its faults. It was not as smooth-running as the slant six (even in the low-compression standard versions), and was definitely noisier, even with the hydraulic lifters. It never came close to equaling the slant six's durability and reliability.

A commonly heard theory for the introduction of the hemi is that the slant six was just too reliable. A germ of truth in this is that low volume dealers (as most Australian Chrysler dealers were) must depend on their service department and parts sales to show a profit. If your top sales model (by far) doesn't need much service, you could be in trouble.

While this is possible, a more likely reason for the hemi engine was that Chrysler had to do something to upgrade its stodgy image. Both Ford and Holden had performance versions of their six-cylinder powerplants on the performance market, and Valiant's new hemi blew them all away, and the V-8s as well. This did much to improve Chrysler's image and led to some of the best sales years in its history.

it attracts a lot of attention and no end of inquiries — including questions about the block heater, an option not normally seen in California.

We thoroughly enjoyed our test drive in the Valiant, partly because it conjured up memories of the Dodge Dart that we owned, more than 20 years ago. It's more lively than one might expect of a 28-year-old, six-cylinder car. (We weren't entirely prepared for that, since our old Dart was powered by the 180-horsepower V-8.) The engine is quiet, smooth and very responsive, and the car cruises quietly at freeway speeds. The TorqueFlite transmission shifts almost imperceptibly. Steering is a bit on the slow side, but pleasantly light. The body is tight, squeak- and rattle-free. Front bucket seats are very comfortable, and rear knee room is remarkably generous for a car of this type.

On the downside, we are not enthusiastic about the Valiant's brakes. Jim Sinclair observes that in high-speed stops, they work very well, down to 25 or 30 miles an hour — at which point they exhibit a tendency to fade. We had exactly the same experience with our old Dart, and found ourselves in a somewhat hairy situation, on more than one occasion.

The suspension system, consisting of torsion bars up front and leaf springs at the rear, is truly superior. The ride is a little firmer than most of the competition, and very comfortable; and han-

dling is excellent. As a matter of fact, the Valiant's slant six engine results in a better-handling car than our old Dart V-8. The eight-cylinder cars outweigh the sixes by 180 pounds, model for model; and virtually every additional ounce is situated directly over the front wheels. Thus the V-8's handling could be tricky, for unless the driver was thoroughly familiar with the car's characteristics, it was altogether too easy to break the rear end loose. (Of course, it was possible to have fun with it, too, putting the car deliberately into a controlled skid and then pulling it around with a touch of the throttle.)

The MoPar compacts of the 1960s were fine cars, and the unusual nature of the Canadian model makes our driveReport car all the more appealing. ☞

Top: Dash contains easy-reading gauges, pushbuttons for tranny. Left: Even the "Park" position was controlled from the dashboard. Below: A must in the rugged north, an engine block heater.

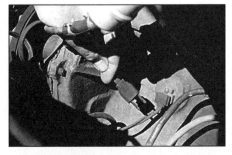

Acknowledgments and Bibliography
Automotive Industries, *March 15, 1964;* Langworth, Richard M., The Complete History of Chrysler; Slant Six News, *various issues;* Wright, Jim, "Dodge Dart," Motor Trend, *February 1963;* Zavitz, R. Perry, Canadian Cars, 1946-1984; "Chrysler's Slant Six," Motor Trend, *December 1964;* "A Pair of Barracudas," Car Life, *March 1967.*
Our thanks to Dave Brown, Durham, California; Walt McCall, Windsor, Ontario, Canada; Jack Poehler, Editor, Slant Six News, Salem, Oregon; National Automobile Museum, Reno, Nevada, Jackie Frady, Executive Director; Perry Zavitz, London, Ontario, Canada. Special thanks to Jim Sinclair, Santa Clara, California.

1965 PLYMOUTH

The Encyclopedia Britannica *describes the barracuda thus: "swift and powerful...bold and inquisitive...potentially dangerous to man...."*

Where cash is short, ingenuity often tends to flourish. Errett Lobban Cord proved that, time and again. So did the Graham brothers.

Another case in point is Plymouth's Barracuda. When the word got out (and seemingly, in Detroit word always gets out!) that Ford was developing a new "sporty" car, Chrysler Corporation's product planners saw a potential market for a Plymouth-built competitor for the car that would be known as the Mustang.

But Chrysler's research and development budget was a limited one. Whatever was to be done must be accomplished with a minimum cash outlay, using existing components to the maximum possible extent. And so, just as Ford was employing the mechanical components of the Falcon in developing the Mustang, Plymouth similarly based its new model on the Valiant.

Chrysler, however, went one step beyond Ford in requiring double duty of existing materials. For, while the Mustang had all-new sheet metal, the forward half of Plymouth's new Barracuda was — apart from an attractively restyled grille — pure Valiant. The newcomer even bore the Valiant name for the first year of its production. The title was perhaps a little cumbersome. Officially it was the Plymouth Valiant Barracuda.

What Chrysler Corporation had done, of course, was to rapidly develop a fastback rear section, grafting it to the Valiant front. Quickly, simply, inexpensively they had made ready their little "sporty" car, and an attractive job it was! They even beat Ford to the punch, for although its development started much later than that of the Mustang, the Barracuda was in the dealers' showrooms on April 1, 1964 — 16 days before the Mustang appeared!

Easily the most striking feature of the first-generation Barracuda was its enormous rear window. Measuring over 2,070 square inches, it was the largest such piece of glass ever

BARRACUDA

By Arch Brown
Photos by Vince Manocchi

installed in an automobile. It was also, as Barracuda owners were to discover, by far the most difficult to clean — at least on the inside.

The standard engine for that first Barracuda was the 170-c.i.d. version of Chrysler's slant six, but few cars left the factory so equipped. More popular was the larger, 225-inch six, but the overwhelming favorite, accounting for more than 90 percent of Barracuda production, was the optional V-8.

The latter was a brand new engine, provided for all of Chrysler's compact car lines. Introduced in January 1964, it was basically an under-bored version of the company's popular 318-c.i.d. block. In the interest of saving both weight and space, revisions were made to the intake manifolds and cylinder heads. Both durable and responsive, the new engine rated at 180 horsepower.

In some respects the Valiant chassis was better suited to the "sporty car" application than that of the Falcon. Its torsion bar suspension provided superior handling characteristics, for instance, particularly in cornering, and

although the brake drums were of smaller diameter than those of Ford's "pony car," the lining area was 20 percent greater. A further advantage was the Barracuda's faster steering ratio.

In addition to the tapering tail, the Barracuda was distinguished by special wheel covers with simulated knock-off hubs. Its handsome grille would be borrowed, in 1965, by the entire Valiant line. Inside, bucket seats were provided in front, and the bench-style rear seat could be folded flat like that of a station wagon, providing a luggage area — or sleeping space — measuring nearly six feet in length. Thus, the Barracuda combined much of the utility of a station wagon with the flair of a sport coupe.

Incidentally, the Barracuda outweighed the conventionally styled Valiant "Signet" hardtop coupe by just over a hundred pounds, evidently as the result of that huge stretch of rear glass. As we shall see when we come to the driving impressions, that extra weight may have been a significant plus.

Plymouth had been through a rough patch. For years it had been the industry's number three seller, behind Chevrolet and Ford. For a time, circa 1940, it had even threatened Ford's hold on second place. But a series of quality-control problems, followed by a succession of garish designs in the early sixties, had bumped it down as low as eighth place in 1962. A totally restyled Valiant and an attractively facelifted standard-sized car, both backed up by Chrysler's revolutionary new five-year/50,000 mile warranty, combined to push Plymouth back up to fifth place in 1963, and then to fourth the following year, behind Chevrolet, Ford and Pontiac. Much better, but still....

All of which is to say that the Barracuda's sales of 23,443 units during that abbreviated first year, while far below the record figures racked up by the hot-selling Mustang (see sidebar, page 104), were — by Plymouth standards — encouraging. And in 1965, its first full year of production, the Barracuda was actually the best-selling model in Plymouth's entire line!

There was little change in the handsome fastback that year. The 170-c.i.d.

Originally published in Special Interest Autos #82, Jul.-Aug. 1984

A GRAN TURISMO
FROM HAMTRAMCK

Above: From certain angles, fastback styling gives Barracuda a truncated appearance. *Right:* Stylized "V" in rear window trim is a reminder of car's Valiant origins.

1965 Barracuda and Mustang Fastbacks Compared

	Barracuda	Mustang
Price (8-cylinder)	$2,571	$2,697
Engine, type	ohv V-8	ohv V-8
Bore/stroke	3.625 x 3.3125	4 x 2.875
Displacement	273 cubic inches	289 cubic inches
Horsepower @ rpm	180 @ 4,200	200 @ 4,400
Torque @ rpm	260 @ 1,600	282 @ 2,400
Compression ratio	8.8:1	9.3:1
Carburetor	2-V	2-V
Transmission (automatic)	3-spd. + torque conv.	3-spd. + torque conv.
Ratios (:1)	2.45/1.45/1.00	2.46/1.46/1.00
Maximum ratio at stall	2.20	2.02
Differential	Hypoid	Hypoid
Ratio	2.93:1	2.80:1
Drive axles	Semi-floating	Semi-floating
Steering, type (power)	Integral	Linkage
Ratio (overall)	18.8:1	21.7:1
Turn circle (curb/curb)	37'2"	38'2"
Brakes, type	Hydraulic, drum	Hydraulic, drum
Drum diameter	10 inches	10 inches
Lining area	153.5 square inches	127.8 square inches
Tire size (standard equipment)	7.00 x 13	6.95 x 14
Suspension, front	Indep., torsion bar	Indep., coil spring
Rear	Semi-elliptic	Semi-elliptic
Shipping weight	2,930 pounds	2,720 pounds
Wheelbase	106 inches	108 inches
Overall length	188.2 inches	181.6 inches
Overall width	70.1 inches	68.2 inches
Overall height	53.9 inches	51.5 inches
Bhp per c.i.d.	.659	.692
Pounds per bhp	16.3	13.6

Primary source: *Automotive Industries,* March 15, 1965

six was dropped and so was the Valiant name, though the V-shaped logo continued to appear just below the rear window. In all other respects the Barracuda carried on as before. No point in messing around with a winning combination! That year 64,596 of the smart little cars were produced — including, of course, our driveReport car. It would prove to be the Barracuda's all-time record.

The sporty little Plymouth was again relatively unchanged for 1966, except for a revised grille that was no particular credit to its designer. But the following year there was an all-new Barracuda. Or rather, three of them. A redesigned fastback was offered, featuring a much smaller rear window. There had been complaints about the rear-seat passengers getting fried by the hot summer sun, beating down through that vast expanse of glass! And no doubt the cost of manufacturing that huge window had a bearing on the decision to create something of more modest dimensions.

New to the line for 1967 were a convertible and a hardtop coupe — body styles which were simultaneously deleted from the Valiant line. The hardtop, especially, had an Italian flair to its styling, and its understated good looks

Above: Parking/signal lamps were styled to look like serious driving lights. Below: Barracuda was the first true fastback from a U.S. manufacturer since the style was abandoned by GM in the early '50s.

made it very nearly as popular as the flashier fastback. Like the Valiant, the Barracuda boasted a two-inch-longer wheelbase that year — 108 instead of 106 inches. Overall it was four-and-a-half inches longer than the model it replaced. Fourteen-inch wheels were adopted for all three Barracudas that year, giving the cars a sturdier look. The Valiant, meanwhile, clung to the 13-inch variety.

Increasingly, the Barracuda was cultivating a performance image. The big-block Chrysler 383 became available with the Formula S package in 1967 (see sidebar, page 108), and in 1968 the lead-footed driver could even have the hemi-head 426 as part of a super-stock competition package. The 318, meanwhile, replaced the 273 as the Barracuda's base V-8.

Sales, which had slipped badly in 1966, picked up with the introduction of the restyled 1967 models. But then demand slackened once again. By 1969 volume was down to half the figure of two years earlier. Sales of the Mustang, meanwhile, while far below the peak of 1965-66, were holding steady, and Chevrolet's new entry in the field, the Camaro, was doing nearly as well. Nor were Plymouth's other car lines faring

much better than the Barracuda. The division fell from fourth to sixth rank in the industry that year, as both Buick and Oldsmobile forged ahead.

1970 found the Barracuda totally restyled once more. Two configurations — the hardtop coupe and convertible — were offered, each in three distinct trim lines: Base, Gran and 'Cuda. At midyear a coupe with fixed quarter windows was added to the Base series as a price leader. The smaller slant six, now displacing 198 cubic inches, became the standard engine for this model only. And in a departure from

what must have been thought of as the Barracuda tradition, no fastback was offered.

Styling of the 1970 Barracudas was reminiscent, in a sense, of the Mustang, for it followed the same long hood, short deck theme. The public evidently liked it, for sales received a 73 percent shot in the arm! Plymouth division in general was riding high that year. 1970 was not a good year for the industry in general, but Plymouth, paced by the popular new Duster coupe, was able to regain third place for the first time since 1959!

Production Figures 1964-1974[1]
Barracuda — Mustang — Camaro

	Barracuda	Mustang	Camaro
1964	23,443	121,538	
1965	64,596	559,451	
1966	38,029	607,568	
1967	62,534	472,121	220,917
1968	45,412	317,404	235,151
1969	31,987	299,824	243,059[2]
1970	55,499	190,727	124,889[3]
1971	18,690	149,678	114,643
1972	18,450	254,964	68,656
1973	22,313	385,993[4]	151,008
1974			

[1]Model year figures
[2]Includes hold-over cars sold as 1970 models
[3]"1970½" model, introduced 2/26/70
[4]"Mustang II" (sub-compact)
Sources: Don Butler, *The Plymouth and De Soto Story*; Jerry Heasley, *The Production Figure Book for US Cars*; Michael Lamm, *The Great Camaro*.

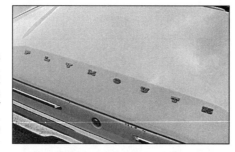

Right: In the rear, it was called a Plymouth. On the sides, Barracuda.
Below: Enormous rear window could really parboil back seat passengers on a sunny day. Below right: Gas filler was unchanged from Valiant. Bottom right: Taillamps are also stock Valiant units.

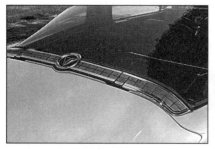

Barracuda Production (by model year) 1964-1974

Year	Fastback	Convertible	Hardtop		Sub-totals	Totals
1964	23,443					23,443
1965	64,596					64,596
1966	38,029					38,029
1967	30,110	4,228	28,196			62,534
1968	22,575	2,840	19,997			45,412
1969	17,788	1,442	12,757			31,987
1970		1,554	25,651	(Base Series)	27,205	
		596	8,183	(Gran Series)	8,779	
		635	18,880	('Cuda Series)	19,515	
		2,785	52,714			55,499
1971		1,014	9,459	(Base Series)	10,473	
			1,615	(Gran Series)	1,615	
		374	6,228	('Cuda Series)	6,602	
1972			10,622	(Base Series)		
			7,828	('Cuda Series)		
			18,450			18,450
1973			11,587	(Base Series)		
			10,626	('Cuda Series)		
			22,213			22,213
1974			6,745	(Base Series)		
			4,989	('Cuda Series)		
			11,734			11,734
Grand Total, 1964-74						392,587

Then, abruptly, the bottom dropped out. 1971 Barracuda production came to only a third of what it had been, just the year before. Plymouth's last convertibles — to date, at least — were built that year; Barracudas, of course. But sales were dismal: fewer than 1,400 rag-tops went out the showroom door.

Predictably, the range was severely cut for 1972. Base and 'Cuda hardtops comprised the entire line, and the high-performance hemi, 440 and 383 engines were no longer offered. Sales, such as they were, remained about level with the previous year. And the Plymouth Division, which had slid back into sixth place during 1971, was unable to improve its position.

Nor was 1973 substantially better. Plymouth sales in general, the Barracuda included, rose a little, but not enough to alter the marque's relative position. Engine options were cut once again with the deletion of the six, an oddly timed move in view of the fuel crisis being experienced by the nation that year. Thus the 318-c.i.d. V-8 became the standard powerplant, and the 340 the only available option.

Even Mustang's sales were dropping in those days. and it wouldn't have been surprising if Plymouth had terminated the slow-selling Barracuda. But, perhaps encouraged by recent sales gains experienced by Chevrolet's Camaro, the division retained the little sport coupes for one more season. They needn't have bothered. Total 1974 production came to only 11,734 cars —surely not enough to be profitable. And so, with the close of the 1974 model year the Barracuda passed into history.

One is left to wonder why Chrysler Corporation's hopes for its sporty little specialty car were never realized.

illustrations by Russell von Sauers, The Graphic Automobile Studio

© copyright 1984, Special Interest Autos

specifications

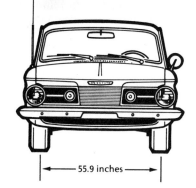

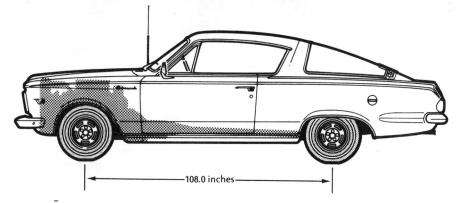

55.9 inches

108.0 inches

1965 Plymouth Barracuda

Price	$2,571 f.o.b. factory, with standard equipment. (Federal excise tax and preparation charges included.)
Options on dR car	Torqueflite automatic transmission, power steering, 14-inch wheels

ENGINE

Type	Overhead-valve V-8
Bore x stroke	3.625 inches x 3.31 inches
Displacement	273 cubic inches
Max. bhp @ rpm	180 @ 4,200
Max. torque @ rpm	260 @ 1,600
Compression ratio	8.8:1
Taxable horsepower	21.6
Valve lifters	Mechanical
Induction system	Ball and Ball 2-venturi carburetor, model BBD 3843S
Lubrication system	Full pressure
Cooling system	Centrifugal pump
Exhaust system	Single
Electrical system	12-volt

TRANSMISSION

Type	Torqueflite 3-speed automatic with torque converter
Ratios: 1st	2.45:1
2nd	1.45:1
3rd	1.00:1
Reverse	2.20:1
Max. ratio at stall	2.20:1

DIFFERENTIAL

Type	Hypoid
Ratio	2.93:1
Drive axles	Semi-floating

STEERING

Type	"Constant control" power steering, integral type
Turns lock-to-lock	3.5
Ratio	15.7 gear; 18.8 overall
Turn circle	37 feet, 2 inches (curb to curb)

BRAKES

Type	4-wheel hydraulic, drum type
Drum diameter	10 inches
Total lining area	145.2 square inches

CHASSIS & BODY

Frame and body construction	All steel, unitized
Body style	2-door "fastback" hardtop coupe

SUSPENSION

Front	Independent, torsion bars
Rear	Semi-elliptical leaf springs, one piece axle
Shock absorbers	Delco-Lovejoy single-acting hydraulic
Tires	6.95 x 14 (79.00 x 13 standard)
Wheels	Pressed steel

WEIGHTS AND MEASURES

Wheelbase	108 inches
Overall length	188.2 inches
Overall width	70.1 inches
Overall height	53.9 inches
Front track	55.9 inches
Rear track	55.6 inches
Ground clearance	5.6 inches
Shipping weight	2,930 pounds

CAPACITIES

Crankcase	5 quarts (with filter)
Cooling system	18 quarts (with heater0
Transmission	17 pints
Fuel tank	18 gallons

INTERIOR MEASUREMENTS

Head room, front	38.3 inches
Head room, rear	36.8 inches
Leg room, front	40.7 inches
Leg room, rear	30.6 inches
Shoulder room, front	54.2 inches
Shoulder room, rear	52.6 inches
Seat height, front	8.0 inches
Seat height, rear	10.3 inches

CARGO AREA (rear seat folded down)

Length	71 inches
Minimum width	43 inches

PERFORMANCE*

Top speed	105.6 mph (average)
Acceleration: 0-30	3.6 seconds
0-40	6.0 seconds
0-50	7.9 seconds
0-60	10.5 seconds
0-70	14.2 seconds
0-80	18.0 seconds
Standing 1/4 mile	17.5 seconds (average)

* From a road test conducted by the British journal Wheels and reported in the May 1967 issue. The vehicle used was a 1967 Valiant sedan with the same engine and transmission as our driveReport car. Final drive ratio, however, was lower: 3.23:1. This car would be about 120 pounds lighter than the Barracuda.

• Was it because it started out as a fastback at a time when that configuration was considered obsolete?

• Or did Plymouth fail to merchandise it aggressively enough?

• Certainly, it was upstaged, especially in the early years, by the Mustang. Could that have been the problem?

It's a mystery, for the Barracuda was both an attractive and a thoroughly competent automobile.

There remains one more speculation: Will the Barracuda one day come into its own as a collectible car? At this point a good example can still be purchased at a very reasonable figure, though the

Mopar's proven torsion bar suspension helps contribute to car's handling.

*Above: Semi-buckets provide comfortable riding up front, while, **above right,** rear seat room isn't quite as commodious. **Right:** In the ponycar tradition, center console was standard. **Below:** Instrument panel, however, is simon-pure Valiant. **Below right:** Outside rear view mirror adjusts with this toggle. **Facing page, top left:** With rear seat down, there's snoozing space for two or a cavernous cargo bay. **Top right:** 273 V-8 was most popular engine choice in Barracuda.*

price has escalated by about 30 percent in the past three years. It's impossible to predict the market, of course, but we think the Barracuda just might take off. It has a lot going for it!

Driving Impressions

There was the familiar feel to Rob Roche's Barracuda when we slipped into the driver's seat — and even more déjà vu a few minutes later when we guided the little car through the streets of North Hollywood and out onto the Hollywood Freeway. Familiar, because in the days when this Barracuda was new, our personal transport was a Dodge Dart V-8, a mechanical twin to our driveReport car.

That old Dart had its faults, most of them duplicated in the Barracuda. But it served us well for some 84.000 miles — and then went on to see our son through graduate school in the years that followed. We've had pangs of regret, from time to time, that we ever let it go!

These cars are fun to drive! They're lively and responsive; step on the loud pedal and you hear music — and with no hesitation! And if they're a bit inclined to understeer, it's no trick to keep them on course. We used to enjoy throwing the Dart into a controlled drift. Never had another car that would do that trick so neatly — or snap out of it so promptly with a flick of the wheel. The whole family loved that car, the first compact we ever owned.

Of course, we wore out the brakes pretty fast. A set of heavy-duty linings — rock-hard buggers they were — remedied that problem, but at a cost,

---

The Formula S Package

Even with its lively little V-8, the Barracuda wasn't fast enough for the performance crowd. Muscle cars were riding high in 1965, and it was important for almost any manufacturer to have one—as an image builder, if nothing else.

And so, in 1965 Plymouth offered a competition package for the Barracuda. They called it Formula S.

There was already a high-performance version of the Mopar 273 engine, a new option available on any of the Chrysler Corporation compacts: Plymouth's Valiant and Barracuda, and Dodge Division's hot-selling Dart. It was known as the commando 273. Thanks to its high-lift/high-overlap camshaft, dome-shaped pistons, dual breaker points, unsilenced air cleaner, high-compression heads (10.5:1 instead of the standard 8.8:1), 4-barrel carburetion and throaty-sounding dual exhausts, the horsepower of Chrysler's smallest V-8 was raised from an already sprightly 180 to an almost screaming 230. Zero-to-60 time was cut from 10½ seconds to 8 seconds, flat!

Somebody at Plymouth was smart enough to see that in order to keep all this power on the road and under some semblance of control by the driver, certain chassis modifications would be advisable. Accordingly, the

Formula S package was developed. In addition to the Commando 273 engine it included:

• Heavy-duty front torsion bars and rear springs.
• A sway bar.
• "Firm-Ride" shock absorbers.
• Goodyear Blue Streak tires.
• Special, wide-rimmed wheels.

As an added fillip, front disc brakes were available as a dealer-installed option. The Barracuda Formula S was as roadworthy as it was quick!

It was also readily recognizable. In addition to rally stripes down the hood and across the length of the top, a Formula S medallion was affixed to each front fender, just behind the headlamp. The Barracuda, already a car that one could scarcely help noticing, became—in Formula S guise—even more distinctive!

Evidently, at least for some drivers, it wasn't fast enough. For 1968 the Formula S buyer had a choice of two powerplants, both larger and substantially more powerful than the original. The first of these was a 340-c.i.d. version of Chrysler's small-block V-8. Basically a bored, high-compression version of the bread-and-butter 318, it produced 275

horsepower at 5,000 rpm, which surely should have been enough for anyone!

But just in case it wasn't, Plymouth managed to stuff a special version of Chrysler's 383-c.i.d. big-block V-8 under the Barracuda's hood. Space problems were said to have restricted the breathing of this monster somewhat, so it developed only (only?) 300 horsepower at 4,200 rpm. The same engine with different manifolding, fitted to the larger Plymouth Road Runner (see *SIA* #75), produced a thundering 335 horsepower. But 300 should have been adequate—even to the all-out performance enthusiast—for the 3,000-pound Barracuda!

The Formula S package went into 1969, its final year (at least under that name) with the same choice of power trains—except that the 383 engine was now up to 330 horsepower, a figure that almost defies comprehension in this day and age of small, fuel-stingy 4-bangers!

But the spotlight that year was on the 'Cuda, which provided a four-speed transmission with a Hurst shifter, along with twin hood scoops and special paint treatment. By the following year the 'Cuda would develop into a full line of upscale Barracudas—and a force to be reckoned with in competition circles!

we'd estimate, of about a 20 percent increase in the stopping distance. We don't recommend the procedure!

Actually, the Barracuda seems to handle more predictably than the Dart did. Perhaps this is related in part to the three-inch-shorter wheelbase (108 inches versus 111 for the Dart). But mostly, we think, it's a factor of that huge back window; 2,074 square inches of safety plate glass, placed directly over the rear wheels, has got to have something to do with holding the back end of the Barracuda in place.

The seat is low, but comfortable. We raised ours an inch, many years ago, by means of a set of small wooden blocks — a procedure we'd recommend to almost anyone. Head room is ample, even for the tall driver, with the seat thus propped up. The Barracuda's buckets provide some lateral support, but not much. Leg room is ample, up front. Unlike our old Dart, which was a sedan, the fastback Barracuda is a bit tight in the back seat, in terms of both head room and knee room. We look upon it as a 2 + 2, rather than a true five-passenger car.

This automobile is no museum piece. It's a working car, and although it's still a very nice unit, after 132,000 miles it shows some of the effects of hard use. Chrysler wasn't using hydraulic tappets on its smaller engines in 1965, for instance, and at idle the valve train makes itself heard. One isn't aware of the clatter at speed, however. And anyway, it's entitled to make a little noise, for so far as Rob has been able to determine, the engine has never been opened.

The front torsion bars have a lot to do with the Barracuda's impeccable manners when it comes to cornering. The ride is firm, free of pitch, and quite comfortable. There's not a lot of body lean, and as we've indicated, the rear end is more inclined to stay where it belongs than was that of our old Dodge Dart.

This car is equipped with Chrysler's optional "full-time" power steering — fast, responsive and rather too light for our taste. Brakes, on the other hand, are non-powered, and a heavy foot is required for a high-speed stop. The Barracuda "rocks" a little over sectioned concrete pavement. Nothing wrong with the shocks, so far as we could determine, but we'd be inclined to replace them —as we did on our own car — with a set of the heavy-duty variety.

There are automatic transmissions and then there are automatic transmissions, and in 1965 Chrysler's Torqueflite was the best of the lot. Perhaps it still is; we make no judgment on that score. But this gearbox shifts smoothly and quickly. There's very little slippage, and acceleration is probably comparable to what a three-speed stick would deliver.

Production Figures 1964-1974[1]
Barracuda — Mustang — Camaro

	Price 6-cyl.	Price V-8	Production*
100 Series			
Sedan, 2-door	$2,004	$2,135	40,434
Sedan, 4-door	$2,075	$2,206	42,857
Station Wagon, 2-seat	$2,361	$2,492	10,822
200 Series			
Sedan, 2-door	$2,137	$2,258	8,919
Sedan, 4-door	$2,195	$2,326	41,642
Convertible	$2,437	$2,568	2,769
Station Wagon, 2-seat	$2,476	$2,607	6,133
Signet Series			
Hardtop, 2-door	$2,340	$2,471	10,999\
Convertible	$2,561	$2,692	2,579
Barracuda			
Sport Hardtop	$2,487	$2,571	64,596

*Production figures include both six- and eight-cylinder models.
Prices are f.o.b. factory, inclusive of federal excise tax and preparation charges.
Sources: *Automotive Industries*, March 15, 1965; Don Butler, *The Plymouth and De Soto Story*

Perhaps it was inevitable that young Rob Roche would buy a Barracuda as his first car. His grandfather owns one, his brother owns one, and his father has three of them — including a gorgeous '68 Formula S (see sidebar, page 108).

Rob is in the Navy now, serving as an aircraft mechanic. But his dad, Dick Roche, is maintaining Rob's Barracuda with tender loving care, as it awaits the day of its owner's return. ❧

Acknowledgments and Bibliography

Automotive Industries, *March 15, 1965; Don Butler,* The Plymouth and De Soto Story; *Jerry Heasley,* The Production Figure Book for US Cars; *Motor Trend, January 1965 and February 1966; Wheels, May 1967.*

Our thanks to Ralph Dunwoodie, Sun Valley, Nevada; Mike Lamm, Stockton, California. Special thanks to Dick and Rob Roche, North Hollywood, California.

Plymouth Pride

Owners compare five prewar Plymouths on the back roads of Vermont.

When Chrysler's entry-level automobile, the Plymouth, was introduced at Madison Square Garden on July 7, 1928, there was little indication that this new car would be largely responsible for guiding the company through the economic woes of the Great Depression of the 1930s. The 1928 Model Q metamorphosed from the Chrysler 52, which originally derived from the Maxwell Four. Four-wheel hydraulic brakes, full-pressure engine oiling system, and aluminum pistons were some of the features that truly made it a good little car. Features that both Chevrolet and Ford would not introduce for nearly a decade. Sales figures for its introductory year were

greater than 66,000. These numbers paled in comparison to what Chevy and Ford were producing. By 1931, Plymouth produced more than 100,000 cars, and by so doing managed to displace Buick for the Number 3 seat in the ever-heated competition for top automobile production. For 1933, Plymouth changed its chassis from a 112- to 107-inch wheelbase. Reaction from the public was disappointing and, as a result, Plymouth quickly set matters straight and offered a 112-inch wheelbase "Deluxe" model, which came in a multitude of colors and an array of optional equipment. After its first 10 years, Plymouth was celebrating the most successful

Originally published in Special Interest Autos #185, September/October 2001

By Robert Gross
Photography by the author

sales rate of any other automobile company in the U.S. By the time the prewar era drew to a close in 1942, more than four million Plymouths were traveling the nation's roads.

To show Plymouth's prewar progression, we selected five variants: 1928 Model Q Phaeton, 1932 PB Convertible Sedan, 1937 Station Wagon (Westchester), 1939 Business Coupe, and a 1941 Coupe. The cars were brought to SIA's world headquarters in Bennington, Vermont, where the drivers of each car evaluated all the cars mentioned above with the exception of their own. Each car was driven through a specially mapped-out driving course in and around the scenic town of North Bennington, which included twisty back roads, long, sweeping curves, mile-long straightaways, and one big hill. Owners were asked to drive each car over the course, paying very close attention to how each car performed. Of particular interest were its handling, ride quality, performance, comfort, styling, character, and desirability. Because each car responded differently from the next, this made for quite an interesting owners' comparison report. When the sun had set and our testing drew to a close, the day had created a newfound sense of insight for our five test-drivers on a variety of prewar Plymouths. Perhaps their knowledge can guide you to a model that suits your taste.

SCOREBOARD

	BE	Bruce B	MB	Bob B
Styling	4	5	3	5
Character	4	5	3	5
Ride Quality	3	3	2	2
Handling	2	3	2	2
Ergonomics	4	3	3	2
Performance	2	2	1	3
Desirability	4	5	3	5

THE COMPARISON
1928 Model Q Touring

Owner: Earl C. Buton Jr.

Life-long Plymouth enthusiast Earl Buton is very proud of his family's pre-war collection. Among his most prized is this two-tone green 1928 Model Q. As with all freshman-year Plymouths, this five-passenger Touring rides on a 109.7-inch wheelbase and relies on a 170.3-cu.in. four-cylinder and a non-synchro 3-speed gearbox for power. I-beam front axle and solid rear axle, all mounted to semi elliptic springs, comprise the suspension. Because of the engine's 45hp, the rear is fitted with 4.30:1 gears and has no problem, as we found out, pulling some very steep hills. The steering is by worm & sector, and four-wheel hydraulic drum brakes are utilized to bring the 2,305-lb. Q to a halt. Optional equipment includes dual-sidemount wheels, trunk and trunk rack, dual taillights and cowl lights.

Bob Esslinger

Plymouths had a lot of chrome in 1928, making the cars look much fancier that they were; more than most other car companies did, anyway. I always liked the open, airy feeling of the touring cars, especially on hot summer days. On the road, the Q had a very choppy ride, better than Chevys or Fords of the same time, but one of the harshest of the cars tested today. The steering is a bit loose on uneven surfaces, but the brakes work surprisingly great, and that's very important. Seating is lower than I preferred and took some getting used to. Overall performance from the engine was very good for a small four-cylinder. The 4.30:1 rear-axle ratio made pulling

hills much easier than I expected. Touring cars are very popular, and I sure wouldn't mind owning this one.

Bruce Buton

The 1928 has nice lines and is well proportioned for a car of its era. Interior is plain. yet fitting for the rest of the car's styling. Nice sloping fenders and the dual sidemounts really set this car off. Down the road it bounces, shakes, rattles, and creaks. You really have to pay attention to the road, as it's not the easiest car to keep between the lines. Seating is comfortable, though the split windshield is cumbersome as it cuts right across my field of view. I missed not having a temperature gauge and thought the placement of the fuel-level gauge at the rear of the car was very unique, if not inconvenient. The throw of the gearshift was very long, almost as long as my arm. Power was somewhat lacking, and the second and third gear ratios are too wide. All this aside, though, I just absolutely love this car.

Michael Baisley

The dual sidemounts, two-tone green paint, and optional wire wheels made the 1928 Plymouth a real sharp car. Being a four-door convertible touring model just added to the beauty. The ride is a little rough and requires both hands on the wheel at all times. Like most cars of this vintage, it usually went where it wanted to, especially on rougher surfaces. Overall though, it was a joy to drive, and its braking was much better than I had anticipated. An open car with the side windows removed gives great ventilation. Especially on hot days. Seating was comfortable and the steering wheel well located. At 45 hp, it's no powerhouse, but it went right along with no fuss at all. Being a touring model and the first year Plymouth, this car is very desirable, though I wouldn't want to take it on a long journey.

Bob Butler

Graceful lines, large round headlights, dual sidemounts, and 20-inch wire wheels. This car looks dynamic. On the road, it has that typical old-car ride, but it sure beats walking. Keeping the car on rough roads proved to be a real challenge. I found myself constantly over-correcting the steering as the car wallowed all over the road. Surprisingly, the engine made plenty of power to pull the big, long hill in second gear. The car was hard to control when braking on a hill. Inside, I found the mirrors to be useless, due to excess vibration. Small doors make entry difficult, and the seat and pedal orientation were rather uncomfortable at times. Though I would love to have a car like this to take to local shows, I would in no way want to drive it on a long trip.

1932 PB convertible sedan

Owner: Bob Esslinger

A short production run, lasting only from April to October, makes the 1932 PB a rather rare bird. Owner Bob Esslinger drives to most any show during the course of a year. In fact, he averages about 3,000 miles annually. Power was up to 64hp from a larger, 196.1-cu.in. four-cylinder. Advertised by Plymouth as "Floating Power," the PB was one of the first cars to use rubber engine and transmission mounts. Aluminum pistons, counterweighted crankshaft, and an oil filter were some of the engine's other mechanical innovations. An automatic clutch, if activated, permitted one to shift the 3-speed transmission using manifold vacuum without the use of the clutch. Its steering was the typical worm & roller system, and the final gear ratio was 4.33:1. Also, to reduce road noise, the PBs came with a "steering shock eliminator" which kept vibrations from the road from transmitting upward to the wheels. Overall, the 1932 PB was an innovative piece of machinery.

Earl Buton

It's nice to have all seats inside the car, as opposed to a rumble seat, like a 1932 coupe. As the only car in our test with suicide doors, the vehicle has a really classy look. The dark blue paint and cream top give it a nice overall appearance. On the road the ride was somewhat choppy. It had a tendency to wander a bit, but it was always safe. The crown in the roads caused it to pull to the right. The seating was rather low, and I slid around on the leather seats through turns. Second gear is very smooth and useful for in-town driving and permitted speeds of 35-40 mph without straining the engine. With only 16 known to exist today, this car is very rare, and one would fit nicely in my collection.

Bruce Buton

Of the cars in the test, the PB takes the cake. From the suicide doors to the trunk, it's one sexy car. Dash layout is simple yet elegant for a Plymouth, though more chrome would have made it stand out. The overall ride with a more powerful four-cylinder and lower center of gravity gave a better feel than the Q. It's very smooth through curves, but it does get to a point where it feels as though it might lose control. Handling was much superior to the Q. Instead of having both hands on the wheel, I was able to control it with just one. Though it's easier to see out of the windshield, there are blind spots on the sides of the car. Rear-view mirrors mounted on the sidemounts are useless. Because of its rarity and great styling, this PB is a

SCOREBOARD

	EB	Bruce B	MB	Bob B
Styling	4	5	3	4
Character	4	4	3	3
Ride Quality	3	3	3	3
Handling	3	3	2	4
Ergonomics	3	3	2	2
Performance	4	3	3	4
Desirability	5	5	3	3

must-have for an early Plymouth four-cylinder collector.

Michael Baisley

Nice convertible 2-door sedan. Great styling with dual horns and twin-sidemount spare tires. Compared to the 1928 Q, the ride was noticeably more comfortable. Corners and S-curves were more manageable, though the car could still get away from you. Because of the small windshield, vision is limited, though side visibility is better than you would expect. Gauges, though small, are easy to read. Plymouth upped the horsepower to 65hp and, compared to the '28, it's a noticeable change. First gear is a little low, though second and third find their way into gear with ease. Early cars such as the '28 Q and this PB are very desirable, but because of their age and basic mechanical layout, their usefulness is limited.

Bob Butler

Suicide doors are a big part of this car's styling. These are huge compared to the 28's, making entry and egress much easier. Fender-mounted spares lend to its character and keep with the traditional lines. The ride quality was much improved over the Q. Smoother over rough roads, and not as cantankerous at speed, the '32 was very driver friendly. Handling seems as though it was also improved over the '28. Far less driver input was required to keep the car on the road. Braking was very responsive, with no pulls or drags. Interior was more spacious and, by design, the 2-door layout gave more room for the driver. Seating was high, which hindered outward visibility. The engine responded well, and the transmission was rather noisy, though it gave smooth shifts. Though the improvements to the '32 over the '28 are very noticeable, they aren't enough to sway me to buy one.

1937 PT50 Station Wagon

Owner: Bruce Buton

Built on a truck chassis, the PT50 station wagon was a very rare woody wagon. Owner Bruce Buton told us that most of the 600 1937 station wagons were built at U.S. Body & Forging in Tell City, Indiana, but because of a massive flood toward the end of the production year, the last 60 or so had to be out-shopped to J.T. Cantrell in Huntington, New York. With straighter body styling and flatter panels, Cantrell-bodied wagons are very different from those built by U.S. Body & Forging. Bruce tells us that the straighter panels made the wagon's restoration a lot easier. Because it's built on a double-drop-frame truck chassis, the gas filler is oddly located in the floor behind the driver's seat. Power comes from a 201.3-cu.in. flathead six that makes 82hp and is mated to a 3-speed gearbox. I-beam with semi-elliptic springs in the front and a hypoid rear axle comprise the rest of the suspension. Instruments include an 80-mph speedometer, odometer, and fuel, amp, temp and oil gauges. Interior, door jambs and steering wheel are painted gray.

Earl Buton

Very boxy, but if you wanted a wagon, that was what you got in 1937. As with all "woodies," this one seemed to attract plenty of attention. The two-toned wood catches your eye immediately. The ride is bouncy but firm and leaves you with a confident sense that you are in control. Steering is very light, with little to no play, and its tight ratio gives a very short turning radius. Seating is very chair-like and provides a comfortable position with good visibility. Though the instruments are mounted in the center of the dash, they are easy to see. With a weight of 2,795 lbs., the 82hp engine is adequate for flat roads and modest hills. Because of their unique wooden bodies, these old wagons are very popular. This particular one happens to be very rare as well.

Bob Esslinger

Woodies are always very popular. This one is a very good-looking car and has a very nice color combination. The ride quality was a bit choppy, especially on one of the rougher roads the car was tested on. It really shows its truck origins. Steering is easy and direct. Though the brakes work well, it seemed to pull to the left. The wagon offers lots of head room and great visibility. With the extra seating, I could fit all my grandchildren. The engine has adequate power, but it seemed to be geared too high. Because it is one of the rare Cantrell-bodied wagons, I find this car to be very desirable. I love woodies, and this PT50 is one of my absolute favorites.

Michael Baisley

I just can't say enough about the styling of the 1937. Because it's built on a truck chassis it is even more unique. The car was quite large inside and could fit a lot of people. Its ride was bouncy like a pickup of that vintage, rightfully so since it was built on a truck chassis. I was impressed with its handling; much more reassuring than its ride. Braking could have been better, but that might be because of its weight. Seating was adequate, and gauge visibility left much to be desired. The woody ran well, and the gearing gave great pickup, especially on some of the back roads we took it on. This is a very desirable car. Not only is it a classy looking vehicle, but its rarity and unique wooden body make it such a wonderful vehicle.

Bob Butler

There is something about a woody that defies explanation: the beginning of the SUV legacy 60 years ahead of its time. Unfortunately, the character and styling exceed its ride quality. The ride is rough, and the rear end has a lot of unsprung weight. On rough roads, there is noticeable creaking and groaning from the upper body. Steering was responsive and required little input. Entry and exit were not easy, and the door openings were partially blocked by the seats. Cab area was tight despite the outward appearance of being large and roomy. The woody was not a power-house, even with the six-cylinder engine. It pulled the big hill behind the '28 Q and wasn't able to close the distance between the two cars. Even with the cramped interior and low power output, I would love to own one. There is still something about that fine woodwork.

SCOREBOARD

	EB	BE	MB	Bob B
Styling	4	4	5	5
Character	5	4	5	5
Ride Quality	3	3	2	3
Handling	3	4	3	4
Ergonomics	3	4	4	3
Performance	3	4	3	3
Desirability	5	4	5	5

1939 P7 Road King Business Coupe

Owner: Michael Baisley

Though the body looked new for 1939, it was actually just a disguised 1938 that used an updated two-piece windshield, fresh front-end sheet metal with flush-fit fender-mounted headlights and reshaped taillights. Plymouths were maturing nicely and the sales figures showed it. Power came from an 82hp, 201.3-cu.in. six similar to the engine that was found under the hood of the 1937 Wagon. Although this was the first year Plymouth offered a column-mounted shifter, this base model P7 Road King has a floor-mounted shifter. Other mechanical innovations included a Safety Signal dash that changed colors as the vehicle's speed increased and coil-spring front suspension. The most affordable of all Plymouths this year was the $645 Road King Business Coupe such as Michael Baisley's, shown here.

Earl Buton

Very smooth lines. Similar to what was being offered by Chevrolet and Ford at the time. With their distinctive fenders and running boards, the 1939s were quite attractive. At speed, the ride was surprisingly choppy. When it hit larger bumps, the car would jump a little sideways, but was never uncontrollable. Compared to modern cars, the brakes are hard, but it seemed to stop just fine. Steering is light, and the ratio was very wide. The chair height and seats were comfortable and the instruments were easy to see. Power was adequate and it pulled the large hill with ease in second gear. The shifter was well located, but it seemed to have a lot of play. While I like this car, It's not as desirable as a rumble-seat coupe or convertible.

Bob Esslinger

I thought the 1939 Coupe was a wonderful-looking car, smooth of line and tastefully styled. On the road it handled very well, even over the rougher sections. Suspension was much better than what Chevy or Ford was offering this year. The car tracked nicely, but the steering was a bit hard when going through turns. Brakes required a very heavy foot and had a tendency to make the car pull to the left. The seat offered a very comfortable driving position, and outward visibility was better than most of the other cars tested. The engine made plenty of power, but I found the gearing to be too high and required the transmission to be shifted often. With a very comfortable ride and its beautiful styling, I think this a neat car.

SCOREBOARD

	EB	BE	Bruce B	Bob B
Styling	3	4	3	5
Character	4	3	3	3
Ride Quality	3	4	5	3
Handling	3	2	4	3
Ergonomics	5	4	4	4
Performance	3	3	4	4
Desirability	3	4	3	3

Bruce Buton

The '39 Plymouth is a great car, but I thought the body lines were out of balance with the styling of the grille. I like the squarish, fender-mounted headlights. They give the car a lot of charm. It's a smooth-riding car and took bumps much better than my 1937. You get a real feel for the rapid advance in technology that was happening in the 1930s. For a short guy of 5' 8", I found the visibility to be better than adequate. Gauges are easy to read, though ventilation could be better. The engine offers great power, and I would feel very comfortable driving it on the highway with today's cars. The gear ratio allows you this option, where my 1937 Wagon rides on a truck chassis and is geared more for low-end torque and pulling hills. A coupe or sedan doesn't usually get my heart pumping, but I could own a '39 Plymouth with pride.

Bob Butler

Body styling is smooth, and the lines are nicely rounded, with no harsh edges. Running boards set off the outside styling, and wheelwells are properly proportioned. Its ride quality is good and it handled itself well on bumpy roads. The springs support the car well, and there was very little body roll going through turns. Steering was a bit heavy. The gear ratio was more suited to highway speeds, and I often found myself contemplating downshifting when pulling a hill. Instruments were laid out in a very driver-friendly arrangement, and all switches were labeled and well within reach. The vehicle had plenty of power and was in line with my expectations. Valve train was slightly noisy at idle but quieted down at about 30 mph. Though I like this car, I don't think I would want to own one. I prefer the styling of the later models better. I would also lean toward a convertible.

1941 P12 Special Deluxe Coupe

SCOREBOARD

	EB	BE	Bruce B	MB
Styling	4	5	4	3
Character	3	5	3	3
Ride Quality	4	5	5	4
Handling	4	5	4	3
Ergonomics	4	5	4	4
Performance	5	5	5	3
Desirability	3	5	3	3

Owner: Bob Butler

Advertised as "The One For 41," the 1941 Plymouth looked very similar to those offered in 1940. Its subtle though very relevant changes included a one-piece "alligator-opening" hood, relocated battery (from under the driver's seat to in the engine compartment), and spring-loaded decklid hinges. The high-end Special Deluxe models such as this pristine example were spruced up with chrome windshield trim, window vents, and striped upholstery material. Using the familiar 201.3-cu.in. inline six, power for the 1941 models was up to 87hp. The three-speed manual transmission took advantage of a column-mounted shifter. As the nation geared up for war production, consumers were in an automobile-buying frenzy. Nearly half a million Plymouths were sold this year, and Plymouth came close to dethroning Ford in the No. 2 spot for total sales this year.

Earl Buton

The best of the prewar Plymouths tested. From the front hood ornament to the rear trunk latch, the whole car fits together gracefully. Its ride is outstanding, with little or no bounce, even on rough surfaces. Front coil springs make it ride like a modern car. Steering was crisp, and the car exhibited little body roll through the turns. Instruments are easy to read, and the switches are well within reach. The seating had too much cushion. A pillow would have given me much better visibility. Performance was outstanding. There was more than adequate power in third gear to pull the largest of the hills on our test drive. Hydraulic brakes stop the car wonder-fully. Though I like the coupe, I would much rather own a convertible of the same vintage.

Bob Esslinger

As far as prewar Plymouths go, this is one nice car. The rounded body panels give it a very smooth look. I love the color too. It's just right for me. Of all the cars, the '41 gave the smoothest ride. It behaved nicely through the turns and tracked well at speed. The back end was a bit light, though. It corners well, and the steering is very light. There was plenty of head room inside, and the gauges were easy to see through the steering wheel. The seats were comfortable, but I would have preferred a higher seating position. The engine offered wonderful low-end power, and it pulled the car up the hills with ease. I really like the color, and the dashboard layout was beautiful. This car is a real head turner.

Bruce Buton

The 1941 Plymouth is a great-looking car with tons of chrome and nice lines for a time when cars were being styled with more streamlined bodies. This car takes a lot from the art deco era and incorporates it into its design. Interior is quite plush, and fitting for the rest of the vehicle. This is the best-riding car of the test. Smooth over bumps, tight into curves. My body wasn't assaulted by the road texture one bit. Inside, it had an easy-to-read dash, well-positioned emergency brake, smooth-shifting column-mounted shifter, and good seating. Power was noticeably brisk and smooth, while the transmission gears were well matched to the engine's speed. Powerful, comfortable, easy to drive, this car has won a spot in my heart; I hope someday I can put one in my garage.

Michael Baisley

The styling of the '41 was very modern looking. Its front-end sheet metal, with one-piece hood, has very classy lines with a beautifully designed grille. The ride was very smooth, comparable to cars of the 1950s and '60s. It composes itself well over rough back roads, with hardly any bouncing. Handling on curves was better than I expected, and it went through S-curves effortlessly. Seating position was comfortable, gauges were clear, and outward visibility was better than I expected. With ample power, it pulled the big hill well in third gear. The 1941, in my opinion, has transitional styling that shows how the early Plymouths shed their skin in anticipation of newer, modern postwar styling. It's a great looker and a magnificent car to drive. I wouldn't mind owning one, but it's not at the top of my list.

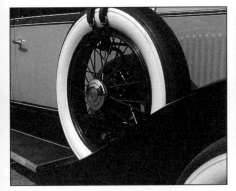

Conclusion

Sporting the most modern sheet metal of the bunch, the 1941 Coupe, with its coil-spring suspension, high horsepower six, and plush interior rated as the overall favorite. Its greatest asset was, without a doubt, its performance, though it ranked high for its plush interior. Although it seemed to fare well on the road, the testers didn't find it to be as desirable as they did some of the others. It also seemed to lack character, according to our testers. Overall though, it was the best one of the bunch on the road.

Hot on the heels of the P12 was the 1937 wagon. And it's no surprise. Everyone loves a woody, especially one as rare as this Cantrell-bodied PT50 wagon. That's why its character and desirability were among the highest on everyone's lists. Styling was also among its strong suits. Its ride quality, on the other hand, seemed to be its Achilles' Heel, and the handling wasn't much better, but that's to no one's surprise since the PT50 was built on a truck chassis.

Next up was the P7. It had as much character, flash, and comfort as the 1941, but it also used many old-style mechanicals, including the revered semi-elliptic suspension and 82hp six. It tied the newer 1941 P12 for interior comfort and ergonomics. It also ranked high for its art deco styling and smooth ride quality. One of its weaker links seemed to be its handling, but that's to be expected in a heavier car that still uses semi-elliptic springs.

At fourth place, the classy PB, with its suicide doors and aura of elegance, rated well with its styling and desirability but was the lowest when it came to interior comfort. Ride quality and handling were also rather low, but when you compare vehicles in chronological order, it makes sense that the newer cars perform better than the older ones—that's called progression.

Bringing up the rear of the comparison was the Model Q. Everyone loved its styling and character and, though it was one of the most desirable cars in the comparison, it was its antique-like mechanicals that brought it down. The testers all loved driving it and thought it was a very charming automobile—especially since it was the first year Plymouth. Unfortunately, its performance was lacking, as was its handling. Perhaps if the test was more evenly evaluated to, say, a 1928 Ford or Chevy, the Plymouth would have come out the victor.

As we stated earlier, there are not really any winners, or losers for that matter. The comparison was designed to show the progression of a few select prewar Plymouths. From 1928 until 1941, as we all learned, there are some definite changes, all of which ultimately helped Plymouth achieve its success and hold the third-place position over all other automobile manufacturers when it came to overall production and sales records. These five examples clearly show Plymouth's prewar parade of progress. ໖

SCOREBOARD					
	1928 Q	**1932 PB**	**1937 PT50**	**1939 P7**	**1941 P12**
Styling	17	16	18	15	16
Character	17	14	19	13	14
Ride Quality	10	12	11	15	18
Handling	9	12	14	12	16
Ergonomics	12	10	14	17	17
Performance	8	14	13	14	18
Desirability	17	16	19	13	14
Total	**90**	**94**	**108**	**99**	**113**

Plymouth Model Year Production, 1928-1978

1928	66,097
1929	108,345
1930	75,510
1931	106,896
1932	83,901
1933	298,557
1934	321,171
1935	350,884
1936	520,025
1937	551,994
1938	289,388
1939	417,606
1940	420,265
1941	542,610
1942	152,427
1946-47-48	1,059,489
1949	520,385
1950	610,954
1951-52	1,007,662
1953	650,451
1954	463,148
1955	705,455
1956	571,634
1957	726,009
1958	443,799
1959	458,261
1960	483,969
1961	356,257
1962	339,527
1963	488,488
1964	552,633
1965	728,228
1966	687,514
1967	638,075
1968	790,239
1969	751,134
1970	747,508
1971	702,113
1972	780,937
1973	**908,790***
1974	745,805
1975	507,338
1976	459,512
1977	473,748
1978	385,068

* Plymouth's biggest single production year

Production figures authenticated by the Plymouth Owners Club.

Plymouth Engines, 1928-1971

Year	Cylinders	Displacement	Bore x Stroke	Output (Gross HP)	Year	Cylinders	Displacement	Bore x Stroke	Output (Gross HP)
1928	I-4	170.3	3.625 x 4.125	45	1950	I-6	217.8	3.25 x 4.375	97
1929	I-4	175.4	3.625 x 4.25	45	1951	I-6	217.8	3.25 x 4.375	97
					1952	I-6	217.8	3.25 x 4.375	97
1930	I-4	196.1	3.622 x 4.75	48	1953	I-6	217.8	3.25 x 4.375	100
1931	I-4	196.1	3.622 x 4.75	56	1954	I-6	217.8	3.25 x 4.375	100
1932	I-4	196.1	3.622 x 4.75	65	1954	I-6	230.3	3.25 x 4.625	110
1933	I-6	189.8	3.125 x 4.125	70	1955	I-6	230.3	3.25 x 4.625	117
1934	I-6	201.3	3.125 x 4.375	77	1955	V-8	241	3.44 x 3.25	157
1935	I-6	201.3	3.125 x 4.375	82	1955	V-8	260	3.56 x 3.25	167, 177
1936	I-6	201.3	3.125 x 4.375	82	1956	I-6	230.3	3.25 x 4.625	125, 131
1937	I-6	201.3	3.125 x 4.375	82	1956	V-8	270	3.63 x 3.26	180
1938	I-6	201.3	3.125 x 4.375	82	1956	V-8	277	3.75 x 3.125	187, 200
1939	I-6	201.3	3.125 x 4.375	82	1956	V-8	303	3.82 x 3.31	240
					1957	I-6	230.3	3.25 x 4.625	132
1940	I-6	201.3	3.125 x 4.375	84	1957	V-8	277	3.75 x 3.125	197, 235
1941	I-6	201.3	3.125 x 4.375	87	1957	V-8	301	3.91 x 3.125	215, 235
1942	I-6	217.8	3.25 x 4.375	95	1957	V-8	318	3.91 x 3.31	290
1946	I-6	217.8	3.25 x 4.375	95	1958	I-6	230.3	3.25 x 4.625	132
1947	I-6	217.8	3.25 x 4.375	95	1958	V-8	318	3.91 x 3.31	225, 250, 290
1948	I-6	217.8	3.25 x 4.375	95, 97					
1949	I-6	217.8	3.25 x 4.375	97	1958	V-8	350	4.06 x 3.38	305, 315

Year	Cylinders	Displacement	Bore x Stroke	Output (Gross HP)
1959	I-6	230.3	3.25 x 4.625	132
1959	V-8	318	3.91 x 3.31	230, 260
1959	V-8	361	4.12 x 3.38	305
1960	I-6	170.9	3.40 x 3.125	101, 148
1960	I-6	225	3.40 x 4.13	145
1960	V-8	318	3.91 x 3.31	230, 260
1960	V-8	361	4.12 x 3.38	305
1960	V-8	383	4.25 x 3.38	330
1961	I-6	170.9	3.40 x 3.125	101, 148
1961	I-6	225	3.40 x 4.13	145
1961	V-8	318	3.91 x 3.31	230, 260
1961	V-8	361	4.12 x 3.38	305
1961	V-8	383	4.25 x 3.38	330, 340
1961	V-8	413	4.19 x 3.75	350, 375
1962	I-6	170.9	3.40 x 3.125	101
1962	I-6	225	3.40 x 4.13	145
1962	V-8	318	3.91 x 3.31	230, 260
1962	V-8	361	4.12 x 3.38	265, 305
1962	V-8	383	4.25 x 3.38	305
1962	V-8	413	4.19 x 3.75	410, 420
1963	I-6	170.9	3.40 x 3.125	101
1963	I-6	225	3.40 x 4.13	145
1963	V-8	318	3.91 x 3.31	230
1963	V-8	361	4.12 x 3.38	265
1963	V-8	383	4.25 x 3.38	305, 330, 360, 390
1963	V-8	413	4.19 x 3.75	340
1963	V-8	426	4.25 x 3.75	415, 425
1964	I-6	170.9	3.40 x 3.125	101
1964	I-6	225	3.40 x 4.13	145
1964	V-8	273	3.63 x 3.31	180
1964	V-8	318	3.91 x 3.31	230
1964	V-8	361	4.12 x 3.38	265
1964	V-8	383	4.25 x 3.38	305, 330
1964	V-8	413	4.19 x 3.75	340, 360, 390
1964	V-8	426	4.25 x 3.75	365, 415, 425
1965	I-6	170.9	3.40 x 3.125	101
1965	I-6	225	3.40 x 4.13	145
1965	V-8	273	3.63 x 3.31	180, 235
1965	V-8	318	3.91 x 3.31	230
1965	V-8	361	4.12 x 3.38	265
1965	V-8	383	4.25 x 3.38	270, 315, 330
1965	V-8	413	4.19 x 3.75	340, 360
1965	V-8	426	4.25 x 3.75	365, 425
1966	I-6	170.9	3.40 x 3.125	101
1966	I-6	225	3.40 x 4.13	145
1966	V-8	273	3.63 x 3.31	180, 235
1966	V-8	318	3.91 x 3.31	230
1966	V-8	361	4.12 x 3.38	265
1966	V-8	383	4.25 x 3.38	270, 325
1966	V-8	426	4.25 x 3.75	425
1966	V-8	440	4.32 x 3.75	350, 365
1967	I-6	170.9	3.40 x 3.125	115
1967	I-6	225	3.40 x 4.13	145
1967	V-8	273	3.63 x 3.31	180, 235
1967	V-8	318	3.91 x 3.31	230
1967	V-8	383	4.25 x 3.38	270, 280, 325
1967	V-8	426	4.25 x 3.75	425
1967	V-8	440	4.32 x 3.75	350, 375
1968	I-6	170.9	3.40 x 3.125	115
1968	I-6	225	3.40 x 4.13	145
1968	V-8	273	3.63 x 3.31	190
1968	V-8	318	3.91 x 3.31	230, 290
1968	V-8	340	4.04 x 3.31	275
1968	V-8	383	4.25 x 3.38	290, 300, 335, 350
1968	V-8	426	4.25 x 3.75	425
1968	V-8	440	4.32 x 3.75	350, 375, 390
1969	I-6	170.9	3.40 x 3.125	115
1969	I-6	225	3.40 x 4.13	145
1969	V-8	273	3.63 x 3.31	190
1969	V-8	318	3.91 x 3.31	230
1969	V-8	340	4.04 x 3.31	275
1969	V-8	383	4.25 x 3.38	290, 330, 335
1969	V-8	426	4.25 x 3.75	425
1969	V-8	440	4.32 x 3.75	350, 375, 390
1970	I-6	198	3.40 x 3.64	125
1970	I-6	225	3.40 x 4.13	145
1970	V-8	318	3.91 x 3.31	230
1970	V-8	340	4.04 x 3.31	275, 290
1970	V-8	383	4.25 x 3.38	290, 330, 335
1970	V-8	426	4.25 x 3.75	425
1970	V-8	440	4.32 x 3.75	350, 375, 390
1971	I-6	198	3.40 x 3.64	125
1971	I-6	225	3.40 x 4.13	145
1971	V-8	318	3.91 x 3.31	230
1971	V-8	340	4.04 x 3.31	275, 290
1971	V-8	360	4.00 x 3.58	255
1971	V-8	383	4.25 x 3.38	275, 300
1971	V-8	426	4.25 x 3.75	425
1971	V-8	440	4.32 x 3.75	335, 370, 385

Engine figures authenticated by the Plymouth Owners Club.

Plymouth Clubs & Specialists

For a complete list of all regional Plymouth clubs and national clubs' chapters, visit **Car Club Central** at **www.hemmings.com**. With nearly 10,000 car clubs listed, it's the largest car club site in the world! Not wired? For the most up-to-date information, consult the latest issue of *Hemmings Motor News* and/or *Hemmings Collector Car Almanac*. Call toll free, **1-800-CAR-HERE**, **Ext. 550.**

PLYMOUTH CLUBS

Plymouth Owners Club
P.O. Box 416
Cavalier, ND 58220-0416
701-549-3746
Dues: $24/year; Membership: 3,700

Slant 6 Club of America
P.O. Box 4414
Salem, OR 97302
503-581-2230
Dues: $25/year; Membership: 2000

Winged Warriors/ National B-body Owners Association (NBOA)
216 12th Street
Boone, IA 50036-2019
515-432-3001
Dues: $25/year: Membership 500

PLYMOUTH SPECIALISTS AND RESTORERS

Antique De Soto-Plymouth
4206 Burnett Drive
Murrysville, PA 15668
724-733-1818
1938-60 NOS mechanical and trim parts

Brad's NOS Parts
P.O. Box 2988
West Columbia, SC 29171
803-755-0066
New mechanical and electrical parts

Jacks Auto Parts
1783 Route 9 North
Howell, NJ 07731
732-431-8050
New electrical and mechanical parts

Jeff Carter Auto Restoration
20815 52nd Ave W, Suite 2
Lynnwood, WA 98036
425-672-8324
Specializing in Mopar restorations

Phoenix Graphics
5861 Kreyne Rd. Suite 10
Tempe, AZ85283
800-941-4550
Body and engine decal kits

Pro Antique Auto
50 King Spring Rd.
Windsor Locks, CT 06096
860-623-8275
1929-64 mechanical and trim parts

Valley Vintage Auto Parts
P.O. Box 486
Brunswick, OII 44212
440-355-4085
New and used parts and accessories

Year One
P. O. Box 129
Tucker, Georgia 30085-0129
800-932-7663
NOS and repro body and trim parts